Colonial Entanglement

Colonial Entanglement

Constituting a Twenty-First-Century

Osage Nation Jean Dennison

ILLUSTRATIONS BY

BUFFALO NICKEL CREATIVE

FIRST PEOPLES

NEW DIRECTIONS IN

INDIGENOUS STUDIES

THE UNIVERSITY OF

NORTH CAROLINA PRESS

CHAPEL HILL

Publication of this book was made possible, in part, by a
grant from the ANDREW W. MELLON FOUNDATION.

Set in Chaparral and Myriad types
by Integrated Book Technology

The paper in this book meets the guidelines for permanence and
durability of the Committee on Production Guidelines for Book
Longevity of the Council on Library Resources.

The University of North Carolina Press has been a member of
the Green Press Initiative since 2003.

Library of Congress Cataloging-in-Publication Data
Dennison, Jean, 1979–
Colonial entanglement : constituting a twenty-first-century
Osage nation / Jean Dennison ; illustrations by Buffalo Nickel
Creative.
    p. cm. — (First peoples : new directions in indigenous studies)
Includes bibliographical references and index.
ISBN 978-0-8078-3580-7 (cloth : alk. paper)
ISBN 978-0-8078-7290-1 (pbk : alk. paper)
1. Osage Indians—Politics and government. 2. Osage Indians—
Legal status, laws, etc. 3. Osage Indians—Government relations.
4. Tribal government—United States. 5. United States—Race
relations. 6. United States—Politics and government. I. Title.
E99.O8D38 2012
323.1197'5254—dc23   2012007568

To my parents, whose faith in me has never faltered.

Contents

Acronym Guide

BIA: Bureau of Indian Affairs. *See* OIA

CDIB: Certificate Degree of Indian Blood

An official document issued by the U.S. government certifying the percentage of biological ancestry an individual has in a federally recognized American Indian nation. New applicants must submit legal documents, such as a birth certificate, to the BIA illustrating biological descent from someone listed on a base roll. The U.S. government generally created the base rolls during the allotment period, with little input from American Indian nations. While these rolls remain controversial, many American Indian nations use them as part of their own citizenship criteria, including requirements for a certain percentage of blood.

OGRC: Osage Government Reform Commission

A group of ten Oklahoma-based Osage headright holders appointed by the OTC to survey the Osage people and write a constitution reflecting those opinions. They were sworn in on March 3, 2005, and served through the adoption of the 2006 Osage Constitution on March 11, 2006. The group consisted of Tony Daniels, a judge for the Miss Oklahoma pageant; Doug Revard, a retired Oklahoma district judge; Edward Lookout, the grandson of the last hereditary chief of the Osage; Joe L. Conner, a Ph.D. in experimental/clinical psychology; Jerri J. Branstetter, a corrections counselor; William S. Fletcher, the primary litigant behind the 1994 Osage sovereignty case; Priscilla H. Iba, a teacher of the Osage language who volunteered at the Osage Tribal Museum; Mary Joe Webb, a member of the Tulsa Catholic Diocese Synod Commission; Charles H. Red Corn, an award-winning novelist; and Jim Norris, a retired senior Health Services officer for the Indian Health Service.

OIA: Office of Indian Affairs

This agency is housed within the U.S. government and is responsible for the government's relationship with American Indians, American Indian nations, and Alaska Natives. Officially created as the OIA in 1824, its original duties involved negotiating treaties with American Indian nations. The department was moved from the Department of War to the Department of the Interior in 1849 with its name changed in 1947 to the Bureau of Indian Affairs. Today, it focuses primarily on the administration and management of the lands held in trust, providing services and assistance based on treaty obligations. It also operates court, law enforcement, and detention facilities on American Indian lands.

ONO: Osage Nation Organization

A group officially founded in 1964 that argued that the 1881 Osage Nation Constitution had been illegally terminated by the BIA and thus still represented an active government. In addition to advocating a return to this governing structure, this group was motivated by a desire to move Osage citizenship away from the headright system toward a minimum one-fourth blood quantum requirement. The ONO was unsuccessful in its reform efforts due to its insistence on a minimum blood requirement for citizenship and the perception that its intent was to do away with the headright system altogether—a system that was providing annuitants with a substantial income each quarter from oil lease revenues. One of its founders, Charles H. Lohah, is the current Supreme Court chief justice within the current Osage Nation.

OSA: Osage Shareholders Association

A group of Osage annuitants organized on September 20, 1994, in Pawhuska, Oklahoma, for the purpose of encouraging efficient management of the Osage Mineral Estate, protecting the federal trust relationship with the Mineral Estate, encouraging better management of the Mineral Estate by the BIA, and calling for laws to protect the Mineral Estate against theft, fraud, and conflicts of interest. OSA meetings are attended by about thirty and occur approximately once a month, depending on current issues of concern. This group took a vocal stand against the 2006 Constitution and has led initiatives against its passage and for its reform.

OTC: Osage Tribal Council

The governing body of the Osage Tribe from July 1, 1907, when it was established by an act of Congress, until July 1, 2006, when the 2006 Osage Constitution went into effect, with the exception of a three-year window in the 1990s. The OTC was originally intended to last for only twenty-five years, until the Osage people would, according to BIA projections, be acculturated into mainstream U.S. society, eliminating any need for Osage governance. Through various creative tactics, the OTC was able to extend the Mineral Estate until 1958 and then to 1983. In 1978, the OTC convinced the U.S. government to change the language about the duration of the Mineral Estate from "until otherwise provided by an Act of Congress" to "in perpetuity." When the OTC was established in 1907, its members included all Osage listed on the 1906 roll. Those Osage born after July 1, 1907, however, were not added to the roll and could not vote for or hold office in the OTC, until they themselves became annuitants, usually by inheriting a share in the Mineral Estate upon a parent's death. The OTC was made up of a chief, assistant chief, and eight council members, who met biweekly to pass resolutions pertaining to the business of the Nation.

Acknowledgments

In writing this book, I incurred many debts, most especially to those Osage who have allowed me to share their perspectives and histories. The early encouragement and patience of the 31st Osage Tribal Council, Julia Lookout, Leonard Maker, Kathryn Red Corn, the Osage Government Reform Commission, Hepsi Barnett, and the Osage Language Department made this research possible. The stories told and the questions asked by various Osage provide the substance of this book. To all these people I will forever be in debt.

While at the University of Florida, I was fortunate to find a group of professors and graduate students who nurtured my academic growth. Peter Schmidt continually impressed me with his insights, while his thoughtful reviews and questions kept me on track. Marilyn Thomas-Houston's support and unwavering confidence in my abilities during my six years at the University of Florida kept me at the university. Through their excellent seminars, Brenda Chalfin and Stacey Langwick provided me with the central theories that inform this book. Without their guidance, I would have been at a great disadvantage. The importance of the critical perspectives provided by Rob Freeman, Roberto Barrios, Lauren Fordyce, Jai Hale Gallardo, Ryan Morini, and Scott Catey cannot be overstated.

My research and writing was supported by Osage Nation higher education scholarships, University of Florida fellowships, and University of North Carolina at Chapel Hill fellowships and a postdoc, in addition to major grants from the National Science Foundation and Wenner-Gren. I offer thanks to these funding sources and to the people who helped make these great opportunities available. I would also like to thank my parents, Gene and Sally Dennison, who provided room and board throughout various stages of the research and writing process. Their home on the Oklahoma prairie has been both my inspiration and my sanctuary.

The research for this book was born out of this support, supervision, and generous funding, but the writing grew out of ongoing conversations among current scholars in the fields of anthropology and American Indian studies. This process has shown me the richness of peer review as a tool of collaboration and enrichment. Through the University of North Carolina Press I was fortunate to receive extensive and well-targeted feedback from

Kevin Bruyneel and Pauline Strong, both of whom inspired me to push my analysis of the Osage reform process deeper. In addition to the official peer review, feedback from and conversations with my Indigenous studies colleagues Mark Rifkin, Audra Simpson, Robert Warrior, J. Kēhaulani Kauanui, Jessica Cattelino, Joseph Genetin-Pilawa, Garrick Bailey, Steven Rubenstein, and Mario Blaser were essential to this manuscript and my professional development.

Throughout my time at the University of North Carolina at Chapel Hill, I have benefited a great deal from my colleagues in American Indian studies and anthropology. Perhaps most clearly, I am indebted to Valerie Lambert for her steadfast guidance, her unwavering support, and her critical reading of the manuscript. I also greatly benefited from the mentorship of Dorothy Holland, who was always willing to share her astute understandings of academic culture while facilitating many essential brainstorming sessions on a range of topics, including the title of the book. May all young academics be so lucky to have such devoted mentors.

In American Indian studies at UNC–Chapel Hill, I also benefited from the conversations and critiques of Keith Richotte, Michael Green, Theda Perdue, Malinda Maynor Lowery, Tol Foster, Jenny Tone-Pah-Hote, Dan Cobb, and Kathleen DuVal. In the anthropology department, I had similar insightful interactions with Jocelyn Chua, Arturo Escobar, Don Nonini, Silvia Tomášková, Anna Agbe-Davies, Amanda Thompson, Dana Powell, and Courtney Lewis. Many other faculty at UNC–Chapel Hill provided the community support and provocative discussion essential to any book project. These include, but are certainly not limited to, Sara Smith, Michal Osterweil, Neel Ahuja, Nina Martin, Ariana Vigil, Emilio del Valle Escalante, Joseph Jordan, Andrea Benjamin, Laura Halperin, and Jennifer Ho.

This book benefited greatly from its editors, who generously gave their time. Special thanks to UNC Press editorial director Mark Simpson-Vos, who provided thoughtful and time-intensive feedback, helping my manuscript mature into the book it is today. From his reading of the earliest draft to his choice of reviewers, and, most importantly, to the First Peoples manuscript development workshop, Mark nurtured my scholarship, refined my vision, and facilitated the discussions necessary to help me best articulate the issues at stake in the 2004–6 Osage reform process. Much of this would not have been possible without the generous support of the Mellon Foundation's First Peoples: New Directions in Indigenous Studies university press collaborative grant. I would like to offer thanks to all those who made this opportunity available to junior authors in the field of Indigenous studies.

In addition to Mark, many others have assisted me with the editing process, including my mother, Sally Dennison, whose eternal dedication to and patience with my writing has made my career in academia possible. Additionally, my husband, Michael Ritter, has provided not only an unwavering source of patience and support during this process but also several tireless weeks editing various drafts. Without their editing, support, and countless lessons in grammar, this book would never have been possible.

Several Osage thoughtfully reviewed the manuscript at various stages. In directing me to essential readings, as well as in critiquing its weak points, Veronica Pipestem greatly assisted me with an early version. Priscilla Iba's multiple reviews flagged several points for revision, in addition to challenging me to further articulate both the successes and the challenges of the reform process. Charles Red Corn, Leonard Maker, Jami Powell, and Joe Conner also provided important feedback and guidance on drafts of the manuscript.

Finally, I would like to acknowledge the limits of this book. While I strove to capture the complexities involved in the current Osage political situation, it must be recognized that words can only provide glimpses of experience. Not only is there the fact of my limited experience due to my youth, but also it is simply not possible to write about and understand all of the diverse and changing ideas surrounding historical and current manifestations of Osage politics. My hope then, is that this book is understood as a beginning.

Introduction

Late one night in March 2004, I received a call from my father. He told me that he had been "up on the hill," the area in Pawhuska, Oklahoma, where the Osage Tribal Council (OTC) chambers and other offices of the Osage Nation are located. He explained that there had been a lot of discussion about reforming the requirements for voting. I laughed and told him that people had been talking about reforming Osage citizenship my whole life and most of his. He replied that this time was different, that the OTC had introduced a bill in the U.S. Congress to finally settle the Osage citizenship problem, which, due solely to their status as headright holders, gave only 4,000 of the possible 16,000 Osage descendants the right to vote in Osage elections. This system had been in place since the 1906 Osage Allotment Act (34 Stat. 539), when the United States government allotted the Osage reservation surface lands but left the subsurface nationalized among the Osage. A share of the proceeds from this subsurface, known as a headright in the Osage Mineral Estate, was given to each person on the roll, and this headright was required in order to vote in subsequent Osage elections.

My father further explained that congressional field hearings had just been held in Tulsa. At these hearings, various people of Osage descent had argued that the Osage, like all other federally recognized American Indian nations in the continental United States, needed to be able to determine their own citizenship and government. It now looked like the U.S. House would pass the bill and send it on to the Senate.

"Somebody needs to document this," my father said, always scheming for ways to bring me back to Oklahoma. That night, however, he made a convincing case, and our phone conversation was the catalyst for this book.

In the summer of 2004, as I began preliminary research on the Osage government reform bill (Public Law 108-431), which was moving through the U.S. Congress, I understood myself as an Osage. I had not yet, however, considered exactly what that meant for my political identity. I had spent the first eighteen years of my life in Oklahoma but had never been eligible to vote in Osage elections. Shortly after turning eighteen, I left Oklahoma for college, before political participation had become important to me. I had been told that I would inherit half a share in the Osage

Mineral Estate and thus half a vote in Osage elections upon my father's death. Since this did not seem like a desirable trade-off, I had been content to engage Osage politics through my father.

After researching the history of this reform bill, however, and especially as the reform process evolved, it became clear that my simple understanding of Osage political identity did not fully reflect the complex histories and debates that surround Osage citizenship. During my first months back in Oklahoma, informal visits with a variety of people who worked for the Osage Nation or lived on the reservation began to help me understand how complex these issues really were at this moment of transition.

During these discussions, my own heritage was occasionally the topic of conversation. Since my grandfather had been an "original allottee," meaning he had been listed on the 1906 Osage allotment roll, and since my father had willed his half-headright to me upon his death, I would one day inherit the right to vote in and run for OTC elections. This meant that most everyone I talked with regarded me as a nonvoting Osage. There were other factors beyond Osage descent and headright holding, however, that some Osage used to categorize me. Since I had grown up off-reservation and now lived out of the state, many on-reservation Osage thought that I was less impacted by Osage life. I also did not easily fit within the phenotypical markings associated with being Indian; in particular, I have light skin. Because of these and other notions surrounding belonging, my relationship to the Osage Nation was occasionally questioned.

During an OTC meeting a couple of months into my research, I sat next to a woman I recognized as a program director for one of the Osage youth services programs but with whom I had not yet had any interactions. She asked me about some of the video footage she had seen me recording during the Osage Sovereignty Day celebration and then mentioned how much last-minute work she still had to do on her sons' clothes for the upcoming *In-Lon-Schka* dances, a ceremonial dance held in each of the three Osage districts on separate weekends in June. "Were you at the dances last year?" she inquired. When I responded that I had been, she then asked, in a way that will be familiar to many American Indians, "Who is your family?"

Knowing that the real question she was asking concerned who my Osage relations were, I explained that my father, Gene Dennison, was an Osage attorney who lived in Skiatook and that my grandfather, Bus Dennison, had farmed and lived on his Skiatook allotment lands.

Somewhat frustrated, she continued, "To me you have an accent, an eastern accent." I was a little taken aback by this, having grown up in Tulsa, about fifteen minutes from the reservation, but I responded that I had gone to college in Ohio and had married an Ohioan. Finally, she seemed satisfied; she had succeeded in placing what she recognized as my foreignness. "It is an Ohio accent," she said with authority. By continuing to study me, she had eventually found a characteristic that marked if not my whiteness, then certainly my difference from her.[1]

Because my research was "back home," I was occasionally forced to inhabit such uneasy spaces, making me deeply attuned to the debates about what the Osage Nation had been in the past and should be in the future. These debates were personal, in the sense that some included me within their definitions of Osage citizens while others did not. They were, however, also deeply revealing, bringing various issues from the landscape of my life into stark relief. I saw new meaning in the condescending comments from my grandfather about the "Oh-Nos," members of the Osage Nation Organization, which was formed in the 1960s in an earlier attempt to change citizenship standards, who were supposedly going to take away his share in the Mineral Estate, or comments from my father about what "trouble" we were in when a "full-blood stepped up to the microphone." These scattered fragments, along with notions about my own "Osage blood," were given new shape and deeper context. They now fit within a larger puzzle, which my research helped me piece together. Perhaps most importantly, I realized early on that there was far more than cultural and political identity at stake in these debates. We as an Osage Nation were reasserting our sovereign rights over our citizenship, government, and territory, and in the process we were trying to figure out exactly what we wanted this to involve.

The primary issue under debate during the Osage Nation's 2004–6 reform process was what shape the new Osage Nation should take. On the one hand, there was an almost one-hundred-year legacy of the Osage being primarily a group of headright holders in a Mineral Estate. On the other hand, this term "Osage" was sometimes used to signify various people who shared particular "biological" and/or "cultural" traits. Finally, for those people most active in the 2004–6 Osage reform process, using sovereignty to increase Osage control was the most important goal of reforming the Osage Nation in the twenty-first century. Throughout the reform process, various participants deployed their own situated histories, desires, facts, and lived experiences in an attempt to bring their vision of an Osage future into being. It is these chronicles, truths, and contestations that are the primary concern of this book.

The 2004–6 Osage governmental reform process revealed many of the central topics of national debate in the twenty-first century, especially those surrounding the issues of biology, culture, natural resources, and sovereignty. While some scholars have argued that the nation-state is being replaced by region-based polities,[2] such as the European Union, most agree that the nation "remains the decisive locus of membership even in a globalizing world. . . . [Current trends] indicate, rather, the resilience and continued relevance of the nation-state model. Nationalism is remarkably flexible."[3] It is this flexibility that is the focus of my book. While the specific term "nation" has a limited history within the European context and is most likely directly tied to the process of colonial conquest and the building of empires,[4] the concepts behind this term, and its usage within this book, are more far-reaching.

From anthropologist Audra Simpson, I understand nationalism as an "awakening of dormant collectivities . . . toward a more contingent and planned project."[5] This project of national reawakening was what the 2004–6 Osage reform process was all about. In the chapters that follow, I will be using the debates surrounding the 2006 Osage Nation Constitution to consider the various forces at work in the ongoing processes of national reform happening across the globe. Understanding what these processes allow, as well as the ideas they employ, is vital to this project. This book speaks to the way in which the 2006 Osage reform process reconciled the various rhetorics surrounding Osage bodies, practices, resources, and authorities into a national narrative.

Constitution

The opportunity I had to witness these vital discussions firsthand allows for a unique perspective on the constitution, a fundamental component of nations today. At its most basic, a constitution is nothing more than a "rational agreement" over a set of preferred "default options" intended to "reduce the complexity involved in some choices."[6] Constitutions represent the decisions that have been made on the classic political theory dilemmas of belonging and authority that go back as far as polities themselves. Constitutions often appear to consist of fully unified philosophies but are better understood as more or less frozen images of ongoing debates. I argue for an ethnographically grounded theory of constitutional writing as a politic of contestation.[7] Nations must always be forged out of various conflicting imaginings of the polity, which national documents, such as constitutions, must attempt to reconcile.

In the case of the Osage, the writers of the 2006 Constitution had to find ways to make sense of layered and at times conflicting biology-, practice-, resource-, and sovereignty-centered notions of their national self. In this way, I will show how constitutional writing is a process that attempts to fuse various histories, meanings, identities, and bodies, creating new material and political realities. This process of bringing together disparate components into a single mass is what nationalism is all about. Through this book, I aim to expose the possibilities, limitations, and consequences of such a coalescing process, as articulated by variously situated Osage.

While constitutions must be understood as both a creation of and part of what reinforces "imagined communities" in the Benedict Anderson sense, they must also be understood as enabling "hegemony" in the sense of Antonio Gramsci: "a problematic, contested political process of domination and struggle."[8] The fragility of these hegemonic forms necessitates the constitutional documents that have gained popularity across the globe. I argue that the constitution must be understood as a container, always striving to encompass more than it can reasonably hold. It must also, however, be understood as a boundary, keeping particular bodies and authorities at bay. This kind of focus on constitutions keeps us from ignoring the stakes involved in national formations. As Antoinette Burton points out, "We need to pay more attention to the question of who needs it, who manufactures the 'need' for it, and whose interests it serves."[9] Constitutions create far more than debates. Livelihoods, authorities, and physical structures all manifest from these decisions; governments are formed and strengthened, thereby changing global dynamics.

Throughout this book, I have chosen to focus primarily on the rhetoric behind nationalism rather than the structures it produces, investigating how the 2006 Osage Constitution itself was debated and eventually came into being. In focusing on the debates behind the constitution rather than the infrastructure created by the constitution, this book provides a unique perspective on the most pervasive governing device of the twenty-first century. The contestations behind the 2006 Osage Constitution become evident through the ethnography of the reform process, elucidating complex negotiations that are often concealed by ratified documents. While constitutions are never static entities, require constant enactment, and most often have built-in provisions for amendment, the authorities they privilege and those they constrain are often hard to locate ethnographically. In moments such as the creation of new governing documents, however, the debates and contentions become more evident, providing a space to hear what is actually at stake in writing a constitution.

As Winston Nagan and Craig Hammer point out, "In the hands of observers rather than lawyers, constitutions are nothing but codified expectations of authority . . . written in contradistinction to the prospect of continuous (even violent) conflict over how power and authority are to be constituted and exercised."[10] Through investigations of how understandings of the Osage as "a race," "a culture," a group of "shareholders," and "a sovereign polity" were used to argue against and to substantiate the 2006 Constitution, this book interrogates the primary realms in which authority was contested and the Osage Nation was reconstituted. By looking at how these conflicting notions of Osage nationhood were silenced by, subsumed within, excluded from, and deployed throughout the 2006 Osage Constitution, it is clear that such a document could never represent the breadth of debate occurring within a nation at any given time. Instead, constitutions must be seen as a coalescing of discordant viewpoints, where both inclusion and exclusion have complex consequences for the internal validity of the nation.

Entanglement

In its focus on the rhetoric at stake in twenty-first-century constitutional writing, this book must also contend with the ongoing settler colonial process in which the Osage reform process took place. Following the work of Patrick Wolfe, it is clear that in the United States and other settler colonies, the process of conquest has been neither completed nor abandoned. Instead, the "logic of elimination" continues as the primary "organizing principle," using various tactics to gain access to indigenously controlled territory.[11] Rather than seeing racial or other devices of differentiation as a motivation for conquest, Wolfe rightly points out that these are part of the logic of elimination, in that they are used to deny prior rights to land. Few moments of the 2004–6 Osage reform process can be viewed as wholly outside of this logic, which works, above all, to deny future possibilities for an Osage Nation.

The challenge that motivates this book is to produce a record of this moment of national reform that calls attention to the inherent power dynamics within the ongoing colonial context without erasing the agency that national reform entails. The Osage, like all people across the globe, draw on a wide variety of rhetoric to form understandings of self and nation, but some of these seem to work against and even contradict Osage nationalism. As Paul Chaat Smith has argued, it is "only when we recognize that our own individual, crazy personal histories, like those of every other Indian person of this century, are a tumble of extraordinary contradictions, can we begin making sense of life."[12] These contradictions are never straightforward, but rather they work on multiple levels—most importantly, they define what can be imagined for the future. In fact, the term "contradiction" itself does not quite do justice to the way in which various forces are entwined with Osage life. Such complexity can be seen not only across Indian Country but throughout the world and must be understood as a fundamental part of how power dynamics function in reality. I utilize the term "entanglement" to highlight these moments of complexity and follow how they serve to at times bolster and at other times hinder national capacities.

My usage of entanglement has been inspired by both academic and Osage sources. Achille Mbembe defines colonial entanglement as including "the coercion to which people are subjected, . . . a whole cluster of re-orderings of society, culture, and identity, and a series of recent changes in the way power is exercised and rationalized."[13] Pushing against what she sees as the "discrepancy between prescription and practice" in many colonial histories, Ann Stoler argues for presenting "more tangled stories of colonial expansion," where even the most personal of moments are fraught with debates over political discourses.[14]

For their part the Osage and all American Indian nations have long understood the colonial process as at once devastating and full of potential. Osage ribbon work, born out of eighteenth-century trade with the French, is perhaps the ideal metaphor of colonial entanglement. Using the raw material and tools obtained from the French, Osage artists began by tearing the rayon taffeta into strips and then cutting, folding, and sowing it back together to form something both beautiful and uniquely Osage.[15] In picking up the pieces, both those shattered by and created through the colonial process, and weaving them into their own original patterns, Osage artists formed the tangled pieces of colonialism into their own statements of Osage sovereignty.[16] Osage ribbon work reminds us that it is possible to create new and powerful forms out of an ongoing colonial process.

In positioning this logic as an entanglement, my goal is to avoid either ignoring or empowering the colonial forces with which colonized peoples must contend. Furthermore, this approach allows for understanding set-tler colonial forces as having a varied, dynamic, and uneven impact across space and time and even within a small population such as the Osage.[17] It is not always easy to see or extricate oneself from this logic, but when viewed from a distance, it is impossible to deny. The term "entanglement" also serves to negate the easy divide of colonized and colonizer, illustrat-ing the ways few can escape the logic of settler colonialism that permeates these spaces. In each of the nodes discussed throughout this book, we see how various Osage maneuvered within this entanglement, attempting to bring about their own vision of an Osage future.

It is the ongoing colonial process that makes this notion of nationhood so precarious. As Nicholas Dirks has pointed out, "Nationalism was rec-ognized both to have constituted the single most important site of resis-tance to colonialism, at the same time that it provides the most salient demonstration of the power of colonialism to reproduce itself, spawning myriad clones in new nations throughout the postcolonial world that have often been as repressive as the worst colonial regime."[18] The nation-state model with its power dynamics and internal workings is anything but ideal, but it is currently the primary tool for exerting sovereignty. In this sense, I agree with Ann Curthoys when she posits that the rejection of the nation is likely a luxury of empire: "Are the critiques of national history strongest in those national intellectual cultures where 'the nation' has been relatively secure and where interest in that nation's history has long extended beyond its borders? Is the rejection of 'nation' a luxury, mainly for those intellectuals who inhabit powerful or at least populous nations? Is the desire to go beyond national history only possible when there is little—in terms of historians' influence on nation politics and policy—to lose?"[19] Given these tensions, the nation is clearly a necessary entanglement. The key is making something out of this structure that does not mirror the oppression of the colonizer.

Each of the chapters in this book represents additional nodes of entanglement. Reform, blood, culture, minerals, and sovereignty each presented the writers of the 2006 Osage Constitution with unique dilem-mas. In the reform chapter, I discuss the complex colonial history that has deeply unsettled Osage governance, creating the need for governmental reformation. I also give an overview of the constitutional writing process, discussing the obstacles that citizen engagement more widely contends with, as well as the specific problems the colonial process created for twenty-first-century Osage reform. I then move to a discussion of blood, investigating how this racially charged metaphor has changed and been changed by various Osage understandings of relation over time. Looking specifically at the debates about "blood quantum" and "lineal descent" during the reform process, I investigate the entanglement of the Osage body. In chapter 3, I turn to the colonial histories behind the concept of culture and the ways in which it was deployed throughout the reform process. Despite external pressure and internal desires for the inclusion of practices labeled as cultural, I discuss the reasons why these recognized "cultural" markers were excluded from the 2006 Osage Constitution.

The final two chapters of the book focus primarily on the political authority of the Osage Nation. Chapter 4 interrogates the colonial entanglement created by the Osage Mineral Estate trust. By looking at its impact on both the writing and the implementation of the 2006 Osage Constitution, this chapter seeks to make sense of why some Osage felt more comfortable leaving Osage affairs in the hands of non-Osage. Chapter 5 investigates the arguments for the further enactment of Osage sovereignty and is directly at odds with the opinions discussed in the Minerals chapter. After exploring what sovereignty means for the Osage most active in the 2004–6 Osage reform process and how these notions were constituted, this chapter concludes with a discussion of how non-Osage landowners and the Oklahoma Tax Commission labored to deny Osage sovereignty and attempted to reassert their own authority over the territory.

Each of these chapters represents a fundamental component of how constitution writing is a deeply entangled process, particularly in this colonial moment. Each also catalogs some of the differing ways in which various Osage defined themselves in the present and imagined an Osage future. The writers of the constitution labored to centralize authority, identities, and property over the Osage population and territory within a single governing structure. They did this against the desires of some Osage who felt that certain realms of authority, whether economic, as in the Mineral Estate, or cultural, as in particular Osage practices, should remain outside the authority of the newly reconstituted Nation. This negation of various components of authority is a key theme throughout the book. The 2006 Constitution, however, had to do more than stand up to internal debates over the location of authority; it also had to contend with colonial forces that sought to deny or reorient national realities. In both the internal debates about what should ultimately constitute the Nation and in the external debates about how much authority and resources the Osage should be able to wield, national reform must be understood as a deeply entangled process.

Even as I attempt to shed light on the various forces at work in the writing of the 2006 Osage Constitution, I, like all authors, am myself deeply situated. Above all, my perspective must be understood as an Osage nationalist who hopes, sometimes beyond the evidence, that increased Osage control can improve our future capacities. Utilizing various personal narratives at the beginning of each section, I attempt to locate my own position, not so that readers may see past my situated perspective but so that they can see through it.[20] Like any subject position, however, I do not inhabit this position in any uniform or neat way but struggle to come to terms with my own internal entanglement. In this way, I lay claim to, rather than hide from, epistemological and methodological complexity. Combined with other situated Osage perspectives, this book attempts to complicate unifying narratives about American Indians in general and Osage in particular, showing the way in which the colonial entanglement leads to many differently situated perspectives.

In highlighting debates over general findings, I strive to tell a particular kind of story about American Indians. Specifically, my study interrogates general categories, whether "mixed-blood Osage" or "Osage annuitant," focusing on how these categories are constructed, narrated, contested, and changed over time. Rather than using these or other demographic categories to understand how Osage were making sense of the reform process, Osage discussions will be placed in the foreground as a way of showing the complexity of these debates. While doing my research, I repeatedly looked for categories, such as "people with a quarter or more Osage blood," to represent certain positions, but the picture was always far messier. Instead of making sense of the Osage reform process through such categories, this book interrogates a large selection of Osage oratory, investigating where these ideas were coming from as well as what they meant for the future of the Osage Nation.[21]

This book considers a broad range of evidence, including colonial policies, local histories, authorized and unauthorized stories about the reform process, biological "facts," emotions, and personal experiences in order to map out Osage national rhetoric within the context of the 2004–6 citizenship and government reform process. Rather than attempt to create a single lived Osage reality, I follow the diverse ways various Osage incorporate differing ideas into their own notions of self and nation, creating multiple lived realities. One of the models I draw on to communicate this is Donna Haraway's notion of diffraction, about which she says, "Diffraction patterns record the history of interaction, interference, reinforcement, difference. Diffraction is about heterogeneous history. . . . Diffraction can be a metaphor for another kind of critical consciousness . . . one committed to making a difference and not repeating the Sacred Image of Same."[22] These diffraction patterns complicate simple ideas of "Indian," "Osage," or "colonized," focusing instead on the ways in which these categories are continually negotiated. By moving the focus of academic writing away from a taxonomic approach, diffraction works to explicate rather than to generalize.

Another fundamental internal entanglement of this text is my training as an anthropologist. Drawing from a long strand within anthropology, I focus an anthropological eye on the political processes at work within Indian Country. Originally published in 1933, Alexander Lesser's study of the Pawnee, for example, looks at the ways the continuing colonial process impacts Pawnee government, religion, and everyday practices. Perhaps most importantly, he is able to do this while at the same time highlighting Pawnee Nation agency and endurance. Change is depicted as a fundamental, rather than antithetical, component of Pawnee lifeways. As he writes in his introduction, "The controlled consideration of the [hand] games in their changing forms has made it possible to consider the meaning and processes of change, and the inevitability of founding ethnological methodology on a metaphysic of history."[23] This approach of using the changing practices of American Indian nations, both political and everyday, to understand not just the colonial context but also the larger processes of change across the globe has inspired my study of the 2004–6 Osage reform process.

The writings of Beatrice Medicine have also had a lasting impact on my understanding of anthropology. Born in 1923 on the Standing Rock reservation in South Dakota, Medicine was an avid critic of early anthropology and its orientation toward "collecting, displaying, and storing material objects in museums. . . . The recording of music and language grossly obscured the dynamics of Indian interaction and laid the foundation for the 'apathetic, defeated Indian.'"[24] Like Vine Deloria Jr., however, Medicine felt that anthropologists were among American Indians' "greatest hope for the future."[25] Medicine was fascinated with American Indian usage of "confrontation" and "conciliatory acts" as "adaptive strategies to resist total assimilation into a dominant social system."[26] Above all, her anthropology sought to open up future possibilities for American Indian peoples. Because of her legacy, an increasing number of North American Indians are entering academia, gaining training in anthropology, and writing on issues of importance to their own communities. Audra Simpson and Valerie Lambert are two key figures who have influenced my approach to twenty-first-century Osage reform.

Simpson works with the Kahnawake Mohawk and focuses on narratives of self, home, and nation. She writes: "The culture and issues of native peoples can best be examined in terms of the lived experience of nationhood. In order to appreciate that experience, one must take account of the shared set of meanings that are negotiated through narrations—through the voices and structural conditions that constitute selfhood."[27] Simpson focuses on a plurality of experiences and narrations surrounding Kahnawake practices. She analyzes the "utterances, conversations and discourses that work in concert to shape the collective fate of the community and enable forms of recognition and membership *within* the polity of Kahnawake."[28] Focusing on the ways settler state politics are at work within the lives of Kahnawake people, Simpson understands these colonial politics as a crucial, although hardly all-determining, aspect of her research. Seeing Kahnawake citizenship as always more than a fixed identity, Simpson works to understand the various local and colonial factors involved in these negotiated processes of internal and external recognition.

In a similar vein, Lambert writes that anthropologists should center their research and writing on key events. Using Sally Falk Moore, she calls for the study of "events that provide evidence of 'the ongoing dismantling of structures or attempts to create new ones,' that reveal 'ongoing contests and conflict and competitions,' or that expose the 'complex mix of order, anti-order and non-order' that characterize ethnographic realities."[29] The 2004–6 Osage reform process was just such an event. Building on the work of Lambert and others, this book works to understand the continuous production and negotiation of various categories, and in doing so, its goal is to open up possibilities for an Osage future rather than to foreclose a future by defining the Osage in any sort of static form.

Lambert also focuses on the "ways by which living Choctaws are exercising Choctaw tribal sovereignty."[30] In order to do this, she looks at how tribal history, local political movements, economic development, election politics, race, identity, and relationships with the State of Oklahoma and the U.S. government are all interwoven within the daily practice of Choctaw sovereignty. Like Simpson, she refuses to freeze Choctaw citizenship or nationhood into something static, but instead she understands them as "sufficiently flexible and polysemous that they can be selected, assembled, and deployed in different ways and with different meanings at different points in time. . . . [They] are not fixed, but are best understood as claims that are negotiated and renegotiated, institutionalized and reinstitutionalized, over time."[31] By focusing on the issues of importance to indigenous peoples, these anthropologists have provided the central orientation for my treatment of the Osage reform process.[32]

Throughout the text I have attempted to choose the words with the baggage I most prefer to carry. Some of these choices are obvious, while others are subtler. When at all possible, it is certainly best to use specific terms, such as "Osage" or "Choctaw," but sometimes it is important to refer to larger trends affecting indigenous peoples throughout America. The term "Native American" arose as a reaction to the term "Indian," which was seen as a colonial word beginning with Columbus's confusion about landing in India. Despite this critique, I have chosen to use the word "Indian," primarily because it was the word most commonly used within the Osage community, and "Native American" has just as many of its own problems and dangerous connotations tied to things such as the environmental movement. Most frequently, I use "Indian" as part of the phrase "American Indian," to at least place the context on the proper continent. I will also occasionally use the word "indigenous," particularly when talking about the larger global population of people affected by settler colonialism.

"Tribe" is another term of contention within the literature and has long been used to talk about American Indian polities. Unlike with the term "Indian," however, the arguments against this term are far more compelling. Albert Hale, former president of the Navajo Nation, had this to say when discussing dangerous terminology: "So I beg you, those of you who are in academia, when you are writing papers, watch out for these things. Don't refer to us as tribes when you're trying to build our nationhood, or advance our sovereignty. Refer to us as nations."[33] As Hale points out, "tribe" has long been used by the settler state to demean indigenous peoples and deny indigenous authority. Membership, he argues, does the same thing. Citizens belong to sovereign nations, while you can be a member of any number of clubs or groups with little real authority. Thus, despite common Osage usage of both "membership" and "tribe," I have decided on the terms "citizenship" and "nation" as the most descriptive and productive glosses.

Deciding on what term to call those people who hold a headright in the Mineral Estate was another deliberative process. While the most common phrase used during the time of the reform process was "shareholder," it was utilized, often unconsciously, as part of a larger political strategy. In the same way that members belong to clubs and citizens to nations, shareholders are most often associated with corporations. Such a connection is misleading because it implies ownership of property, when, in fact, the Mineral Estate is owned by the Osage Nation and held in trust by the U.S. government. Holding a headright means that you will receive a percentage of the monies produced from the natural gas, oil, and minerals extracted from the subsurface of the reservation. Those people holding headrights were therefore annuitants, in that they received benefits from the extraction of natural resources from the reservation. In choosing "annuitant," I also hoped to separate the larger group of around 4,000 Osage descendants from the members of the Osage Shareholders Association, which during the reform process was never more than several hundred.

Grammatical tense is another common problem with which writers of anthropology frequently struggle. Early anthropologists have been strongly criticized for writing in the "ethnographic present," which is the continuous use of the present tense, because this creates a sense that the population being described exists within a frozen time during which change does not occur.[34] For this reason, most of this book is written in past tense. The use of past tense is, however, also dangerous, because American Indians have far too frequently been located in a distant past and denied the ability to exist in the current moment. My best solution to these problems has been to reference the specific period I am talking about, namely the 2004–6 reform process. I will also occasionally switch into present tense in order to make the point that these are issues that are still important to Osage people today and will likely remain so into the future.

The final stylistic aspect I struggled with throughout was how to situate my relationship to the events taking place as both an Osage experiencing "our reform" and an academic writing about "the reform." As a solution, I have left the personal narratives beginning each section in first person and attempted to make the rest of the text read from a distance more common to an academic text. Having stated this, there were times when such a perspective limited communication, when I chose to switch, sometimes jarringly, back to first person. These moments are intended to signal the ways in which this text hopes to be more than a record of the

2004–6 Osage reform process. Following critical race theory, "It not only tries to understand our social situation, but to change it, it sets out not only to ascertain how society organizes itself . . . but to transform it for the better."[35] If settler colonialism works to foreclose future possibilities for indigenous populations, this book interrogates those foreclosures in search of the best path to take the Osage Nation into the future.

Chapter 1 **Reform**

WAIT YOUR TURN/MEAT PIES VS. CHICKEN
DUMPLINGS/SECRET MEETINGS/THIS IS MY
LAST MEETING/TRAINED MONKEYS/
FORFEIT THE PROCESS/FOLLOW THE
PLAN/SKEPTICISM/NO FAITH IN OUR
CAPACITY/HURRY IT UP/SLOW IT DOWN/
NOT ALL OF US ARE UNDERSTANDING/TIME
LIMITS/CRITICISM AND NEGATIVE
STATEMENTS/CONFLICT AMONG THE PEOPLE
RESTRAINTS OF GRAMMAR/

REFORM

One of the first people I met when I began my research in the summer of 2004 was Leonard Maker, the head of the Planning Department at the Osage Nation. A small, middle-aged man with long Osage lineages on both sides of his family, Maker quickly impressed me with his grasp of Osage history, both ancient and recent, as well as his willingness to talk openly about Osage politics. Walking into his office for our first meeting, I was struck by the transient state of the room. There were boxes piled everywhere and books stacked up on each shelf of the bookcase. Watching me as my eyes scanned the room, Maker commented that every couple of months he had been moved to another location, so he had stopped bothering to unpack. As one of the smallest programs, he was repeatedly moved to make room for the expansion of other programs, such as those concerning Osage education and health care. With the opening of casinos, the Osage government began investing more money into its service programs, but it had little space to house all of its new employees. Maker did not have a large staff or even a stable project, so he was moved from one office to another, sometimes in his home town of Hominy, and other times in Pawhuska, the capital of the Osage Nation. Some of the buildings had the quality of the hurriedly erected prefab structures that litter twenty-first-century reservations, with thin walls and hollow floors. Others had ancient shag carpeting and lead in the paint, with the homey feeling that only older buildings can have.

In many ways the state of Maker's office could be read as symbolic of the state of the Osage Nation at the beginning of the twenty-first century—a patchwork of well-worn and temporary structures all exceeding their capacity. Even though it was clearly a moment of great expansion and excitement, there was also a sense of bracing anticipation, as if the floor was about to shift beneath our feet. The reform process promised much-needed change, but also insecurity, as we reimagined what our Nation ought to look like in the twenty-first century.

In the chaos of his office, I noticed his dry erase board. Scrawled across its clean white surface was a detailed schematic. Maker was in the midst of planning a process of governmental reform. Public Law 108-431, "To reaffirm the inherent sovereign rights of the Osage Tribe to determine its membership and form of government," had just passed the U.S. House and was now being debated by the Senate. Attorneys for the Osage Tribal Council had crafted this bill to fulfill a campaign promise the councilors had made to expand membership beyond annuitants in the Osage Mineral Estate.

The Osage have a complex colonial history, which has possibly made them unique among the federally recognized American Indian nations in the continental United States. In the 1906 Osage Allotment Act (34 Stat. 539), when the reservation was allotted, the Mineral Estate underneath the reservation was separated from the surface lands. This meant that while the land was allotted to individuals, the subsurface oil and gas remained in national ownership. The proceeds from the sale of oil and gas were to be distributed evenly among all 2,229 people listed on the 1906 Osage allotment roll. Many people today hold only partial shares in the Mineral Estate because their parents' or grandparents' shares were divided among multiple siblings. Additionally, one-quarter of all headrights left the Osage Nation before laws were in place forbidding non-Osage from holding more than a lifetime estate, meaning that after the individual's death, the headright would be returned to a descendant of the 1906 allotment roll.

The goal of the 2004 legislation, however, was to allow the Osage Nation to reform not only its citizenship standards but also its government, which was operating under a single council system established by U.S. law. Maker was developing a plan for reform that could be immediately implemented if the bill became law.

As I sat down to talk with Maker about his plans for the reform process, he explained how he expected the reform to proceed—and also the histories leading up to this moment and what was at stake in writing a twenty-first-century Osage constitution. In a similar way, this chapter will provide a context for the Osage reform process. By foregrounding an understanding of Osage history and the process through which reform took place, this chapter will investigate the tensions that surrounded the process itself. In considering not only the challenges inherent within citizenship-based reform but also the role various U.S. policies have played in creating the issues that plagued the reform process, it becomes clear that the process of reform itself is deeply entangled.

A History of Entanglement

The Osage first encountered Europeans, specifically the French, in 1673. According to historian Willard Rollings, it took only twenty years of contact to fully equip the Osage with horses and guns, allowing them to control westward trade on the prairie-plains of what would later become

Arkansas, Missouri, Kansas, and Oklahoma. By the late eighteenth century, the Osage controlled the trade not only between the French and the western American Indian nations but also among the different European frontiers.[1] In 1795, when the French built a trading post in the area, they were able to convince half the Osage to resettle near the Arkansas River, allowing for the easier exchange of trade goods. While this in some ways gave the French more control over the Osage, it also increased Osage control of trade in the area.

In 1803, the American government acquired this area from the French as part of the Louisiana Purchase, and the Osage's trade advantage, and thus authority in the area, was heavily threatened by the removal of eastern American Indian nations into Osage territory. Lewis and Clark sent Osage representatives to Washington in the hope of smoothing the way for Indian Removal.[2] After his first meeting with the Osage delegation, Jefferson wrote a letter to the secretary of the navy, Robert Smith, describing them as "the finest men we have ever seen" and saying, "We shall endeavor to impress them strongly not only with our justice and liberality, but with our power and therefore shall send them on to see our populous cities, Baltimore, Philadelphia, New York and Boston . . . because in their quarter we are miserably weak."[3] In addition to this strategy, Jefferson proposed in a speech to the Osage a few days later that they increase the interaction between the "two great nations" through trade and an Indian agent.[4] These two strategies of entanglement would drastically change Osage lifeways.

Jefferson's plan for this area was to increase the numbers of trading posts and to provide unlimited credit, encouraging Indians to run up large debts, which could later be used to acquire Indian land. These efforts, however, only strengthened Osage authority, giving them more control over trade in the area. In 1808, therefore, territorial governor Meriwether Lewis banned all trade with the Osage and ordered the Nation to move to a site on the Missouri River. At this new site, threatened with war and an end to all trade, two of the three Osage groups were forced to sign a treaty, according to which they ceded 50,000 square miles of land in exchange for a new trading post and an annuity payment of $1,500 per Osage citizen. By 1814, the U.S. government was able to control all trade with the Osage, making the Osage vulnerable to the wishes of the American government.[5] Control of trade and greater access to guns and horses allowed the U.S. government to gain the upper hand in negotiations with the Osage in a very short period. From 1808 until 1839, there were seven treaties under which the Osage lost control of over 151 million acres of land, gaining only minimal compensation.[6]

On the American side, acquisition of Indian land was typically justified in terms of meeting the needs of the growing American population, but it was also connected to notions of "civilization." As the 1865 Osage treaty reads, "The remaining proceeds of sales shall be placed in the Treasury of the United States to the credit of the 'Civilization fund' to be used under the direction of the Secretary of the Interior for the education and civilization of Indian tribes residing within the limits of the United States."[7] In this way, the Osage were forced to contribute to the building of colonial schools across America, including Carlisle Indian School and Haskell Institute.

From the beginning of the treaty process, it was clear that the existing form of Osage government was not suitable for negotiating the changes under way. On the one hand, Osage governance was decentralized, meaning that there was no one leader who could speak for all Osage in negotiation with European nations and later with the U.S. government. Many Osage were disgruntled that each of the treaties was signed by only a small fraction of the Osage leadership but had severe ramifications for all Osage. Furthermore, the loss of land and the dispersal of the annuity checks led to drastic changes in daily routines, rendering older forms of governing authority unworkable for current lifestyles. Finally, in negotiating the colonial situation, some Osage were persuaded by ideas of "civilization" in circulation, giving older practices an air of "savagery." With all of these factors working in unison, it was clear that by the late nineteenth century, Osage life had become deeply entangled within colonial systems of expansion.

In a final attempt to escape the ongoing territorial expansion of the United States, the Osage were persuaded to sell their lands in Kansas and buy back a small tract of their Oklahoma lands in what was by then known as Indian Territory. They were assured that here they could live free from invasion by white squatters. Instead of allowing the promised isolation, however, the federal government immediately began a whole new series of invasive tactics, this time focused on dismantling the Osage governing structure. For Vine Deloria and Clifford Lytle, a central aspect of the colonial process was the destruction of many of the American Indian governments. Frustrated by the slow and deliberative process by which most of these nations made decisions, the U.S. government began creating more "workable" councils, which could quickly make decisions that supported federal mandates.[8] By creating small "tribal councils," the Office of Indian Affairs (OIA) not only tried to take control of the decision-making processes across Indian Country but also often succeeded in destroying the ways of life that were supported by older governing structures.

Hoping to avoid these OIA-created governments, the Osage passed the 1861 Constitution (see appendix 1).[9] This effort succeeded for almost fifteen years, but in 1876, the OIA created the first federally created Osage Council. In 1877, the OIA's Osage agent, Cyrus Beede, described his creation of this structure, including his selection of Osage to sit on the council. He argued that the earlier system had created much jealousy and that the leaders did not always maintain complete control over their populations. He concluded by saying, "Another year's experience proves the wisdom of the course adopted on taking charge of the agency, in the selection of an executive committee, consisting of governor, chief councilor, and business committee of five, making seven persons selected from among the leading men of all the different factions. These seven men, regardless of character, are recognized as the representative men of the tribe, and through them its business with the agent and government is transacted."[10] In this annual report, it is possible to see the intentional colonial entangling of the Osage Nation. In addition to being transferred to increasingly smaller land bases and witnessing the extinction of the buffalo and other resources, the Osage people had to endure Beede, who appointed his own leaders, "regardless of character," ignoring their governing structure. By completely disregarding the authority of the existing Osage governance, Beede delivered a powerful blow to Osage autonomy.

The Osage did not passively accept this reconfiguration, in 1881 adopting a constitution that once again allowed them to govern themselves (see appendix 2). According to Terry P. Wilson, this effort to reestablish self-governance was directly motivated by the success of an Osage delegation that, without approval from their OIA agent, Leban J. Miles, traveled to Washington, D.C., where they negotiated for treaty annuities to be paid mostly in cash. By taking over the OIA's annuity payments, which served as a tight control mechanism, the Osage delegation reasserted their ability to speak for themselves, rather than through the agents of the OIA. This 1881 Constitution was copied directly, almost verbatim, from the 1839 Cherokee Constitution, with its three-part government, democratic elections, and autonomous boundary control. The Osage thus adopted a governing structure that was fundamentally recognizable to the U.S. federal government, in the hope of being left alone to manage their own affairs.[11]

For Osage scholar Robert Warrior, the 1881 Osage Constitution was a classic example of the Osage practice of "moving to a new country." Following the Osage practice of accepting radical change as part of ensuring a strong Osage future, the Osage set out to reestablish their autonomy. Warrior writes: "The 1881 constitution sets out the parameters of a self-determined, self-imagined, autonomous Osage Nation. They undid the lie that Indian people were not capable of living out the challenges of modernity."[12] This Osage willingness to change was predicated on the insistence of maintaining themselves as a distinct people. The implementation of the 1881 Constitution shows how change was accepted as a necessary part of survival rather than a threat to some sort of fundamental Osage identity linked to an immemorial past.[13] In describing the 1881 constitutional government, Agent H. B. Freeman wrote: "The Osage regard themselves as a nation with a big 'N.' . . . This government is a very real thing to the Osage."[14]

No matter how real the government was to the Osage, in 1900 the OIA dismantled the 1881 Osage Constitution, once again establishing a tribal council–style government, with officials appointed by the OIA. Secretary of the Interior Ethan A. Hitchcock justified this move by criticizing the Osage Nation government's disputed elections, an unwillingness to listen to agency recommendations, a poor choice of elected officials, and what he saw as a profligate use of tax monies.[15] The most threatening clash, however, was over the ongoing policy of allotment.[16]

The federal policy of allotment officially began in 1887 with the Dawes General Allotment Act, which called for the widespread surveying of native tribal lands. Once the surveys were completed, these lands were parceled out, usually in 160-acre tracts, to individual Indians. The remaining lands were then opened up for white settlement, reducing 2 billion acres of Indian-controlled land to 150 million acres.[17] This large-scale policy of allotment was justified at the time by both the federal government and an array of humanitarian organizations, including the Indian Rights Association, the Indian Protection Committee, and the Friends of the Indians, as a solution to the "Indian problem." Allotment, it was argued, would create American citizens by allowing each Indian to become propertied and thus a full part of American society. Euro-Americans saw the breakup of tribal lands as allowing Indians to move beyond the problems supposedly created by tribal structure and adopt "civilization."[18]

Like several other American Indian nations in Indian Territory, the Osage owned their land in fee simple and were thus exempted from the

1887 Dawes Act, which had forced this breakup of tribal lands.[19] Interior secretary Ethan A. Hitchcock went to great lengths, however, to ensure that Indian Territory was allotted, allowing for Oklahoma statehood. In the case of the Osage, this included the cessation of the Osage National Council's official government, which had spoken adamantly against allotment. Hitchcock also appointed allotment-friendly Osage to a body he termed the Osage Tribal Council (OTC), with whom he insisted on conducting business after 1900.[20] In the end, the OTC, led by Chief James Bigheart, was able to negotiate a better allotment, whereby the entire Osage reservation was split among those people listed on the 1906 roll and whereby the Mineral Estate under the entire reservation remained in trust as OTC property. This allotment differed from the usual practice of allotting a small portion of the territory and opening up a majority of the land for white settlement.[21]

During this period of allotment, the U.S. Congress attempted, and failed, to transform the sovereign Osage Nation into a group of individual landowners who held a property interest in a Mineral Estate. Specifically, the OIA created the OTC to administer these natural resources, which was originally intended to last for only twenty-five years, until the Osage people could be absorbed into the mainstream society, eliminating any need for a tribal government. While not successful, this system has had a lasting impact on Osage governance and citizenship.

Through various creative tactics, the OTC was able to extend the Mineral Estate until 1958 and then to 1983. In 1978, the OTC was able to convince the U.S. government to change the language concerning the duration of the Mineral Estate from "until otherwise provided by an Act of Congress" to "in perpetuity."[22] Even as the OTC was fighting Congress to maintain its recognition, an increasing number of Osage were alienated from the annuitant-controlled government. Section 1 of the Osage Allotment Act declared that the 1906 roll constituted the legal "membership" of the Osage Tribe. Voters were, however, originally only males over the age of twenty-one.

In addition to creating the OTC, the Osage Allotment Act recognized three tracts of communally owned lands known as the Pawhuska, Hominy, and Grayhorse Indian villages. These tracts of trust land were left intact for the exclusive use of Osage Indians, to be managed by the federal superintendent of the Osage. Over time, regulations were established in the Code of Federal Regulations (CFR) for the governing of these villages, including a committee of five individuals to oversee the "health, safety, and welfare of the inhabitants" of each village. These boards nota-bly consisted of any Osage descendant living in the designated areas, not just Osage annuitants. Their responsibilities primarily focused upon the maintenance of property in the area and determining who could live within the area. In the case of the Hominy and Pawhuska Indian villages, responsibilities included the establishment of casinos in conjunction with the OTC. With the establishment of the 2006 Osage Nation government, however, authority over these casinos went entirely to the Osage Nation.

In 1942, the OIA changed election procedures for Osage voting to in-clude the women listed on the 1906 roll and any descendant of the 1906 roll who had inherited a share in the Mineral Estate.[23] In 1958, with lobby-ing from the OTC, the OIA again changed voting policies, making the Osage vote dependent on the percentage of the headright held. For example, when three siblings inherited equal shares of one parent's headright, each was given only a third of a vote in tribal elections. This did not change whom the OIA considered legal Osage citizens, however, only who had a vote in OTC elections. The 1906 act limited the status of actual citizenship to those people whose names appeared on the roll. Despite this limitation, Osage descendants, both annuitants and non-annuitants, were included in federal programs, grants, and services, which deeply confused the issue of whom the federal government actually recognized as an Osage.

In 1953, the Osage, along with over a hundred other American Indian nations, including the Menominee and the Klamath, faced termination through House Concurrent Resolution 108, because they were seen as successfully "assimilated" into American society. The federal government had long been trying to "get out of the Indian business," but this period of termination was its most straightforward and "successful" attempt. The Osage, understanding the importance of federal recognition, sent repre-sentatives to Washington, where they were able to successfully negotiate for continued recognition by promising to pay their own operation costs through Osage Mineral Estate proceeds. The fear of termination inspired by both the termination era, as well as the battles required to maintain the Osage Mineral Estate, worked as entanglements throughout the reform process. Fear that the federal government would use blood, cul-ture, or land as a means to deny the status of Osage nationhood repeat-edly surfaced throughout the reform process and continues to be a point of contention within the new government.[24]

During the 1960s, Leroy Logan, Anthony Daniels, Raymond Lasley Sr., Charles H. Lohah, and several other Osage descendants, some with and some without headrights, formed the Osage Nation Organization (ONO) to address the issue of the growing number of disenfranchised Osage. The central argument of the group, officially established in 1964, was that the 1881 Osage Nation had been illegally terminated by the OIA and was therefore still a legitimate government. In addition to advocating a return to this governing structure, this group was motivated by a desire to move Osage citizenship away from the headright system toward a minimum one-fourth blood quantum requirement. The ONO was never successful in its reform efforts, due to its insistence on a minimum blood requirement for citizenship and fears that its real intent was to do away with the headright system altogether—a system that was providing annuitants with a substantial income each quarter from oil lease revenues. Rather than bringing an end to the OTC, this movement resulted in rallying many Osage behind the federally imposed system.

In the 1970s, the effort to change Osage citizenship led to a constitutional referendum, which failed by a small margin; and then in 1978 the matter was taken up in the court case *Logan v. Andrus*, with mixed results. Several nonshareholding Osage descendants filed a suit in federal court, arguing that the OTC did not represent them or their interests and thus should not be considered the primary governing body of the Osage Nation. The trial judge held that the 1881 Constitution had been illegally abolished, saying, "The Secretary of the Interior was attempting to exercise legislative power when he purportedly abolished the government of the Osage Nation in 1900, and thus such action was beyond the scope of his authority and of no legal effect."[25] Nevertheless, the court decided that because the OTC had been in place for over seventy years, it now had general legislative authority over the nation. Thus, even though the OIA had illegally abolished the Osage Nation, the OTC was now considered the only active government of the Osage people. In an appeal, the legislative authority of the OTC was reaffirmed.[26]

The issue of a constitutional convention again surfaced in the 1980s with OTC chief Sylvester Tinker spearheading a law that recognized the continued validity of the 1881 Constitution. He ran on a reelection platform of hosting a constitutional convention but was summarily defeated in the following election. Again taking matters into their own hands, in 1986, Charles Pratt, Juanita West, Leonard Maker, and a sizable group of Osage descendants began organizing around the reinstatement of the 1881 Osage Constitution. After holding a three-day convention, Charles Pratt, a non-annuitant, was elected primary councilor of the Osage National

Council, as the head of the organization was called. In addition to arguing that the 1881 Constitution had been illegally abolished by the OIA, the organization also argued that "that damnable act [the 1906 Osage Allotment Act] took away our national sovereignty, divided the right to vote in tribal matters, struck out any reference to accountability of elected tribal officials, and effectively tied the hands of the Osage Nation to develop both its human and natural resources."[27] A fundamental part of this movement, according to Maker, was that the successor to the OIA, the Bureau of Indian Affairs (BIA), had stated in several letters that the Osage Nation actually consisted only of the survivors of the 1906 roll (see appendix 4). Maker and others feared that when the last original allottee died, federal recognition of the Osage Tribe would die with them.[28]

Several Osage annuitants involved in the Osage National Council, including Billy Sam Fletcher, brought the issue of a preexisting Osage constitutional government to federal court again in 1990.[29] In 1992, the case resulted in a court-mandated process that created a new constitutional government, which was viewed by many as an amendment of the 1881 Osage Constitution. In October, the court formed the Osage Commission and ordered it to prepare a draft of a governing document to be presented to the Osage people for ratification. This organization was funded by the BIA and was required to consist of seven people: two current OTC elected officials, Fletcher and another Osage descendant from the 1906 roll, two members of the BIA, and an arbitrator. The Osage Commission conducted public hearings in eight states and fourteen cities and held a referendum vote requesting specific direction as to how the Osage people wanted to define national citizenship, protect the headright interests, and structure the new government. A majority of Osage voters, which included non-annuitant Osage descendants, approved the final 1994 Constitution, which created a three-part government with the legislative branch termed the National Council (see appendix 3). Since the 1994 Constitution was a court-mandated negotiation, the BIA had more authority than many Osage felt was appropriate. Additionally, given the role of the OTC in the negotiation, the OTC was left completely alone. The 1994 government assumed that the OTC would focus on the minerals and that the new National Council would handle all other Osage affairs.

Several problems quickly developed between the OTC and the National Council. First, there was no clear delineation of duties within the 1994 Constitution, and many departments, businesses, and individuals were uncertain which council to consult when issues arose. Because the OTC had managed affairs for so long, the challenges of changing to a new structure only further complicated these interactions. Another problem was that the buildings, equipment, and other possessions had ambiguous ownership, with the result that both sides made claims to them. A final problem arose when the OTC argued that the National Council was meddling in OTC affairs through the creation of laws that could potentially impact the Mineral Estate. During the 2004–6 reform process, these issues were still fresh for many Osage, who hoped that the new constitution would clearly spell out the duties of each group and thereby avoid these earlier problems. In a Pawhuska community meeting, for example, an Osage annuitant turned to this 1994 constitutional system to provide guidance for the 2004–6 reform:

> People who don't know their history are bound to live the same things over and over again. . . . I was on the tribal council with Mr. Red Eagle in 1994 when we had a constitution. . . . The tribal council was glad to shift all those responsibilities and duties over to the national council; we took care of the minerals. . . . But we've got to learn from mistakes. I am saying let's make sure the Osage Tribal Council does not break any rules of the National government. Let's make sure that the rules are written in such a way that that doesn't become necessary, because this was the downfall of our last government.[30]

Based on her experience of the relationship between the OTC and the National Council in 1994, this speaker articulates the need to have a clearly defined system for these two bodies so that they can function together.

In 1997, the 10th Circuit Court of Appeals reversed the 1992 ruling because the OTC had sovereign immunity and could not have its general governing powers stricken by the U.S. court system. In recognizing the OTC as the legitimate Osage government, this ruling extinguished the 1994 Osage Constitution and returned voting power solely to those holding a share in the Mineral Estate.[31] Meanwhile, because of the OTC's focus on the Mineral Estate, it lagged behind other American Indian nations in its development of casinos, language revitalization, and other national services. The OTC struggled to assert its full sovereignty primarily because of the long-standing threat to Osage authority. Instead, it focused on the most secure areas of its authority, such as the Mineral Estate and the management of federal grant monies.[32]

This tribal council structure, as with other American Indian nations, created an environment that focused on short-term rather than long-term progress. According to research by Stephen Cornell and Joseph Kalt, this lack of foresight often translates into a series of negative impacts,[33] many of which were evidenced by the Osage case. One of the most destructive impacts was nepotism, as relatives were hired who desperately needed work but were unqualified for the positions. This practice thus led to a decline in productivity, sustainability, and even to embezzlement. Another even more rampant problem involved planners focusing more on applying for whatever grants were available than on considering the long-term needs of the community; as a result, other organizations set the priorities for the Nation. This inadequate structure led to nepotism, micromanagement, and decreased internal and external confidence, which resulted in very few lasting successful projects. Cornell and Kalt conclude that this small council structure "is fatally flawed, it seldom works, and it should be abandoned."[34]

There was a large turnover of elected officials in 2002, when the OTC was again up for election. Jim Gray, who ran for chief, and many of the elected councilors ran primarily on a platform that sought to change the requirements for citizenship. The motivation for change was both the growing number of disenfranchised Osage, who had not yet or never would inherit the right to vote, and the lingering insistence by the BIA that the Osage Nation consisted only of the original allottees, only one of whom was still alive. Since the 1906 act very clearly stated that the Osage roll ended on July 1, 1907, there was a very real concern that the U.S. government might decide to dissolve recognition of the Osage Nation when the last person listed on the roll passed away. Given that there was only one original allottee left, this was an imminent problem. As Gray explained, "In a narrow interpretation of the 1906 law, you could have drawn the conclusion that only the original allottees were members of the tribe because they closed the rolls. So, obviously we wanted to expand that in any way we could."[35] According to Leonard Maker, the OTC originally wanted to pass a bill that only changed citizenship but left voting rights and governance tied to the headright system. The BIA, whose support was needed to pass the bill, discouraged such an approach, saying that all Osage citizens needed to be fully enfranchised and thus that a government separate from the OTC had to be created.[36]

The 31st Osage Tribal Council held community meetings and retained pro bono lawyer Wilson Pipestem to write the legislation and lobby Congress for a bill that would allow for not only citizenship reform but also the possibility for reforming the entire governmental structure. This process involved the OTC holding a sixty-day comment period during which it solicited feedback for reform. According to Gray, during this comment period the OTC gathered "broad consensus among the population": "You need to go beyond the membership criterion and really re-define in a large sense what the Osage nation will be for the next hundred years."[37] Out of this process came Public Law 108-431, "An Act to Reaffirm the Inherent Sovereign Rights of the Osage Tribe to Determine Its Membership and Form of Government," which was passed by the 108th U.S. Congress and signed into law in December 2004 (see appendix 5).

The Process

In May 2005 I concluded my pre-research obligations at the University of Florida and made the eighteen-hour drive across the southern United States to Oklahoma to begin my full-time research on the nascent Osage reform. This process had officially begun in February 2004, when the OTC appointed ten people to the Osage Government Reform Commission (OGRC). I had already returned to Oklahoma several times, receiving permission from the OTC to document the reform process and conducting interviews for the Osage Tribal Museum during the first annual Osage Sovereignty Day celebration in February. Before I was even fully settled into my parents' garage apartment in Skiatook, I began attending the weekly OTC meetings and talking to various Osage, including Leonard Maker and reform commissioner Priscilla Iba, about the initial progress of the reform. I was, however, nervous about meeting the rest of the members of the OGRC, who had yet to hear about my research project but whose willingness to give me access was essential to the success of my research.

As I parked in front of the large aluminum-sided structure, which looked much like the Alco building next door, I was not sure I had come to the right place. The sign on the Main Street of Pawhuska read, "American Legion Post 198," and there was no evidence of the Osage Nation's recent purchase of the building. The heavy metal doors opened into a large open room with concrete floors, florescent lighting, and long tables stacked with chairs. The walls were bare and looked like they had recently been primed for painting. To my immediate left was a door that had a printed sign, which read, "Osage Nation Cultural Center." When I poked my head in this door, I saw a woman working on a computer, and I asked if she knew where the OGCR was located. Without turning from the computer she pointed behind her, toward the back of the room. I lugged my camera equipment across the large room, weaving my way between the tables, until I came to a door in the back of the room with a small sign: "Welcome to the Osage Nation Government Reform office."

Three new desks sat in the corners of the room, and a long table with ten chairs took up most of the middle area. The walls were completely blank except for one lonely calendar, and the bookshelf and file cabinet stood empty. I approached a woman at the nearest desk and asked if I could be added to that day's agenda. She smiled and assured me that there would be time at the beginning of the meeting for public input. As I tentatively began setting up my camera, the commissioners and the official Osage Nation Tribal Museum videographer arrived, taking their positions. After commissioner Tony Daniels gave the opening prayer, Priscilla Iba, who was running the meeting in the absence of the chair of the OGRC, Billy Sam Fletcher, asked for any public comments.

When the only other visitor in attendance declined, I introduced my family, my research, and myself in what I hoped would be a convincing sell, stammering on about the importance of the process and the need for both a documentary video and a book memorializing this moment. Glancing nervously at each other, the commissioners were clearly less sure about the importance of such extensive documentation, especially the one-on-one interviews I was requesting. They already had one cameraman trained on all their public meetings and said they wanted to think about how involved they were going to be in my research project. Commissioner Joe Conner requested I let them review materials prior to publication, which I readily agreed to. At one point I stated that I was not looking to uncover any dirty secrets, but I was quickly cut off by Mary Joe Webb, who stated, "I don't mind telling my dirty secrets. Those are my good points," giving everyone a much-needed laugh. I awkwardly concluded that I believed the OGRC held a lot of knowledge, and that I wanted to take advantage of that knowledge as much as possible.

Turning back to face each other, the OGRC then began to work through the agenda they had in front of them. That day's meeting, like many that followed, jumped from topic to topic with little coherence. The members were clearly unsure of how the reform process should proceed or whether they shared any common ground from which to achieve the enormous task of surveying the Osage people and writing a constitution based on this feedback. One topic would be introduced, but discussion would quickly morph into another topic, as the commissioners struggled to make sense of everything that was at stake in this moment. In fact, it took the OGRC many months to begin working as a cohesive group and toward a common goal. Quickly, however, the members accepted my presence as their most tireless observer and as someone who could occasionally provide insight into what was happening around the nation, particularly at the OTC meetings that I was regularly attending.

From that first meeting, I was deeply skeptical about the potential success of the process. There were thirteen months remaining before the next OTC election, which seemed like a very short time frame in which to write a constitution, much less gain input from the Osage public about what this constitution ought to look like. Chief Jim Gray had set this time frame because of the upcoming election. While it is true that many American Indian governmental reforms have been stymied as a result of newly elected governing officials, it is also true that real community engagement takes time.[38] Governmental reform, particularly in Indian Country, most frequently starts with a document prepared by a lawyer or consultant and usually includes only a limited amount of citizen input.[39] From the start, Maker envisioned something different for the Osage. He hoped to create a process that would engage the Osage citizenry, but he felt the need to get it done while he had the support of the OTC, which he could be sure of only for another year.

In the interview I conducted with him before the reform plan was fully drafted, Maker spoke at length about his ideas for the reform process: "The best solution is obvious, it is a constitutional convention, where you have delegates who come representing the various groups of Osage on the reservation. Traditionalists, non-traditionalists, people who don't live on the reservation, shareholders, non-shareholders, young people, old people, all have the opportunity to participate."[40] However, by the time the plan was signed into law by the OTC, the section calling for a constitutional convention had been removed. Instead, it called for the creation of the OGRC, whose ten members were to be appointed by and accountable to the OTC.

When I asked Maker about these changes, he said that some of the OTC officials doubted that a random selection of Osage would be knowledgeable enough to write a constitution. Furthermore, they also felt the need to maintain some control over the reform process. As Maker told me in an interview: "Through the plan, they were delegating substantial authority to these members of the commission. And then the commission itself had to be people that the Council were comfortable with."[41] The OTC eventually decided to adopt a process whereby each council member nominated two Osage; the OTC then briefly discussed their capabilities and held a vote. From this process, the top ten were appointed to the commission. Mark Freeman, one member of the OTC, expressed his frustrations to me about this process, complaining that they had not taken enough time to make their selections.[42]

There were also tensions between Maker and the OTC over who the OGRC ought to include. The original governmental reform plan, designed by Maker, called for half of the OGRC to be annuitants and half to be non-annuitants. When Maker introduced this plan in front of the OTC, however, the OTC argued that it should instead focus on getting the best people for the job.[43] When all the members of the OGRC ended up being annuitants, it seemed more likely that the motivation for changing the comprehensive plan was a fear that non-annuitants, those who had not yet inherited or never would inherit a headright, might create a government that was somehow harmful to the Mineral Estate. While this move won the support of some Osage annuitants, it caused widespread concern that the OGRC did not accurately represent the wider population of potential voters.

This was neither the first, nor would it be the last, of the challenges the Osage Mineral Estate created for the 2004–6 Osage reform process. The OTC had spent the better part of the last hundred years catering to annuitants and focusing on the Mineral Estate. This legacy meant that most of the people participating in the reform process had a hard time even imagining the Osage Nation without the Osage Mineral Estate at its center. In an interview I conducted with Hepsi Barnett, the program coordinator for the OGRC, after the passage of the constitution, she argued:

> We could not get away from this issue with government reform—we couldn't. Ok, it was like, let's put this issue to rest; your shares are protected, they were protected by the Federal Government, they are protected by this constitution. So they are protected; end of story. In my mind there were so many other issues that I felt like, now we can move on, we can really wrestle with some of the finer details of how to make this three branch system Osage. But we never got there, and so in terms of the influences, that was the elephant in the room all the time. Regardless of how much education we attempted it was difficult to not always have the conversation come back to that.[44]

Whether it was a concern over the protection of their shares, or a concern about how decisions affecting the Mineral Estate would be made within the new government, or a concern about how this process might affect the stability of the relationship with the U.S. government, concerns surrounding the Mineral Estate dominated the process of reform.

The legacy of the Mineral Estate also worked to limit participation in the Osage reform process. Despite efforts made by the OGRC to involve the non-annuitant Osage, it was an uphill battle. In addition to feeling insufficiently represented by the OGRC, there was also a 100-year legacy of not being formally involved in the Osage Nation, of being told to "wait your turn." Because it was usually older Osage who had inherited headrights, the annuitant system had fostered alienation among younger Osage, as well as among Osage who would never become annuitants. Furthermore, because so much of the OGRC's community and business meetings was spent talking about the Mineral Estate, many non-annuitants grew frustrated with the process. Finally, college education and employment take many younger people away from the reservation, and the needs of young children further discouraged others. The problem of full citizen participation was not unique to the Osage reform process—it is the most-cited concern of American Indian and other governmental reformers.[45] The high poverty level among American Indians is also an inevitable contributor to these problems.[46]

These were not the only colonial entanglements that the OGRC had to navigate. Another fundamental obstacle was determining who was supposed to be included in the reform process. Given all the complexity involving the issue of citizenship, Maker's plan for reform did not clarify who was included in the phrase "the Osage People," but it did stipulate that the OGRC needed to create a registration process for the proposed constitutional referendum based on existing lists, which needed to be certified. These included "the CDIB [Certificate Degree of Indian Blood] list, membership list, newsletter list, [and] other lists."[47] Now that the U.S. Congress was no longer determining who participated in Osage politics, the OGRC had to decide the criteria for inclusion. As Maker pointed out during our first interview, "It is a chicken and egg question, who decides who the Osage are to participate [in the reform process]?"[48] For Maker, lineal descent from a past Osage population was the most obvious means of establishing citizenship. "Assuming that everybody, most of the 20,000 people that we say are of Osage descent, *are* of Osage descent, then those are the people we want to be represented."[49] The question for Maker, and other Osage, was whether or not everyone listed on the 1906 roll was really of Osage descent.

All members of the OGRC were middle-aged Osage annuitants residing in Oklahoma, but they came from many different backgrounds. The OGRC included Tony Daniels, a judge for the Miss Oklahoma pageant; Doug Revard, a retired Oklahoma district judge; Edward Lookout, the grandson of the last hereditary chief of the Osage; Joe L. Conner, a Ph.D. in experimental/clinical psychology; Jerri J. Branstetter, a corrections counselor; Billy Sam Fletcher, the primary litigant behind the 1994 Osage sovereignty case; Priscilla H. Iba, a teacher of the Osage language who volunteered at the Osage Tribal Museum; Mary Joe Webb, a member of the Tulsa Catholic Diocese Synod Commission; Charles H. Red Corn, an award-winning novelist; and Jim Norris, a retired senior Health Services officer for the Indian Health Service.[50] With such vastly different life experiences, it would be months before the commissioners learned to trust each other and value the different skills they each offered.

When the OGRC began its process, it was handed the Comprehensive Plan developed by Maker and passed unanimously as an ordinance by the OTC, which made it law. Some of the commissioners went so far as to joke that Maker had also written a constitution, which he would hand over to them when it was time. This kind of humor reveals the sense in which some of the commissioners initially felt that the reform process was outside of their control. This was also evidenced by the resentment among the commissioners as well as the confusion about their precise role in the process. Maker recognized early on that this had become a problem for the OGRC, telling me in an interview: "One of the first issues was that the Commission itself was unaware the extent to which they had been authorized to carry out the project. . . . I think there was uncertainty for about a month on their role, and to a certain extent they are still trying to decide whether or not they are a policy making body or whether they are a hands-on management entity."[51] This uncertainty manifested itself most often in long circular debates over issues either too large or too small to be dealt with by the ten-member commission. The most famous of these was what was termed their "meat pie" debate—a two-hour debate early in the process over what food ought to be served at the community meetings.

The one issue most frequently returned to was how the OGRC should best go about the process of engaging the Osage people. In many of the early meetings and informal discussions, it debated the possibility of hosting a convention. Once, when Maker was in attendance, he quickly interrupted, saying, "That's why I laid out some guidelines in the plan, so whoever got on the Commission would be guided, in a sense. Down the road, it's already there; the milestones are already there. We're not going to argue about whether or not we are going to have a constitutional convention. Those decisions were already made by the Council when they decided to go down this road."[52] In insisting on sticking with the plan, Maker hoped to keep the process moving forward. He had developed the plan and had been charged by the OTC with keeping an eye on the OGRC, and he frequently expressed his frustration with the OGRC for spending so much time debating the process. The commissioners, however, had not been part of the earlier discussions about the reform and were struggling to understand how they might take ownership of the process.

The first major task before the OGRC was the "June packet," a mailer designed to inform the Osage public about the reform process and educate them on the various possibilities for Osage Nation governance and citizenship. As part of Maker's plan, the OGRC was instructed to "develop informational materials pertaining to the Osage government and the issues involved in the reform process for dissemination and distribution to prospective voters." The problems with the June packet were so difficult that it did not end up being distributed until September, and then only as part of a larger *Osage News* edition, in which government reform was among many other subjects covered.

When several members of the OGRC initially began drafting the June packet, it quickly became clear that the group did not yet have the trust necessary to delegate tasks. In a business meeting immediately prior to the May 12, 2005, community meeting in Skiatook, Oklahoma, several of the group members were accused of trying to do all the work themselves and of excluding others from participation. This small group had wanted to get the process of writing the packet materials under way, but others felt they had not gone through the proper channels to take the work on themselves. This divide was further complicated by group differences in education, residence on and off the reservation, racial phenotypes, and members' connection to Osage cultural practices. This lack of trust stopped the writing of the June packet altogether and led some members of the OGRC to insist, with little result, that Maker should write these documents himself.

The OGRC was still struggling to get the newsletter off the ground when Hepsi Barnett was finally brought on board in June as the program coordinator for the OGRC. Since receiving her master's degree in public administration from Harvard's Kennedy School of Government, Barnett had been working as a project manager at the New Mexico State

Supreme Court. She was, in addition, a non-annuitant Osage descendant from Fairfax, Oklahoma, and thus she had much to offer the commission. Slightly younger than most of the commissioners, Barnett brought much-needed optimism and persistence to the reform process. Throughout her time as the program coordinator, she worked tirelessly to see the process through.

On June 11, 2005, Barnett called a working session, which was not advertised as a regular business meeting and thus was not open to the public. As a result, it came to be known as "the secret meeting." This represented one of the first, but certainly not the last, conflicts between Maker and Barnett. Maker strongly supported holding open meetings, knowing that the Osage public would quickly grow skeptical of a process that was happening behind closed doors. Barnett, however, intended this meeting to build group cohesion and felt that a closed meeting was needed to ease concerns among the commissioners and build a productive environment. Having worked on the Harvard Project on American Indian Economic Development, Barnett felt strongly that what the commissioners needed was some time alone to develop a positive rapport.[53]

When I arrived at the meeting, I was told that I was welcome to stay but that it would benefit the whole group to have some time off-camera. Barnett began the meeting with a discussion of the newsletter. As was the trend with the OGRC's prior discussions, the commissioners quickly lost focus by delving into a larger discussion of what it would mean for the Osage Nation to take full control over the Osage reservation, including the Osage County court and educational systems. Barnett, in what would become her mantra for the reform process, pointed out that these were not the issues that a constitution had to decide; it just had to leave possibilities open for future lawmakers. The commissioners were, however, not persuaded, and they continued their discussions about the reservation. After a few minutes, Barnett again broke in, this time with a planned activity.

Barnett divided the group, including me, into two sides and gave each person a number from one to three, which referred to the following questions: "1. What specifically can the OGRC do, or what is needed, to ensure that the objectives in the comprehensive plan are met? 2. What reform issues require more attention and why? 3. What are the strengths that you bring to this process and how can they better be utilized?" From this prompt, we each took turns asking the person across from us our assigned question and answering their question in turn, before moving down the line. This strategy introduced many ideas that were later used in the formation of working groups. At the time of the meeting, however, it was anything but a breakthrough. After the exercise, the commissioners' discussion immediately returned to their deep-seated skepticism about the process, particularly the difficulty of raising public interest and accomplishing their tasks within such a short period.

One of the commissioners, echoing others, said, "What happens here is going to last and that is what scares me. I don't see the point in doing this in a year. We can do it, but it is too big to rush through. I drive home after every meeting saying, 'This is my last.'" This brought a huge laugh and many nodding heads from around the room. Barnett responded by arguing that from the current discussion it was clear that the resources brought to the table by those sitting around the room were as valuable as any group that could be assembled. She also argued that the constitution only needed to be "bare bones" and that the rest of the government would be filled in by legislation. Once again the commissioners balked, saying there was neither time nor public interest and that there was too much at stake.

Until this time, Priscilla Iba had been quiet, but now she turned slowly to the group and said, "I don't intend to fail. We have all sat around like trained monkeys, but now it is crunch time." The confidence and critique in her statement silenced the room and led to a palpable realization that it was time to either give up on the process altogether or put the full force of their effort behind making the reform successful. Revard agreed, saying, "We have to quit being so emotional. We need to take the bull by the horns and treat this like a business." The commissioners then agreed that working groups would be the best way to divide up the immense amount of work and move forward.

This agreement alone, however, did not provide the full confidence necessary to complete the process. The OGRC still needed to actually begin the work in earnest. On June 20, 2005, the OGRC held a business meeting in which the June packet was again on the agenda:

COMMISSIONER 1: Our next item on our business meeting is the June packet. Anybody have any input?

C2: It was my understanding we would all receive copies of what was going in by email. I didn't receive anything. So I think we have to table that issue until Leonard [Maker] gets back. He was going to prepare them and deliver them to us and we don't have them.

C1: So the June packet—we will table that until our next meeting or when Leonard gets back. We'll move forward then to the survey.

C3: I did bring some possible questions. I think that whatever's going on we have to start working on it whether it's in groups or whatever. It's going to need to go on. I think it's something we can be working on while other things are going on.[54]

This seemingly mundane negotiation was actually a significant turning point for the OGRC, as it began taking ownership of the reform process and building trust among the members. In taking over the work and not waiting on Maker to deliver the material, the OGRC slowly gained the momentum necessary to complete the daunting task of writing a constitution based on citizen feedback. Over time, members gained enough confidence to actually change the reform plan, adding a referendum that gave Osage voters a choice on the major issues within the constitution, including blood quantum, the role of the Mineral Estate, and the tripartite government structure (see appendix 6).

Buying into the process was just the first step; the commissioners were then left with not only completing the process but also convincing the majority of Osage voters that their concerns had been taken seriously during the process. One of the first and most enduring challenges was in explaining why there would not be a constitutional convention. During a meeting for Osage employees to discuss the upcoming referendum vote, one of the program directors said that these questions should have been created within a constitutional convention rather than by the members of the OGRC themselves. In response, one of the commissioners stated, "We are having this referendum vote in lieu of a constitutional convention because of the deadline we were given to get this process done. Our alternatives have been to give people surveys, public forums, and this referendum. And then in February, there will be a vote on the ratification of the constitution that will contain these elements."[55] The Osage public generally supported reform but were skeptical of the process, a skepticism that was rooted, as the remainder of this book will show, in the authority at stake in reform.

Concerns about the concentration of authority and representation are endemic to reform efforts, particularly when written documents such as constitutions are the intended end product. The difficulty of obtaining true and enthusiastic community involvement has plagued many recent constitutional reforms in Indian Country, including that of the Cherokee

Nation of Oklahoma, the Hualapai Nation, and the Northern Cheyenne Tribe. Even when the constitutional convention model is used, Eric Lemont reports that "almost uniformly, tribal members relate that they either were unaware that their nation was undertaking governmental or constitution reform or did not feel there was an appropriate forum within which to learn and comment on the process."[56] While there are strategies for increased community engagement, such as the negotiated rulemaking model,[57] these are very time consuming and would have a hard time working in diverse and far-flung communities, especially when the populations exceed a couple thousand.[58]

Governmental reform is inevitably going to privilege certain perspectives. In this way, constitutions must be understood not as the holistic narrative of a people but as, at best, a negotiated rendering of many highly contested and shifting debates. In the case of the Osage and other colonialized nations, these debates become even harder to navigate. A lack of trust, histories of exploitation, mistrust of governments, limited faith in one's own capacities, jealousies, and disenfranchisement from full governing authority have all weakened American Indian nations' potential for successful reform, not to mention actual governance.[59]

In an attempt to deal with these obstacles, Maker's plan called for the development of informational materials and a website, as well as the use of community meetings, workshops, symposia, and a survey to "solicit citizen suggestions and recommendations."[60] While the OGRC would eventually circulate a questionnaire, design a webpage, hold a referendum vote, and conduct a legal symposium, much of the feedback it received came from the community meetings it hosted across Oklahoma, Texas, and California. The OTC had a long history of holding these "community meetings" in order to communicate with the dispersed Osage headright holders, particularly during elections, when feedback was desired, or when a contentious issue needed to be addressed. During the reform process, these community meetings were intended to serve the dual purpose of informing potential Osage citizens about the reform process while also gathering opinions about what they wanted to see in government reform. Given that these meetings had a long tradition among the headright holders, and that these annuitants had much to lose in terms of their quarterly payments and authority, it is not surprising that they formed the majority of the attendees.

The OGRC hosted over forty community meetings, each of which lasted approximately two hours. Occasionally, its job was easy, as when participants had prepared their comments or even researched solutions to the issues the reform was trying to address. More frequently, however, the audience was not aware of the topics being covered ahead of time and expected that the community meeting was going to be more of an information session than an opportunity for citizen participation. One younger non-annuitant expressed his frustration with the progress of one community meeting in the following exchange:

> M1: I get tired of hearing all these people talk about losing their headrights or blood quantum. I want to see something happen. I'm 33 years old and we've been talking about this as long as I can remember.
> COMMISSIONER 1: What do you want to happen?
> M1: I want this to hurry up.
> C2: Talk to us. Tell us what you want. We don't know if you don't talk.
> M1: You're talking about this government. Not all of us are understanding the various governments that are possible, the constitution versus what you've got now?
> C3: Resolution.
> M1: Right. So how can we tell you what we want when we don't know what it is? I don't have anything to say. I know a constitutional government is made up of three branches, but that's pretty much all I know about it. So how can I talk to you about something if I don't even know about it?[61]

Because the Osage population was not given guidelines on how to prepare for these meetings, meeting participants were often only able to offer spontaneous reactions rather than informed opinions. Many of these meetings became little more than listening sessions, which did not allow for ample consultation and engagement. Since the pertinent material, such as possible options for an Osage governance structure, was not available prior to the community meetings, participants in these meetings tended to give only vague responses, especially during the early stages of the reform process.

In order to hear from as many voices as possible, the OGRC decided to limit the time of each individual's comments. When they attempted to enforce time limits, however, the commissioners were frequently met with opposition, since it is customary for Osage elders to use interrelated and sometimes drawn-out stories rather than to speak in succinct sound bites. One elder was stopped mid-sentence and mid-thought when he heard the buzzer signaling the conclusion of his allotted time. Others in the audience offered up their time to let him finish, but the elder insisted on sitting down, illustrating that such time limits were inappropriate and damaging to the process.

One member of the OGRC described these community meetings as both the most challenging and the most rewarding part of the reform process: "It was really challenging to sit through some of those town meetings and just be hit up side of the head every once in a while with criticism and with negative statements. I hadn't dealt with that much criticism before."[62] As illustrated by the health care town hall meetings held by members of the U.S. Congress in the summer of 2009, the community meeting format sometimes creates a venue that is dominated by the loudest and most critical voices. During the Osage reform process, these voices were usually those of the annuitants, who stood to benefit the most from maintaining the status quo and who thus attempted to use the community meeting format to derail the reform effort.

While community meetings can sometimes be hijacked by the loudest voices in the room, they can also offer an important space for a critique of the process itself. At a community meeting in Hominy, Oklahoma, immediately before the passage of the 2006 Osage Nation Constitution, a well-respected Osage elder who had served many years on the OTC stood up and gave a fifteen-minute speech about the problems he saw with the reform process, touching on a wide range of issues, from the confusion about the elements of the potential constitution to how the OTC had served the Osage well for generations. Referring to the constitution, he stated, "I can't see that its going to help us any better. It will make conflict among the people."[63] While it would be easy to dismiss the rambling speeches and insufficiently supported arguments that are a part of the community meeting format, these statements frequently mark a deeper angst that has to be addressed if a constitution is going to gain popular support. This elder's predictions of confusion and division among the Osage under the new system have proven prescient. Short of abandoning reform altogether, however, such testimonies gave few ways for the OGRC to move forward, making the community meeting a challenging forum for constitutional reform.

Several years later, Maker acknowledged the problems with these meetings, saying that he had hoped that the commissioners would turn to specialists for help rather than relying so heavily on the community meetings for input. He saw these meetings more as informational sessions than as opportunities to gather substantive feedback.[64] This process did allow, if not completely ensure, a substantial amount of community engagement, in the sense that anyone was welcome to come and give his or her opinion, and well over a thousand people did. Many aspects of the 2006 Osage Constitution, including the structure of the government and the criteria for citizenship, did follow more or less directly the wishes of the majority of Osage who spoke at the community meetings. There were, of course, many other opinions that called for other ways of imagining the twenty-first-century Osage Nation that were not included in the constitution.

In addition to the community meetings, the OGRC circulated a questionnaire, which was mailed out to all descendants of the 1906 roll who had addresses listed with the Osage Nation, which consisted, at the time, of approximately 7,000 people. Of these, 1,378 filled out at least a portion of the thirty yes-or-no questions and the three additional comment sections. Almost all of the issues on the questionnaire, including whether or not government reform was needed, had a clear majority support.[65] Some of this, however, was a result of the wording of the question, which reflected the fact that the commissioners were nonspecialists. For example, question number two asked: "Are you in favor of a representative democracy with a 3 (Executive, Legislative, Judicial) branch form of government?" This was followed by question number three: "If you answered 'NO' to question 2, what form of government do you prefer?" With this wording, the tripartite form of government was the only real option provided. In the way the questions were framed, it seemed apparent that the designers of the reform process already had particular models for governance in mind.

Barnett and the commissioners, hoping for additional community guidance, decided to add in a referendum vote. Maker argued vigorously against this addition, saying it would delay the process and add the unneeded expense of another election. Instead, Maker proposed a phone poll, which he ended up conducting through an Oklahoma University–based polling group, going over the head of the OGRC and instead gaining approval directly from the OTC. In addition, he hired professionals to help him revise the questions drafted by the OGRC. Maker argued the phone poll could help him reach the non-annuitant view, which had not yet been fully assessed in the reform process. Maker delivered the results of the phone poll in a report on the progress of the OGRC in which he criticized members for their slow progress, circular discussions, and noncompliance with the reform plan. He went on to suggest the formation of independent youth and constitution-writing committees to complete the remainder of the work. The results of the phone poll, as related in the report, were different from the questionnaire results, with significantly more respondents wanting Osage officials to reside on the reservation, in addition to a minimum blood quantum for citizens—two proposals that Maker himself supported. The circumstances surrounding the phone poll made Barnett and the commissioners deeply skeptical not only of the poll's results but also of Maker's relationship to the process.

This moment became the breaking point between Maker and the members of the OGRC, as they requested that the OTC relieve him of his duties as their liaison to the OTC. Maker, for his part, was convinced, based on the results of the phone poll, that a large majority of Osage would support the constitutional reform and as a result began focusing his attention on the transition process. Barnett and the commissioners persuaded the OTC to fund the referendum vote, citing the need for more official citizen engagement; 1,650 people participated in the referendum vote and showed clear support for all but one of the sixteen questions. Not surprisingly, the one issue still without clear consensus was how the Osage Mineral Estate was going to be handled in the new government. The OGRC conducted another round of community meetings in an attempt to deal with this issue and sought the opinion of twelve Osage lawyers in a legal symposium on December 16, 2005.

Beginning on January 6, 2006, the OGRC, its staff, and several consultants, including Osage lawyers and elders, gathered for a three-day writing retreat in a Tulsa, Oklahoma, hotel. In preparation for the retreat, Barnett had hoped that the OGRC's working groups would each draft portions and that she would be able to combine those parts into a draft constitution. As in the writing of the referendum questions, however, the commissioners used the committee meetings more as spaces for debate and research and as a sounding board for various perspectives than as drafting sessions. Some materials did come out of these sessions, including suggestions on how the three branches would function. Several of the individual commissioners also wrote and submitted various pieces for consideration.[66] Barnett then created the first draft of the constitution by combining these materials, other constitutions, the referendum results, information from the community meetings, and documents, including draft constitutions, submitted by various Osage.[67] Many of the sections of this draft constitution had multiple options, and little was in a formally written state.

At the writing retreat, and in the weeks that followed in Pawhuska, the commissioners, Barnett, and various consultants sat around a table with this draft projected on a screen in front of them. They debated its contents line by line, rewriting as they went. Most of the commissioners were present for the entire month-long writing process, and other individuals came and went, adding their opinions to the group writing process. In between each session, Barnett and the lawyers for the OGRC spent countless hours compiling the decisions made in the large group and working out exact details. The entire drafting process took place within the span of three weeks, with several of the sessions including five or six hours of debate on topics ranging from simple word choice to more complicated discussions of how the judicial branch should be organized.

From the very beginning of the reform process, several Osage had expressed an interest in writing the preamble, and they had each submitted their drafts to Commissioner Charles Red Corn, who had agreed to compile their efforts into a single draft version. At the beginning of the meeting slated to draft the preamble, Red Corn stated: "On the first couple of paragraphs, I wrote that more in the form of poetry than following grammar and I sent it to some poets and to writers and none of them really had a problem with it. . . . They all thought it was very well put together and they understand that if you're going to put the restraints of grammar [in] you're going to lose a lot of feeling and a lot of meaning."[68] Later in the meeting, however, it became clear that, much like the rest of the constitution writing process, each word was going to be scrutinized by everyone present, including myself:

> PARTICIPANT 1: Would it read well if we took the "ing" off "acknowledging"?
>
> P2: I think that goes with "giving thanks for their strength." The trouble with that is that "acknowledging" might be the only way we can start this next part. We're going to acknowledge that 1881 constitution and acknowledge some other things. It depends on how we can come up with this next . . .
>
> JEAN DENNISON: Can we end it with "giving thanks for their wisdom and strength" and then add "acknowledging our ancient tribal orders" in the next sentence?[69]
>
> P3: That's the way it was and [P1] changed it.

P1: You can start a new sentence with "We give thanks."
P4: I want to say that through this constitution, I would just start
   with how it was done where it says "paying homage."[70]

In addition to illustrating how I was occasionally caught up in the process, this excerpt is also a typical example of the problems that develop when trying to write any document as a group. While it was helpful to discuss larger concepts in groups, the actual writing was a very challenging and time-consuming process. In this dialogue, the participants in the writing process are not only dealing with larger issues, such as how to acknowledge the 1906 act, but are also attempting, in a large group, to deal with the style of the writing.

Out of this process came a document that at times lacked elegance. It was, however, reflective of the majority of opinions expressed by Osage participating in the reform process. On March 11, 2006, the OGRC hosted a vote, with 1,454 people voting for the constitution and 728 voting against it, leading to the passage of the 2006 Constitution by a majority of 66 percent (see appendix 7). After the passage of the constitution, it became clear that there was a vocal minority, consisting primarily of members of the Osage Shareholders Association (OSA), who were going to continue to discredit the new constitution. The OSA was created as a watchdog group to monitor the Mineral Estate and the distribution of its proceeds. Only a very small percentage of Osage annuitants were members of the OSA, and even fewer regularly attended its meetings or agreed with the severity of its politics. Those active in the OSA tended to be cynical about Osage governance in general, a fact only heightened by fears that a change in the governing structure would, if not directly then certainly indirectly, change the dynamics of authority and threaten the proceeds they currently received from mineral production on reservation lands. During the reform process, one headright paid around $6,000 a quarter, and so, depending on the percentage of one's headright(s), this could represent a substantial amount of income for an individual.

Members of this group cited a range of problems with the reform process, including low voter turnout, the problematic distribution of absentee ballots and other election materials, and, of crucial importance, a fundamental disagreement with the way the Mineral Estate was incorporated into the 2006 Osage Constitution.[71] On the OSA online forum, these issues led some Osage to call for restarting the process, arguing that merely amending the 2006 Constitution would not sufficiently address the document's problems.[72] Furthermore, some of these postings expressed a concern that the bar for creating amendments to the constitution was set too high and used this as a reason to call for restarting the process. As the constitution states, "Every petition shall include the full text of the proposed amendment, and be signed by qualified electors of the Osage Nation equal in number to at least twenty-five (25%) percent of the electorate." However, since the electorate consists of every person with a membership card in the Osage Nation, which in 2011 had exceeded 15,000 card-carrying citizens, only 2,182 of whom had voted in the 2006 election, many people found the possibility of an amendment by petition unlikely.

These obstacles are not unique to the Osage reform process but are common problems in governmental reform efforts, particularly when dealing with such powerful forces as the ongoing settler colonial process inevitably creates. As Americans continue to settle the territory of the United States, they utilize a host of strategies that attempt to deny the continued presence of indigenous authority over the land.[73] The Osage case provides insight into how one group grappled with the fundamental questions in all political assemblages, those of belonging and authority, given this external struggle for territorial control. The following chapters will explore four areas on which Osage debates centered: blood, culture, minerals, and sovereignty. Each chapter will focus on how various Osage articulated their hopes for the future of the Osage Nation, the entanglements created by the settler colonial process, and how the writers of the constitution coalesced these ideas into the 2006 Constitution.

Chapter 2 **Blood**

ALL LINEAL DESCENDENTS OF THOSE OSAGES LISTED ON THE 1906 ROLL ARE ELIGIBLE FOR MEMBERSHIP IN THE OSAGE NATION

BLOOD

On July 1, 2005, I arrived, as usual, at the Osage Tribal Council chambers just before 9:00 A.M. The over-air-conditioned wood-paneled room where the OTC's meetings were held had a domed ceiling with a skylight, a state-of-the-art recording system, and murals covering the walls. The murals were intended to tell the history of the Osage from past to present. They started on the left with the children of the sky coming from the stars and joining the people of the land, water, and earth in a move to a new territory. They ended with Osage of various phenotypes and dress standing in front of the OTC building itself.

Drawing out my pen and paper to take notes on the day's affairs, I found my seat in the small audience section, where folding chairs had been set facing the u-shaped tables for the councilors. Most of the other people in attendance were program directors, who were there to give their monthly reports to the OTC. The program directors generally used these meetings to update the OTC about the developments in their programs, but they also occasionally asked for additional funds, gained approval of grants in progress, or sought guidance on personnel or other problems they were having. At each Monday committee meeting, the OTC heard from the various Osage Nation programs, which were spread out evenly throughout the month.[1] Any issue requiring additional funds or a change in policy would then be voted on during the next bimonthly Wednesday business meeting.

As soon as the day's committee meeting was convened and the prayer said, the Certificate Degree of Indian Blood (CDIB) Department asked for an executive session, requiring all nonelected officials to leave the room.[2] Waiting out the forty-five-minute executive session, which we had been told would be no more than five minutes, several of the program directors and I discussed the progress of their programs, their frustration with the council-style governing structure, and what the CDIB Department could possibly be up to. They were indignant about the way the OTC micromanaged their affairs and demanded that they wait, often for over half the day, to give their monthly reports. They complained that problems were only addressed after they had fully developed and that there was no mechanism for Nation-wide strategic planning. We guessed that the executive session had something to do with a rogue CDIB employee, since personnel issues were the main reason executive sessions were usually held.[3] It turned out we were only partially correct.

I was later told by various sources that this meeting was called because the Bureau of Indian Affairs (BIA) was no longer signing the CDIB cards of those descendants whose ancestors were listed in the 1906 roll but who were believed not to have Osage blood. This was particularly significant since, shortly after the Office of Indian Affairs (OIA) created the 1906 roll, Osage leaders went before the secretary of the interior as part of a formal hearing to dispute 200 of the names listed on the roll based on lack of connection to the Osage Nation. Some of these individuals had moved off the reservation, while others were Indians from other Nations, such as the Kaw. The Osage leaders argued that these names had been fraudulently added to the roll in order to gain access to Osage lands and other resources, but the appeal was not sustained. The current OTC was thus left with the dilemma of whether or not to act on this opportunity, which appeared to confirm that the OIA's roll had been wrong since 1906. If true, the federal government could be held responsible for massive losses of land and Mineral Estate proceeds that had gone to "non-Osage" allottees and their descendants.

In the following weeks, the OTC met repeatedly with the Osage Government Reform Commission (OGRC) about the list of "non-blooded Osage," trying to decide if and how this would impact the list of Osage eligible to participate in the reform process. Through conversations with the Osage BIA superintendent, the OTC eventually realized that there had not been any change in BIA policy. It was determined that an Osage woman in the Osage CDIB Department had begun inserting the word "adopted" on CDIB card applications when she had evidence that the ancestor had not had Osage blood, either because they had been adopted into the Nation prior to allotment or because they had been placed on the 1906 roll "fraudulently." When the BIA superintendent of the Osage Nation received these CDIB applications, she refused to sign them because of this insertion, not realizing that these people were lineal descendants of those listed on the 1906 roll. As a result, this policy caused weeks of consternation not only for the OTC but also for the OGRC, which was trying to determine the voting requirements for the November referendum election. This single issue, in fact, stymied the OGRC, leading to months of circular discussions about whether Osage blood was an essential aspect of being Osage and how this blood could best be traced.

Clustered around the long table in their Pawhuska office, the OGRC members frequently debated the importance of Osage blood. This issue was at the center of all discussions about whom the commissioners were supposed to represent, who should be eligible to vote, and ultimately, what the constitutional requirements for citizenship would be. While few of the commissioners openly questioned the centrality of blood, Chair Billy Sam Fletcher, one of the last remaining Osage full-bloods, frequently expressed his concern with a strictly biological definition of Osage citizenship. In response to another commissioner's comment—"You should have Osage blood to be an Osage. That speaks for itself"—Fletcher pointed out that,

> in times past, Osage on the battlefield didn't kill children; they brought them home and adopted them. A lot of our Osage people are descendants of those encounters. Some people recognize that. My parents always told me there were people who were Osage [because] their ancestors were taken in a battle when they were children. In my own mind I didn't have any conflict if that was the case. And the descendants of those people had been on the allotment rolls. . . . In my own mind, if you adopt a child, like Korean or Vietnamese children, they become citizens of the United States by their adoption and it doesn't matter where they are. So if you adopt this child as your very own, then that's fine.[4]

Fletcher is here arguing that a shared biological relationship is not fundamental to the creation of an Osage citizen. In making his case, he venerates past practices of Osage incorporation as well as the citizenship criteria of the United States. Such uses of the United States as a model are also telling because they give evidence of the fact that for many Osage the United States maintains authority as *the* nation to emulate.

Before Fletcher had finished his comments, however, several of the reform commissioners interrupted and responded in unison, "But is that person really Osage," insisting on the importance of a shared bloodline in the creation of Osage citizens.

This debate over who qualified to vote in the upcoming November referendum was fundamentally about how the Osage Nation should be bounded. All nations struggle to delineate their citizens, particularly in moments of reconstitution. Blood, biology, and race have often played a significant role in this process. Antoinette Burton and others have amply demonstrated that "a blurring of the vocabularies of nationality and race is a founding strategy of the modern [nation] state and, as such, it should be impossible to inquire into the modern state without attending to its creation in a global context of colonialism and racism."[5] Many nations across the globe have racial components in their founding narratives and/ or in their current immigration policies. Race works to build cohesion and solidarity, fusing a diverse group along powerful, if fictive, understandings of biological unity.

In addition, the indigenous body has long been a site of colonial power, where race served to justify colonization, giving existing notions of inferiority and savagery scientific authority. The ongoing process of settler colonization continues to use race, if in more subtle ways. In the insistence that indigenous populations are primarily a group marked by biology, rather than a polity with control over a territory, settlers are able to further entrench their own claims over the land. Through such processes of colonial entanglement, the indigenous body has become a site of consequence and contestation.[6]

Through its issuance of CDIB cards, the BIA certifies not only who is of Osage descent but also how much blood each individual has according to its own records. This model of lineal descent endows those people on the 1906 roll with a fundamental substance that can only be passed to biological kin. For the purposes of American Indians, this substance is almost always referred to as "blood." "Blood" has a long and highly contested history and must be understood as a shape-shifting discourse that sometimes furthers the project of conquest, specifically in the ways it masks the colonial power dynamics at work. At other times, however, American Indians deploy blood in more complex and perhaps even anticolonial ways, which work to undermine an easy reading of this metaphorical substance.[7]

In these debates, it is important to think of blood less as a physical substance and more as a phenomenon. Bruno Latour writes about such phenomena: "When a phenomenon 'definitely' exists this does not mean that it exists forever, or independently of all practice and discipline, but that it has been entrenched in a costly and massive institution that has to be monitored and protected with great care."[8] In this way, blood is certainly a phenomenon that continues to exist and is used by many different institutions. Discourses use blood in diverse ways, connecting it to various regimes of power, privilege, and belonging. The deployment of blood takes multiple forms and often works on multiple registers at once. Today, an understanding of blood as the material by which physical traits are passed from one generation to the next no longer has full scientific legitimacy. Genes have generally come to take blood's place as a marker of heredity and as a source of scientific inquiry. For many people across the globe, however, blood still has real authority as a marker of citizen bodies. In order to make sense of this power in the context of the Osage Nation, I will here scrutinize the various discourses surrounding blood.

While refusing to accept these deployments as either natural or spurious, I will investigate how various discourses of blood were intertwined in the debate about what the constitution of an Osage Nation should include in the twenty-first century. During the 2004–6 Osage reform process, blood played a dominant role in defining the Osage Nation through the creation of an Osage constituency. Blood is, however, not an inevitable way of defining citizens, indigenous or otherwise. This chapter will trace this concept of blood, including its historical roots in the colonial process, its connection to discourses of race and nation, and its use within the 2006 Osage Nation Constitution.

The Phenomenon of Blood

Historian John Joseph Mathews, who was born in 1895 to a Euro-American father and an Osage mother, recorded the most frequently told Osage origin story in the following way: "When the newly-arrived-upon-earth children of the sky, represented by the *Wah-Sha-She*, the Water People, the sub-*Hunkah*, the Land People, and the grand division the *Tzi-Sho*, the Sky People, came upon the Isolated Earth People, the indigenous ones, the four groups formed a tribal unit, and were anxious to lead the Isolated Earth People away from the earth-ugliness of their village, saying that they were thus taking them to a 'new country.'"[9] This origin story does not attempt to create a single lineage for the Osage people but speaks instead about the unification of four separate groups. This Osage origin story does not privilege a single shared body or a unifying substance but instead a process of unification through a shared change in location. Here it is the country or territory that is used as the primary marker of inclusion.

In determining Osage citizenship, the Osage also cite Francis La Flesche, a citizen of the Omaha Nation who conducted research on the Osage around the turn of the twentieth century. According to La Flesche, an individual was Osage by virtue of citizenship in one of the Osage fireplaces (also referred to as clans), which one could either inherit from one's father or be adopted into. La Flesche documents various ceremonies, including a process by which a *dá-gthe* (war captive) becomes a *Shó-ka* (ceremonial messenger) and a part of the group: "The *dá-gthe* becomes a member of the family of his captor and of his gens [people related through their male ancestors]. He can marry within the tribe, and because of his ceremonial office (tribal *Shó-ka*) he is respected and honored and is always welcome at the 'table' of every family in the tribe. He is clothed as well as fed by the families of the tribe and is regarded and spoken of as *Ó-xta*, one who is a favored person."[10] According to Osage historian Willard H. Rollings, when outsiders were adopted they were placed into one of the twenty-four clans, which meant that if they had children they would be considered part of the clan, and thus of the group as a whole, in the same way as other Osage children.[11]

From these historians, it is clear that the biological relationship between parent and child has not been the sole method used to establish Osage citizenship. Instead, one's location within a clan-based governance structure was of primary importance, but so too was one's residence within Osage-controlled territory. In his book on customs and myth, Louis Burns writes at length about the ceremony surrounding adoption and its symbolism as a "new birth." He argues that adoption was common, leading to rapid population growth during periods of geographic expansion and warfare.[12] One recorded example of such an expansion occurred in about 1812, when five lodges of Missouris, a total of about 100 people, fled an ongoing war with the Sac and Fox and joined the Osage.[13]

The development of racial ideologies came out of simultaneous changes in economy, religion, and world structure but can be most clearly tied to the colonial process.[14] Following Albert Memmi, Jean-Paul Sartre, and Ronald T. Takaki, Ann Stoler writes: "Racism is an inherent product of the colonial encounter, fundamental to an otherwise illegitimate access to property and power."[15] In the colonial process, race serves to create differently shaped bodies, including the civilized European body and the primitive indigenous body. These bodies developed through the growing fields of biology, economics, religion, literature, and social science. Fundamental to this idea of race was the concept of blood, which was believed to literally transmit racial qualities from one generation to the next. Blood eventually came to function as the central mechanism through which supposed biological, religious, economic, and political traits were passed from one generation to the next.[16]

"Blood mixing" became a central quandary of early American colonialists, as it did in other colonial contexts, as a result of the profound differences assumed about primitive and civilized bodies. Essential to discourses such as manifest destiny, which argued that whites had been destined by God to civilize the entire American continent, is the notion that American Indians are primitives, not capable of properly owning or developing land. While early settlers thought American Indians too could be civilized, scientific notions of the nineteenth century worked to further entrench notions of savagery as biological, and thus immutable.

Race worked its way into the most personal human moments, affecting not just notions of citizenship but also sexual relations, love, and marriage.[17] Unlike African blood, which was firmly believed to have a "polluting" nature, there was a vigorous debate about the need for, or avoidance of, American Indian blood mixing.[18] In the early nineteenth century, "interbreeding" with Indians became a political strategy through which complete colonization seemed possible. President Thomas Jefferson was one supporter of this approach. In an 1803 letter to Benjamin Hawkins about the Muscogee Creek Indians, he wrote: "In truth, the ultimate point of rest and happiness for them is to let our settlement and theirs meet and blend together, to intermix, and become one people. Incorporating themselves with us as citizens of the United States, this is what the natural progress of things will of course, bring on, and it will be better to promote than retard it."[19] Jefferson's attitude is only one such example from the literature of the day that argued for the dilution of Indian blood. In this way, indigenous peoples and nations would cease to exist, thereby eliminating their claim to the land.[20]

At the same time that Jefferson and others were pushing for the dilution of Indian blood, Osage and other American Indians were trying to make sense of self within the colonial context. Mathews argues that at the beginning of the nineteenth century there developed a noticeable change in appearance among the Osage. "There were young pale-faced people now whose trail you would know from the many footprints, since toes on the left foot would not be pointed in the absolute direction in which the walker was traveling."[21] Mathews goes on to say that some European fathers continued to live with the Osage, becoming part of the Nation by virtue of their residence within the territory. Many became part of the clan structure through adoption and marriage practices. Others, of both European and Osage descent, did not participate in these practices, leaving them outside the clan system and thus outside the current Osage governance structure.[22]

As part of several treaties, including the 1825 Osage treaty, mixed-bloods were singled out and given property within the new reservation areas. The Chippewa treaty of 1826 stated that "half-breeds, scattered through this extensive country, should be stimulated to exertion and improvement by the possession of permanent property and fixed residences."[23] Central to such practices was the idea that because of their white blood, mixed-bloods were more capable of adapting to private property ownership. Conflating blood-based understandings of race with the possession of property, nineteenth-century treaties enforced a very particular notion of what it meant to be civilized and thus what it meant to be Indian.

In 1870, when the U.S. government convinced the Osage to sell their Kansas lands and purchase a reservation in Oklahoma, OIA agent Isaac Gibson added a band called the "Half-Breeds."[24] According to Mathews, the members of this "Half-Breed band" were known as such not simply because of their white ancestry but also because they did not have a clan through which they could be represented politically.[25] Burns concurs with Mathews's assertion that these groupings had little to do with actual percentage of blood: "All mixed-bloods of the latter group [traditional Osage] were counted as full-bloods in population reports, and they were considered to be full-bloods by the true full-blood."[27] Gibson's designation built on and further reinforced a growing rift between two groupings of Osage, which Mathews, Burns, and Terry P. Wilson refer to as the "full-bloods" and the "mixed-bloods." While both groups resided on the reservation and were considered Osage, they lived in different locations and had different lifestyles and different political positions (particularly after the advent of allotment).[26]

In these early discussions of Osage blood, we find provocative slippage between race and practice, blood and politics, clan membership and citizenship, which clearly signals this as a moment of colonial entanglement. The terms used to gloss these complex colonial changes are "half-breed" and "mixed-blood," with their insistence that blood, biology, and even race are really what is at stake in American Indian citizenship. It was, however, residence within the territory that determined Osage citizenship for the purposes of U.S. relocation and Osage self-identification during this time.

In the late nineteenth century, the federal government moved from a policy of removal, which opened up land for white settlement but left American Indian nations mostly intact, to a policy of allotment, where the hope was to eventually do away with Indians, particularly in the form of Indian nations.[28] In 1884, the commissioner of Indian Affairs wrote about the problems of determining the qualifications for allotment as an Indian: "I think it would be for the benefit of all to exclude persons of less than one half Indian blood, and to retain all who are regularly adopted, if Indians, and to add the children of such, but to discourage or prohibit any further adoptions by Indian tribes, especially of whites."[29] While the Indian commissioner did not succeed in creating official policy, allotment rolls almost always contained the blood percentage of each person listed, reinforcing blood-based understandings of Indians.

When it is accepted that allotment was so clearly about obliterating American Indian nations' control over territories, then the rolls created to facilitate this process cannot be viewed as innocuous. In most cases, these rolls have continued to be used by Indian nations as base rolls for citizenship. Providing proof of lineal descent from an individual listed on these rolls has become the standard requirement for tribal citizenship, with many American Indian nations requiring a minimum percentage of blood. Through the implementation of these rolls, the OIA inserted blood relation as the central means of establishing boundaries around Indian nations.[30]

In his 1906 Annual Report, Commissioner of Indian Affairs Leupp stated that policy needed to shift so that the federal government could "manage the affairs of the helpless class with undisputed authority, but, on the other hand, to remove from the roll of wards and dependants the large and increasing number of Indians who no longer needed any supervision from a bureau in Washington."[31] Through the Burke Act of 1906, the OIA could issue "a patent in fee" whenever it was "satisfied of the competency" of "an allottee to manage their own affairs."[32] Competency, as it became known, was tied up not only with citizenship and land but also with the earlier concepts surrounding civilization, including race, blood, Christianity, education, and farming. While the central goal of these policies was still the complete assimilation of the Indian population into the general American citizenry, the immediate, though unintended, effect was to mark people with certain characteristics as competent and thus U.S. citizens and others as incompetent or still American Indians.

Through these policies, we may trace how American Indians became entangled in colonial ideologies of race and civilization. Perhaps most importantly, this period separated American Indian nations from their territory, not just through allotment, which brought increased white settlement of Indian territories, but also through the federal government's self-designated "trust responsibility." Through this policy of issuing competency papers, Indians were again rendered incapable of owning land. Land ownership was viewed as signaling an end to one's Indian status and successful rehabilitation into "whiteness." In this way, citizens of American Indian nations were at once divested of their territories and situated instead as incompetent individuals.

Also during 1906, the Osage were persuaded to allot the Nation's territory. According to several Osage historians, it was the issue of allotment that fully polarized the Osage Nation into two political parties, with the "mixed-blood" party favoring allotment and the "full-blood" party opposing it.[33] In this struggle over allotment, blood came to stand in as a gloss for different practices, political positions, and values. It worked to divide the Osage population into seemingly neat categories of "white" and "Indian," "civilized" and "traditional," "progressive" and "conservative," and "individual" and "communal." While it is clear that these mappings were in fact much more complicated, with political positions being the most telling marker of party affiliation, blood was employed as the referent for these differences.

In 1916, the OIA sent field agents to conduct in-depth field reports on the needs of various reservations. Unlike the reports on the Choctaws calling for tuberculosis treatments, the Pueblos' need for compulsory education, or the Pima Indians' demand for a dam, the Osage report focused on the potential benefits of a blood-based distinction when handling Indian affairs. Throughout his 1917 report, Agent George Vaux deals with the stark contrasts between the Osage "full-bloods" and the "mixed-bloods," in issues ranging from the boarding school, the value placed on money, and the ability to conduct business affairs.

> Broadly speaking, the full-bloods are uneducated in the ways of the white man as respects their ability to conduct their business affairs. A very considerable number of them can not speak English, and but a few can read and write in that language. They appear to be in many respects very trustful of those in whom they have confidence, and in certain directions are easily led. Mixed-bloods, on the other hand, are in very great many instances shrewd business men of ability, and as competent to conduct their affairs as other residents of the United States. Yet under the [Osage] Allotment Act of June 28, 1906, all are treated exactly alike.[34]

Such racialized language must be seen as a fundamental part of the colonial process, both in the United States and in the expansion of colonial empires elsewhere.[35] Ideas of competency, literacy, and financial shrewdness are here seen as deriving from the possession of white blood. In summing up his report, Agent Vaux recommends that "a distinction be made between the incompetent full-bloods and the part bloods [mixed-bloods], and that the latter be given their full share of tribal property and be allowed to do with it as they see fit, while greater effort be made to fully protect the former."[36] Assuming that the Osage use of blood was an exact replica of white uses of the term and not a complex sociopolitical grouping, the agent read these differences within his own racial understandings.

In the following year, the OIA commissioner decided to take the agent's advice, and he applied Vaux's findings to all Indians. Due to the tedious and slow process of individually determining the competency of each Indian, Commissioner Cato Sells turned to blood as a more "efficient way" of assigning American citizenship to competent Indians. As Sells writes, "While ethnologically a preponderance of white blood has not heretofore been a criterion of competency, nor even now is it always a safe standard, it is almost an axiom that an Indian who has a larger proportion of white blood than Indian partakes more of the characteristics of the former than of the latter. In thought and action, so far as the business world is concerned, he approximates more closely to the white blood ancestry."[37] In 1917, Sells issued a "Declaration of Policy in the Administration of Indian Affairs," which gave patents in fee to all adult Indians with less than one-half Indian blood as well as all boarding school graduates, which allowed them to sell their land and automatically made them full U.S. citizens. Indians determined to have over one-half Indian blood could also be declared competent "after careful investigation," but they were unable to sell their last forty acres, which was to be used as a homestead.[38] Sells goes on to discuss the importance of this policy: "It means the dawn of a new era in Indian administration. It means that the competent Indian will no longer be treated as half ward and half citizen. It means reduced appropriations by the government and more self-respect and independence for the Indian. It means the ultimate absorption of the Indian race into the body politic of the nation. It means, in short, the beginning of the end of the Indian problem."[39] While such "far-reaching" policy did not have the desired effect of bringing about the end of American Indian nations, it did remove the restrictions on land, ushering in a wave of white settlement within these areas. Additionally, it also further institutionalized blood as a central component in American Indian recognition.[40]

Again in 1934, as part of the Indian Reorganization Act, the Congress passed legislation that used blood to define specific individuals as "Indians." While the Osage were not subject to the act's provision authorizing

American Indian nations to form constitutional governments, the definitions in this legislation likely strengthened preexisting notions of the importance of Indian blood. Section 19 of the act defined as Indian "(1) all persons of Indian descent who are members of a 'recognized' tribe: (2) descendants of such members living on a reservation: and, (3) all others of one-half or more Indian blood."[41] Perhaps even more important than this third category, Indian blood, through the moniker of descent, is clearly established as a key component in defining Indians, leaving out all other American Indian citizens.

Blood-based configurations such as these have had a lasting impact on American Indian citizenship requirements. U.S. officials used blood to monitor, measure, and categorize Indians in the hope of turning sovereign nations into individual wards. As settlers disrupted the clear territorial boundaries that marked the American Indian nations, the body in general, and blood in particular, became essential to establishing American Indians. Blood is not, however, a natural marker of Indian bodies, but a phenomenon that has taken on force through years of deployment within policy, politics, and everyday interactions. By the twenty-first century, it has become almost impossible to imagine American Indian citizens without using blood as, at least, the initial basis for enrollment. Not all uses of blood, however, work in the same way.

In the context of the 2004–6 Osage reform process, there were two primary deployments of blood. One took the form of a minimum percentage of blood, where discussion was most often focused around race-based calculation, exclusion, pollution, and entitlement. The other was generally known as lineal descent, which was more often used as a mechanism for connecting people separated by location, practice, and racialized categories. By tracing the forces at work within each of these phenomena, we may better understand how various Osage are negotiating blood as a colonial entanglement in the twenty-first century.

Debating Blood

The Osage Tribal Museum, built in 1872 as a chapel, schoolhouse, and dormitory, became, in 1938, the first museum established by an American Indian nation. The sandstone building had been completely remodeled for the museum opening, with each piece of native Oklahoman sandstone brick carefully removed and reused in the reconstruction.[42] In addition to the sandstone exterior, the cupola, the most distinguishing characteristic of the original building, remains to this day. Both facade and cupola completely escaped my notice, however, as I rushed into the Osage Tribal Museum on February 4, 2005.

Having just finished recording the Sovereignty Day's main ceremony and speeches, I dashed through the side door, bypassing the museum's gift shop and gallery. On the stage in the back of the building, which had long ago been converted into an office, I placed my video camera and tripod in front of the blue background I had hung on the beige folding curtain that separated the office from the museum gallery below. I checked my lavaliere microphone for appropriate sound levels before informing Kathryn Red Corn, the director of the museum, who had asked me to conduct interviews on this historic day, that I was ready for our first volunteer.

As the day progressed, I grew increasingly exhausted. While others were enjoying lunch, the day's dance, and fireworks after sunset, I interviewed a steady stream of people. I asked each interviewee what sort of reform they would like to see, in terms of both citizenship and governmental structure. I also asked some variation on the question, "What does today mean to you?" and received a wide variety of answers about the importance of the Osage determining our own future. While all of the answers were powerful, many of them sounded remarkably similar. Most Osage I interviewed wanted a tripartite government and equal voting rights for all Osage descendants.

Toward the end of the day, a woman walked determinedly up the stairs to the office. She had one of her nieces with her, whom she told to sit quietly off-camera and wait for her to finish. As with all participants, I began with the camera turned off, explaining that I was conducting these interviews for the Osage Tribal Museum, but that it was also part of my preliminary research, which was on the reform process as a whole. I handed the woman an informed consent document and explained that, if desired, she could remain anonymous. She could also decline to answer any of the questions and stop the interview at any point. As I continued to explain the material covered on the informed consent sheet, she told me she would like to participate, but with anonymity. Placing the cap over my camera lens, I began the recording by stating that the following interviewee would like to remain anonymous.

I then asked, as I had with all interviewees, "Could you tell me your affiliation with the Osage Nation?" I asked this question primarily because I was curious how different people would describe their relationship with the Nation. Most responded by talking about their family's relation to the

1906 roll, or their employment with the Osage Nation. In her response, this woman said, "I am half-Osage and I live in [town omitted] and if you live in Osage County you probably know who I am. That is me, just generally an Osage woman." From this straightforward response, I knew that this was going to be a different sort of interview.

The next question I asked was, "Would you talk a little bit about what you would like to see for the Osage Nation in terms of citizenship?" She responded that this was something she had "thought long and hard about." She went on to explain: "I would want them to be at least one-fourth or one-eighth because I don't want to be known as the white Osage, blond hair, blue-eyed. Compared with other tribes, our council looks white to me. 'Why do we recognize them as a tribe, they all look white, they don't look Indian, they don't look Osage. They all look white, so why are we as the United States of America recognizing these people when they're not anything?'"[43] While this woman's own status as half-blood might have helped to motivate her desire for a blood-based exclusion, as perhaps did residual political divisions between the mixed- and full-blood Osage parties, this statement reveals more than just a political strategy to gain control. It also illustrates the power of colonially rooted racial ideologies today.

The fractions she listed are most frequently referred to as blood quantums and are the percentage of one's blood based on one's degree of ancestry. According to Eva Garroutte, almost two-thirds of all federally recognized American Indian nations in the United States use some form of minimum blood quantum as part of their requirements for citizenship.[44] This means that where a one-fourth blood quantum is required, people with less than one full-blooded grandparent according to a citizenship roll, or the equivalent, such as two grandparents of half-blood, are not able to enroll in their American Indian nation and are therefore denied citizenship.[45]

During the Osage reform process, blood quantum was occasionally referred to as a potential tool for determining citizenship. In the case of this particular woman, blood quantum and phenotype were connected and deployed as racialized tools of exclusion. Here she marks whiteness as less than one-eighth Osage blood, with blond hair, blue eyes, and not being "anything," whereas she identifies those with at least one-eighth Osage blood as something the U.S. government will recognize as Indian. She, like many other people across the globe, identifies white blood with blue eyes, blond hair, and invisibility, that is, unmarked and normative.[46] In this case, however, whiteness is not privileged in the same way that this neutrality usually affords. American Indian blood is rendered the essential component of what is required for Indian nations to endure.

In discussing such phenomenon across Indian Country, Melissa Meyer points out that "in their purest form, blood quantum requirements amount to a celebration of race," if also turning the tables on racial hierarchies.[47] Meyer, however, goes on to conclude that "measuring fractions of blood and excluding relatives from tribal membership reflects the combined influence of Euroamerican scientific racism and conflated ideas about 'blood' and peoplehood."[48] Historically, U.S. governmental officials have valued blood as a potential tool for diluting an undesirable indigenous presence and for its ability to determine an individual's qualifications for land ownership. While the U.S. government did limit participation in Osage governance to Osage headright holders who had a direct blood connection to the 1906 roll, it never expressly tied recognition to a particular blood quantum. Instead, this entanglement, like others discussed throughout this book, is more complex than a simple mandate. American Indians rework racial notions, entangling blood in their own understandings of relation and survival.

Osage people have repeatedly faced termination, both during the 1950s termination era and as the OTC fought to extend the life of the Osage Mineral Estate. These threats worked along with the discourses surrounding race to instill an ingrained respect for tangible markers of "Indianness," such as blood percentages. During the 1950s in particular, but evident throughout all of these battles for survival, the Osage had to fight against their supposed "whiteness." The result was that white blood was viewed as a contaminant that might, in and of itself, bring about the end of the Osage Nation. Whether or not the above interviewee really believed that the federal government would revoke the recognition of the Nation based on phenotypical appearance alone, the threat of termination was skillfully deployed as a motivating force for creating a minimum blood quantum.

Such an entanglement, however, can have precarious consequences. When viewed as a finite substance, blood delineates nations along racialized lines. Unlike requirements for citizenship in most other nations across the globe, a minimum blood quantum requirement ensures that citizenship will one day no longer be attainable for anyone. Particularly in small nations, marriage with noncitizens is not just inevitable but biologically essential. Therefore, blood quantum is clearly one of the most lasting and productive tools of settler colonial erasure.[49]

J. Kēhaulani Kauanui argues that, in the case of Hawai'i, "blood quantum is a manifestation of settler colonialism that works to deracinate—to pull out by the roots—and displace indigenous peoples."[50] Kauanui illustrates this position by showing that early twentieth-century colonial policies slowly shifted the focus away from Hawaiian land entitlement to the privileging of white property interests through a redefinition of Hawaiian identity. Legislation has worked to deny the Hawaiian sovereignty struggle by linking blood, specifically 50 percent Hawaiian blood, with Hawaiian authenticity and replacing Hawaiian land entitlement with a welfare discourse of pity. This dual erasure of a genealogically based definition of Hawaiian identity and of Hawaiians from the land is clearly a colonial uprooting.

It is through such uprooting, of reducing indigenous people with sovereignty over their own territory to the status of racial minorities, that the practice of marrying outside the Osage Nation came to be associated with disappearance. The entanglement of blood quantum, however, has authority well beyond fears of erasure. It works to change understandings of self and influence interpersonal decisions, such as whom to marry and raise children with. As the Osage interviewee went on to describe, her desire for a minimum blood quantum also came from a desire to maintain a strong Osage Nation:

> I would want there to be a line and then it would make us as a people want to marry our Osage people, take pride in that, and have your kids around other Indians, Osage people. Let's invest in those Osage instead of saying these white people are good. Osage helping Osage, making them better people, investing in that. So in that aspect, yeah, I would want to [have a blood quantum minimum], so then we can keep what we have. It won't be like today, because tomorrow there is going to be a lot less of us. People are going to marry white people and it is just going to spiral down.[51]

Here the logic is that two Osage parents would raise their children around more Osage and with more Osage pride, and they would be more invested in the Osage Nation. Such an argument, however, insists upon a particular biological definition of an Osage and presents everyone else as foreigners to the Osage Nation. Few nations outside of Indian Country have such stringent citizenship requirements, and few requirements could jeopardize the future of a nation more. Thus, the conclusion that "tomorrow there is going to be a lot less of us" should be understood as a consequence of, rather than a motivation for, a minimum blood quantum. The authority of the minimum blood quantum, while certainly compelling, limits Osage citizenship to a very small biological pool.

While other Osage occasionally made calls for a minimum blood quantum, never did a single threshold take on legitimacy, and rarely did even the few people arguing for a blood quantum have a concrete percentage in mind. More often a range was suggested, such as the one quoted above, signifying the fluid nature of these blood quantum requirements even for those desiring a minimum threshold. Instead, it was the "evidence" blood quantum provided, through racial discourses such as phenotype, that seemed to give it authority. In this way, passing on the perceived physical traits of an Indian became a powerful motivator to some Osage, who argued that a blood quantum requirement would make future generations of Osage visibly different from the surrounding white population and thus create a better chance of Osage independence.

Both Garroutte and Circe Sturm write about similar ways blood is deployed in Indian Country, particularly how it is tied to racial signifiers, most notably to phenotype, or "looking Indian."[52] Throughout her work, Sturm shows us how ideas of blood and physical traits are associated with being Cherokee, and also how these ideas are connected with notions of authenticity and culture. Sturm argues that this sort of racial thinking leads to the idea that "as the Cherokee Nation progressively 'whitens,' it runs the risk of losing its distinct racial and cultural identity, the primordial substance of its national identity. In the eyes of the general public, the Cherokee Nation would no longer be a 'real' Indian tribe."[53] These entanglements are not unique to the Osage Nation but are part of the settler colonial experience and are at least partially motivated by outside perceptions of what constitutes an Indian.

One final influence that blood quantum had on the 2004–6 Osage reform process was that it marked entitlement. One member of the OGRC explained to me: "Blood marks your ancestry. Those with more Osage blood had a larger percentage of Osage ancestors who suffered during the colonial process. They should be the ones to first benefit from Osage resources."[54] Such narrations of blood also have a powerful internal logic, especially if American Indian nations are viewed primarily as descendant communities of once great nations, now deserving restitution. While restitution is certainly owed, these are more than simply descendant communities.

American Indian nations are about more than just the past; they are working to build a strong future. Supporting blood quantum means buying into a racial logic born out of the colonial process, which would eventually devastate Indian communities. At an early Pawhuska community meeting, one middle-aged man actively involved in Osage political activities put blood quantum's legacy into perspective:

> To create a [minimum] blood-quantum [for Osage citizenship] is to set the date for when the tribe goes out of existence. Blood quantum is a Federal Government method of defining Osage so that responsibility no longer belongs to them past a certain point. So why do we want to mimic any destructive system of membership that was created to destroy itself? The Bureau of Indian Affairs is in the business of going out of business; we are in the business of ensuring the future. It is our inherent right to determine our membership and our responsibility to ensure it lasts for as long as an Osage draws a breath.[55]

Even though this man had enough blood to pass almost any minimum blood quantum threshold, he saw it as a destructive system, one that would ultimately lead to the extinction of the Osage Nation. Similarly, the commissioner who above argued about entitlement said later the same day: "We are a nation—nations have diversity."[56] Most Osage desired a citizenship standard less dependent on racial categories, like that of the Choctaw, who generally, as Valerie Lambert writes, do not view "the categories of white (or black) and Choctaw as mutually exclusive."[57]

The majority of Osage participating in the reform process did, in fact, reject blood quantum altogether. Of the 1,650 people who voted in the November 2005 referendum, only 236 desired some sort of minimum blood quantum (see appendix 6). During the community meetings, Osage with a wide range of blood quantum percentages repeatedly spoke against the implementation of any blood quantum. Many denied the racial authority that blood quantum seemed to imply. One local lawyer, who had a high percentage of Osage blood, told me: "It is important to remember that Indian nationhood is not a racial or ethnic matter, it is a political status. So blood quantum should be irrelevant."[58] Hepsi Barnett, the coordinator for the reform process, frequently spoke against racial or purely blood-based understandings of Osage citizenship, saying, for example, "What makes us a nation is our political status, it is what keeps us from being just another ethnic group."[59] Such opinions are also supported by thousands of U.S. laws, policies, and court decisions, including the very legislation that created this reform process.[60] In 2004, the U.S. Congress certainly did not mandate or even encourage the use of a minimum blood quantum but instead simply recognized the inherent sovereignty of the Osage Nation to determine its own citizenship. Determining citizenship, however, was not a straightforward task.

During an OGRC business meeting on August 18, 2005, the conversation turned to the interminable issue of the fraudulent names some Osage believed to have been added to the 1906 roll. In addition to the commissioners, Leonard Maker was also present. Maker was a vocal critic of simply using the 1906 roll as the baseline for voting because he felt there were many non-Osage listed on the roll. In the midst of one of the many conversations about the disputed names, Maker argued,

> I have heard that there is enough evidence on file at the BIA to sufficiently document that these people were not Osage. You all need to stop going in circles around this issue and just take a vote. Then you must get started getting stuff done. . . . I used to think this issue of blood was dead, but it has been brought back. It is going to take strength to fix, but we are talking about the identity of the Osage Nation. This is the first time in 100 years that we can answer the questions of who is Osage. Should we just stick our head back in the sand?[61]

Fundamental to Maker's argument is the idea that blood should be the central component in determining not only the upcoming Osage vote but also the "identity of the Osage Nation."

Blood is here less the finite substance debated in the discussions above and more an element passed from generation to generation that signals relation. In Maker's view, the integrity of the 1906 roll is questionable because it was an allotment roll, meaning it made one eligible for 640 acres of land and a share in the Mineral Estate and thus likely included people motivated solely by a desire to gain access to Osage lands and monies. He and others feared that some names were added fraudulently, since the stakes were so high.[62] In this way, Maker saw an Osage blood requirement, however it might be evidenced, as a tool for eliminating those who might have been added to the roll illicitly.

This location of fraud in one's blood was a very powerful force throughout the reform process and is, in some ways, analogous to notions of "illegals" in the United States and other liberal nations.[63] The wrong kind of blood works to pass down an illegitimate status, marking those who are not entitled to the full benefits of citizenship. On U.S. citizenship in particular, Cheryl Harris writes, citizenship law "draws boundaries and enforces or reorders existing regimes of power."[64] Through its ties to particularly shaped bodies, American citizenship has worked to privilege some groups over others at different periods in its history.

While these relations have changed many times, beginning with the specific exclusion of blacks and Indians from early U.S. citizenship, a current and potent example of the connection between race and nation is recent Arizona state legislation—Senate Bill 1070, which many say implements racial profiling to enforce immigration policies, and House Bill 2281, which bans schools from offering ethnic studies classes.[65] In these bills, the State of Arizona is privileging specific phenotypes and knowledge systems. Nonwhite individuals are subjected to increased police interrogation, while white knowledge is returned to its location as sole arbiter of past and present realities. It becomes clear through such extreme examples that citizenship can never be thought of innocently but must be understood as a category with complex dynamics that often has a direct relationship to exclusion and privilege.

Osage debates over citizenship were little different, with millions of dollars of gaming monies pumped into resources for Osage citizens. After much debate, the OGRC decided that anyone with an Osage CDIB card would have a vote in the November referendum election and thus a say in how Osage citizenship should be determined.[66] Chief Jim Gray, who was attending the OGRC's meeting in the hope of putting an end to the circular debates over voting and encourage the OGRC to proceed with the reform process, stated: "The best approach is to include everybody, cast the widest net possible as to the direction of the tribe. You can't limit citizenship before you determine citizenship."[67] Gray here encourages the OGRC to use the OIA's roll as a way of connecting the residents of the Osage Nation, as captured by the 1906 roll, to a current population of people, rather than using blood as a marker of a distinct racial group or ethnicity. Neither blood percentage nor even Osage blood itself are fundamental within this system. Still, however, by saying that the 1906 roll "casts the widest net possible," Chief Gray was assuming that the most fundamental criterion for being an Osage could be found within the bloodline, at least in the sense of its biological relation to the base population created by the 1906 roll.

Throughout the 2004–6 Osage reform process, the concept of blood, mostly divorced from its empirical binds of calculation and phenotypical materialization, was repeatedly referenced as the central concept at stake in defining the Osage. Of the 1,378 people who returned the questionnaire, only 24.4 percent were interested in a minimum blood quantum; however, 85.1 percent answered in the affirmative to the question, "Do you have to have Osage blood to be an Osage?" Here, "Osage blood" is most commonly understood as signaling lineal descent from, or biological connection to, individuals understood as Osage in the past. As stated above, there was a contentious debate about whether or not all individuals on the 1906 federally defined allotment roll had Osage blood. However, 71 percent of Osage participating in the questionnaire felt that the 1906 roll was sufficient for establishing Osage relation. In this way, the category of "Osage blood" was divorced from its connection to race-based exclusion and redeployed as a tool for uniting a population separated by racial categories and geographical distance.

In addition to multiple-choice questions, there were also sections of the questionnaire dedicated to voluntary longer responses, where a respondent was free to include any thoughts they wished. One middle-aged man from Massachusetts shared his reasons for rejecting blood quantum while embracing notions of blood: "The most extraordinary thing about my Osage blood is the knowledge that I am related to every other member of the tribe. To exclude individuals because of their degree of blood is contrary to the idea of tribal membership and a certain path to the ultimate disappearance of the Osage Nation." The central motivating factor in the discussion of blood is again the fear of the "disappearance" of the Osage Nation; but blood quantum is here causal, not preventative.

Strong and Van Winkle find similar reconfigurations of the concept of blood in the work of American Indian fictional authors, including N. Scott Momaday. "Momaday's 'memory in the blood' becomes a refiguring of 'Indian blood' that makes it a vehicle of connection and integration—literally, a remembering—rather than one of calculation and differentiation."[68] Momaday defines blood memory as a comprehension of the connections between one's family/tribal nation and oneself. For Momaday, this comprehension resides in the blood itself and exists outside of Western ways of knowing.[69] Through the concept of "blood memory," blood becomes a system of knowledge that is immeasurable. Here, blood is disentangled from race, releasing the Indian body, and thus nation, from discourses that have attempted to contain it.

As Chadwick Allen argues, Momaday's "blood memory boldly converts the supposedly objective arithmetic of measuring American Indian blood into an obviously subjective system of recognizing narratives—memories—of Indian indigeneity."[70] Through the use of blood memory, blood ceases to function as a taxonomic system of disappearance and instead represents the possibility of connection. Veronica Pipestem, an Osage annuitant, has also written about blood memory, saying it is the "feeling of being surrounded, almost smothered, by that which is right in front of us and inside of us but escapes articulation. . . . Blood memory is elusive because it is so large and it is manifest in so many different things and we are only able to catch tiny glimpses of it at any given time because of its vastness."[71] Blood is used to disrupt colonial systems of knowledge and conquest. It becomes a means of connection that refuses to mark a point of disappearance. Its smothering power eludes colonial typologies.

Perhaps one of the best spaces in which to observe the authority given to the concept of "Osage blood" was an Osage government reform message board during a discussion about whether Osage citizenship should require residence on the reservation. To this question, one woman wrote: "I am Osage. I am proud to be Osage. I do not live in one of the [Osage] districts but my heart is there. My family ties are there. My bloodline ties me ever and forever there. You cannot exclude or ignore me because you don't see me. I am one of you. WE ALL are of one nation."[72] Blood is here used to root oneself to the nation. By positioning both her heart and her family ties within the districts, this woman establishes her connection to Osage territory. Rather than reading this posting as a rejection of the importance of territory, this quote and most of the discussion during the reform process placed a great deal of emphasis on the existence of Osage territory, even as many rejected the idea that there should be a residency requirement for citizenship. Osage blood rooted Osage lineal descendants to the territory and therefore the Nation. "Blood" was used to establish a permanent relationship with ancestors from the Nation, which could not be broken.

In this moment of national reformation, it is not surprising that Osage blood was frequently used as a root system connecting people to the land and the Nation. Unlike blood quantum, which works to "deracinate—to pull out by the roots—and displace indigenous peoples,"[73] blood is here used to make connections among a dispersed nation. Liisa Malkki describes such phenomenon as common to most national projects: "Thinking about nations and national identities may take the form of roots, trees, origins, ancestries, racial lines, autochthonism, evolutions, developments, or any number of other familiar, essentializing images."[74] As Malkki goes on to argue, these images do have their limitations, particularly in terms of creating essentialized images that ignore vast migrations and invasions, processes that have existed the world over. Fundamental to national projects then is the naturalization of particular spaces and categories. The discourses of nationalism bring with it such baggage.

The "blood entanglement," however, goes deeper than its typical essentializing usage within national rhetoric. As Mark Rifkin reminds us, it can never be completely separated from colonial deployments of the term that have worked to limit the possibilities of future indigenous bodies. Insisting on blood relation, or lineal descent, denies all kinship relation except the biological connection of sperm and egg donors. When considering the OIA's implementation of rolls for registration in tribal nations during the allotment period, Rifkin asks: "Can the coordinated assault on native kinship in U.S. policy in the late nineteenth century be understood as an organized effort to make heterosexuality compulsory as a key part of breaking up indigenous landholdings and 'detribalizing' native peoples?"[75] Rifkin's provocation elucidates the fact that one of the central bodily norms hidden within ideas of blood is heterosexual reproduction, where the sexual relationship between male and female is understood as the fundamental moment that brings a citizen into being. Through the use of lineal descent from these allotment rolls, all other kinship relations are hidden and the singular moment of "biological" procreation is thought of as all-determining. Thus, even lineal descent must be understood as a colonial entanglement.

Constituting Citizenship

The ten members of the OGRC knew they had a daunting task ahead of them as they gathered in a hotel on a temperate winter morning in Tulsa. The generic hotel conference room had a wall of windows, covered by a heavy curtain, and several tables placed together to make a long rectangle. After ten months, forty-two community meetings, a phone poll, a questionnaire, and a referendum vote, they now had the formidable job of pulling all of this material together into a workable constitution. To advise them on the day's many decisions, the OGRC had invited the lawyers they had hired for the process, several other Osage lawyers who were volunteering their time, and several elders from around the Nation. With excitement running high, we each took our seats. I positioned myself faithfully beside my camcorder, ready to record the three-day event. As always, the OGRC started with a prayer thanking the heavenly father for making this day possible.

After discussing a name change from the Osage Tribe of Oklahoma to the Osage Nation as well as some jurisdictional issues, the group came to "Article 2. Membership." As the text document projected on the screen scrolled downward, the room became quiet; everyone contemplated the complexities that would have to be addressed. For the past hundred years, the U.S. government had only allowed those with a share in the Mineral Estate to participate in Osage politics. There were at this time approximately 12,000 individuals, including myself, who were descended from someone on the 1906 roll but who had been up to this point alienated from Osage politics. Now that the U.S. government had acknowledged its own lack of jurisdiction in determining internal Osage affairs, the OGRC was left with the task of writing the new citizenship criteria.

It was clear throughout the many discussions of the reform process that almost no one wanted to keep citizenship tied to the headright system. I recalled in particular one interviewee's powerful declaration, shortly after the passage of the federal law: "Today I am an Osage, finally." He went on to explain that his brother had died before ever getting a vote while his mother had multiple headrights and therefore multiple votes. Having registered to vote in the U.S. elections when he was eighteen, he had been deeply frustrated by his inability to participate in "my own tribe's election process."[76] While the 2004 U.S. congressional act did not in fact make this man any more of an Osage than he was before, it did sever the congressionally mandated connection between Osage voting rights and the Osage Mineral Estate, allowing for the possibility of his citizenship. The commissioners sitting around this table, and later Osage voters, would be the ones to decide whether he was, in fact, now a full voting citizen of the Osage Nation.

While it was also clear to the writers of the 2006 Constitution that there was a mandate to change citizenship from the headright system that had been imposed for the last 100 years, it was less clear exactly how this should be done. One of the lawyers hired to assist the commissioners spoke up first: "I think we already have a problem with this. . . . They want the lineal descendancy from '06 and they want some way to contest enrollment."[77] This statement was based on the November 19, 2005, referendum election, in which 87.70 percent of the voters (1,414 people) had said that they would like the 1906 Osage allotment roll to constitute the base roll, with all descendants eligible for citizenship (see appendix 6). In a second question, however, 79.74 percent (1,315 people) had agreed that "membership of people on the base roll will be subject to challenge by the new government if it is proven that fraudulent measures were used to establish membership into the tribe." In other words, while the voters clearly rejected a blood quantum, many still desired a way to limit Osage citizenship to people who had a legitimate claim; it was defining this legitimacy that was the source of considerable tension.

After spending several hours in discussion, the drafters of the 2006 Osage Constitution broke for lunch. But even upon returning, they could not decide the citizenship requirements. The issue would surface repeatedly as the weeks passed but would ultimately not be decided until one of the final drafting sessions on January 23. Although these later meetings were open to the public, the OGRC, their staff, and I (with my video camera) were generally the only ones in attendance, due primarily to a lack of both widespread notification and interest in attending the long, and often tedious, drafting meetings. The primary stumbling block for constituting citizenship was still how to use the 1906 roll to determine citizenship while also addressing concerns about "fraudulent" enrollees. It was decided that not constitutionalizing a base roll would be the easiest way to address the possibility of fraudulent enrollment, allowing the Osage Congress to determine citizenship however it pleased.

Several of the commissioners, however, argued persuasively that nothing should be done about the supposed fraudulent names. They asserted that the second question about fraudulence on the referendum vote was not an accurate representation of Osage opinion because many had reported that they thought it applied to more recent Osage enrollment and not the 1906 roll itself. These commissioners also felt that evidence of fraud was not strong enough to support their disfranchisement, nor did they have the time for the thorough investigation that proving fraud would require. Furthermore, they supported a base roll because they did not think that this issue should keep coming up every time there was a change in administration. Perhaps most convincing, they argued that if voters had any uncertainty about their own citizenship in the new government, they would likely vote against the entire constitution.[78] These arguments were persuasive enough that the OGRC decided to proceed with setting a base roll, ensuring that all descendants of the 1906 allotment roll would gain Osage citizenship upon application.

Citizenship in the final constitution, ratified by Osage voters on March 11, 2006, reflected this complex notion of Osage blood (see appendix 7). Section 1 of the article on membership defined the base membership roll as "those persons whose names appear on the final roll of the Osage tribe of Indians pursuant to the Act of June 28, 1906."[79] Setting the base roll did mean that even if it was proven that someone on the base roll did not have "Osage blood," because the person had been incorporated prior to 1906, his or her enrollment could not be challenged. This decision destabilized a static notion of Osage blood but ultimately resulted in the creation of a new biological pool to which someone had to prove a blood connection in order to be an Osage citizen.

Section 2 of the article on membership stated that "all lineal descendants of those Osage listed on the 1906 roll are eligible for membership in the Osage Nation, and those enrolled members shall constitute the citizenry." Lineal descent from the 1906 roll confined Osage citizenship within colonial rhetoric, which works to limit the definition of Indian polities to particularly endowed bodies. Section 4 of the article on membership, however, began to untangle this colonial legacy by giving the Osage Nation Congress the ability to create laws regulating the "adoption of members," which leaves the door open for a process of naturalization. Through these citizenship requirements, including the rejection of "blood" as the sole means of Osage qualification, the writers of the 2006 Constitution ensured that, while biological relationships were the primary means of defining the polity, the Osage were not a racial group.

Throughout this chapter, I have traced the varied ways that ideas of blood were deployed during the Osage reform process. It is clear that blood cannot be read as a simple substance but must be understood as a complex network of ideas, scientific truths, and racial imaginaries, as well as a root system used to connect distant people to the Nation. Participants in the reform process occasionally used blood as a tool of exclusion, creating a racialized limit for Osage citizenship. In these cases, blood quantum, fraud, adoption, entitlement, phenotype, and racial purity were hard to disaggregate. While these concepts of blood are clearly entangled in various colonial discourses, particularly that of race, blood was seen as a tool for creating a future for the Osage Nation. Nations often require essentialized notions of connection, and blood can be a strong tool for establishing such a relation. Viewed through arboreal metaphors, blood is used as a device to link people to the Osage territory and thus the nation.

Blood was only one of the forces that had to be managed in order to write the 2006 Osage Constitution. Culture was another major entanglement that the OGRC had to make sense of during the 2004–6 Osage reform process. Culture, like blood, is a colonial concept that has been imposed on indigenous people; yet it also serves an important role in imagining an outside to the ongoing colonial process. Like blood, culture is believed to provide the roots for the nation, but during the constitutional process it was also used by some participants in the process as a means of limiting the authority of the new nation. In investigating these tensions inherent in culture, the potential and the dangers become evident. The writers of the 2006 Constitution ultimately denied static notions of culture, which were rooted in colonial discourse, and instead insisted on the fluidity of Osage practices.

KEEP IT SEPARATED. INDEPENDENT. OSAGE CULTURE SHOULD BE MAINTAINED AND TRANSFERRED BY THE PEOPLE THEMSELVES.

YOU ARE NOT HIRING A DRUM KEEPER

IF YOU NEED A GOVERNING DOCUMENT TO TELL YOU HOW TO BE OSAGE, YOU'VE WAITED TOO LATE TO TAKE CARE OF YOUR CULTURE

CULTURE

On a pleasant afternoon during my time at the University of Florida, I joined several graduate students and professors for lunch. We sat outside, enjoying the mild weather and hoping that the afternoon showers would hold off long enough for us to eat a leisurely meal. After discussing some current departmental politics, the conversation turned to my upcoming research in Oklahoma. As I was discussing the grants I was currently writing, a woman at the table, whom I knew only in passing, asked ironically, "But what bubble do you really check?" I was at first unsure what she meant, until she slowly responded, "I have never seen you wear anything . . . cultural . . . so, how do you identify yourself?" She had not just my attention, but that of the entire table, most of whom wanted to see the tongue lashing that would surely follow. At first, I was at a loss. Slowly I managed a frustrated response about the stereotypes of American Indians stuck in the past wearing feathers and beads, trying to put her question squarely in its place.

Later, when I had finished my research and returned to Florida, I was better equipped to address such interrogations. Having participated in my own Nation's reassertion of authority over what it meant to be an Osage today, I had developed a more sophisticated approach to addressing such stereotypes. One day, during my office hours, two graduate students, one of whom had just returned from a long research stint, came in to use the visual lab that is housed in the basement of Turlington Hall. We sat and joked about the length of her fieldwork in her own hometown in Mexico. In the course of the conversation, I mentioned that the U.S. government had registered my father as an "incompetent," meaning that any trust lands or funds he possessed were not subject to state taxes but were managed by the U.S. government. The student from Mexico looked at me and said, "I did not know you were Native American. Is your father a full-blood?"

I responded that he was not and explained that the Osage had never mandated a minimum blood quantum and now configured citizenship through lineal descent from an allotment roll.

Not satisfied, the graduate student continued, "But does he live on the reservation?"

I explained that he had grown up on the reservation and now lived about two miles outside of the reservation boundary; I also said that there were Osage all over the world, with large concentrations off-reservation in Oklahoma, Texas, and California.

With furrowed brow, the graduate student slowly asked, "So do your parents live in a tipi?"

Unable to control ourselves, the other graduate student and I burst into a fit of laughter. The first graduate student quickly explained that as an undergrad she had gone with her anthropology professor to Canada where they had stayed overnight in a tipi. I politely inquired if she had noticed anybody else staying in tipis. She paused and admitted that it was only she and the anthropologist who had stayed in the tipi. She then asked, "But, what about the tipi on college green?"

One of the anthropology professors on campus set up a tipi each year as part of his North American Indian class. The exercise had long frustrated me because of the stereotypes it inevitably reinforced as it sat for the week on campus without any explanation. Finally flustered, I explained that the Osage had ever only stayed in tipis while hunting and, like all American Indians I knew today, lived in houses of all varieties, but certainly not tipis.

Such American Indian stereotypes are common across the globe and play a key role in the ongoing colonial process. Despite the fact that few of the over 500 American Indian nations existing today have ever lived in tipis, such imagery is burned into the modern psyche. The image of the stoic Indian hunting buffalo on horseback has captured the popular imagination and represents not simply the United States' past, but also the static image of American Indians today. American Indian "culture," as such images are often labeled, has been located so deeply in a mythical past that it becomes very difficult to inhabit "culture" today, leaving contemporaneous American Indians looking counterfeit. Like the notions of blood and race discussed in the previous chapter, culture is an equally complex, and perhaps even more captivating, entangled space for American Indians today.

The nebulous concept of "culture" is at once a classification of stereotypes removed from my life and a gloss for experiences that connect me to other Osage. Even at a young age, I bristled at touristic productions, deeply troubled by authenticity and how it affected local understandings of self. My decision to study anthropology was motivated primarily by an undergraduate class I took, Anthropology of Tourism, in which we directly addressed issues of authenticity and explored the complex history of culture.

Culture originated as the unexplainable force that other disciplines had yet to parse and has always been to some extent anthropology's calling card.[1] The concepts embodied in culture have changed over time and are understood by most anthropologists today as shifting nodes within all aspects of life, including governance.[2] Culture, however, all too often takes on a static shape when applied to American Indians, becoming a far thornier issue.

This chapter will begin the process of parsing out cultural entanglements, exploring how the writers of the 2006 Osage Constitution encountered and negotiated it. Osage culture must be understood as a shifting phenomenon remade within different institutions, including the intersecting settler colonial, scholarly, and Osage deployments. At times static and located only in an ancient past, culture can also take on significant life, giving meaning and substance to understandings of self and nation. Culture has proven to be a dangerous colonial tool of conquest used to signal disrupture and disappearance, but it has at times also been used as a precarious means of holding off colonial forces. Culture, and the difference it implies, is a term laden with desires, which can create deep anxieties and dangerous authenticities, as well as a powerful sense of belonging. The most potent danger in the cultural discourse, as with all colonial entanglements, is its potential to limit possibilities for the future of indigenous nations.

Many authors have argued that cultural discourses continue to create ideal types, defining who is and who is not a "real" Indian.[3] One of the early and most direct critiques of anthropologists' use of culture came from Vine Deloria Jr., who writes: "Not even Indians can relate themselves to this type of creature who, to the anthropologists, is the 'real' Indian. Indian people begin to feel that they are merely shadows of a mythical super-Indian."[4] This "mythical super-Indian" works to limit the activities that are a recognizable part of American Indian culture. By focusing primarily on Indians who participate in particular kinds of cultural practice, some early anthropologists contributed to the myth of Indian extinction by denying the ways all peoples have divergent and changing modes of interacting in the world.[5]

The challenges inherent in these static notions of American Indian culture cannot be separated from the colonial process. As historian Nicholas Dirks illustrates, "Culture is a colonial formation" in that it is an "object of knowledge" and way of viewing the world that was formed during the colonial period to justify conquest and rationalize continuing occupation.[6] While the conquerors had "science" to understand the world around them, they positioned indigenous populations in relation to "tradition" and "culture." In order to become fully realized humans, indigenous populations needed white civilization. It was thus this "culture" that marked individuals as "still" Indian. Within this formulation, American Indian culture could only be preserved, not practiced and adapted.

Through notions of authenticity, many of the discourses surrounding culture work to freeze indigenous practices in the precolonial moment and deny indigenous authority today. In the words of Kevin Bruyneel, "The imposition of colonial rule denotes the effort by the United States to narrowly bound indigenous political status in space and time, seeking to limit the ability of indigenous people to define their own identity and develop economically and politically on their own terms."[7] In this way, static notions of culture have been used to erase an indigenous political presence today by relegating authentic American Indian peoples to a mythic past. American Indian culture, it seems, is not under the control of contemporary American Indians.[8] "Culture" has had a devastating effect on the solidification of Indian identity and has limited the possibilities for what Gerald Vizenor terms "survivance."[9]

In addition to colonialism and anthropology, the notion of culture is also deeply entangled with nationalism. Drawing from the work of Eric Wolf and Ernest Gellner, anthropologist Kirk Dombrowski illustrates the way "culture . . . has its roots in the budding nationalist movements of central Europe of the late 1800s."[10] Redeployed from its reference to aristocratic behavior, culture was used to gloss differences in class, race, and religion. As a central component of nationalism, culture serves to unite populations otherwise deeply divided.

As in the case of blood, the discourses surrounding culture become even more complex as they are entangled with the lives of American Indian peoples today. Concerning this increasing complexity, Paul Chaat Smith argues, "For our part, we dimly accept the role of spiritual masters and first environmentalists as we switch cable channels and videotape our weddings and ceremonies. We take pride in westerns that make us look gorgeous (which we are!) and have good production values. We secretly wish we were more like the Indians in the movies."[11] Smith argues that while static notions of American Indian culture can be compelling, the ultimate effect is often devastating. The us/them opposition inherent in colonial ideologies of American Indian culture is particularly dangerous for American Indian national sovereignty. If no authentic Indians remain, then indigenous authority over territory can all the more easily be disregarded.

This cultural entanglement is traceable in many discussions of American Indians today, but it does not always take on the fully static, or historically located, shape of colonial culture. In Scott Lyons's discussion of citizenship, for example, he redefines the concept of *jus sanguinis*, usually described as "blood relation," to include "the possession of language, religion, and culture."[12] He also goes on to say that each indigenous nation should create standards of citizenship that perpetuate what it thinks is most central to its nation. "If I were to revise a constitution by myself, I would probably adopt some hierarchy of membership that would actively produce what I think most Ojibwe want: language revitalization, cultural renewal, some privileging of the land and the people who live there, and the most important goal: economic justice."[13] Here, there is a strong desire for American Indian nations to insert "culture" into their constitutional documents. This is not, however, static practice from the past but cultural renewal, which allows for greater possibilities. Lyons's work illustrates one of the ways "culture" continues to play a formative role in many American Indian peoples' understanding of themselves today.[14]

In turning to the specific context of the 2004–6 Osage reform process, the remainder of this chapter will begin parsing the cultural entanglement in Indian Country today. By its very nature, it must, however, remain incomplete. As with any set of practices, understanding the content of "culture" necessitates personal experience. Words by themselves can never quite do justice to cultural ideas, and words have, especially when it comes to the "culture" of American Indians, frequently done much harm. Any detailed description I could offer of these experiences in action might further ongoing colonial efforts to capture, categorize, and possess all things indigenous. In shifting the focus away from the content of these practices, I will utilize the strategy of ethnographic refusal, so eloquently outlined by Audra Simpson.[15] In this way, I will primarily seek to focus my attention on the deliberations over the term "culture" during the reform process, including how desires for culture were expressed and why it was ultimately determined that "culture" was outside the scope of the 2006 Osage Constitution.

Cultural Desires

On my first day of research, I stopped at the Osage Tribal Museum before heading over to the Osage Tribal Council (OTC) business meeting set to begin at 10 A.M. I had become friends with Kathryn Red Corn, the director of the museum, during the previous summer, and so I made what would become my habitual first stop by the museum to catch up on Osage gossip. James Elsberry, the videographer hired to record all the Osage Government Reform Commission public meetings, worked for the museum. Elsberry filled us in on the recent activity of the OGRC, which included the community meetings that had been held over the last two weeks in Grayhorse, Pawhuska, Bartlesville, and Oklahoma City. It was quite evident that the first community meetings were not going well for the OGRC.

Elsberry described the crowd's palpable hostility at the Oklahoma City meeting the night before, where frustration with the initial stages of the process had been expressed. Speakers had complained about the selection of the commissioners, a process that had taken place behind closed doors, had not allowed for enough application time, and had resulted in the representation of only headright holders. They also grilled the OGRC on how their money was being spent and how elections were going to be supervised. Rather than simply offering their opinions, as the commissioners had expected, those in attendance had interrogated the process itself, expressing skepticism about whether or not this was really a representative process of citizen engagement.

The commissioners were apprehensive when I met them at the Tulsa community meeting the next day. They were holding the meeting in a large conference room at a branch library. The venue was state of the art and was, in fact, almost as large as the area holding books to be loaned. When I later transcribed this and other community meetings, I would deeply appreciate this particular location—most of the other meetings took place in old aluminum community buildings with dreadful acoustics.

Several of the commissioners had arrived early and were arranging the rows of chairs that would face the OGRC when the meeting began. I placed my camera off to the right side, where I could turn the camera on the OGRC and participants as needed. As with the other meetings during this round, following a prayer to lead off the session, Leonard Maker began with a twenty-minute description of the process that had led to the governmental reform effort. Toward the end of his address, Maker stressed the need to hear citizen opinions, especially as they related to how the government might reflect Osage culture: "Some of the information we've had presented to us and we've known ourselves over the years is that a government has to be reflective of its culture; it has to be culturally related. How do we relate this government to the Osage culture? We know that the OTC is not culturally related to the tribe and maybe that's one of its failings. So we want you to think about that. How can we do that? What features of this new government can reflect who we are as a people? Those are the things that are on the table." Even though the OTC had been in place for almost a hundred years, this was a system the U.S. government had imposed. Given the chance to again create a new government structure, Maker drew upon the research of various consultants, as well as a sense of his own Osage identity, to argue that the new constitution could surely find a way of expressing Osage culture. The question for those in attendance was, "What would this look like?"[16]

From the beginning of the reform process, Osage culture and its various referents of tradition, values, and ancient ways lurked as one of the elephants in the room that the commissioners knew they had to contend with in some fashion during the writing of the constitution. During the first annual Osage Sovereignty Day celebration in February 2005, which kicked off the reform process, Chief Jim Gray gave an impassioned speech about the need for government reform and his hopes for the new nation: "We have a culture that has been absent from our tribe as a government. And one of the things I would like to do is be able to recognize the cultural aspects of the Osage Nation."[17] Later in the speech, he returned to cultural themes: "So let us begin the process of working together to create a document which reflects Osage values. The best ideas are under this tent; Osage ideas. Our traditions should be the core of what the ultimate governing documents will be in the coming days."[18] For both Chief Gray and the head of planning for the Osage Nation, "culture" necessarily deserved a prominent role in the Osage constitution.

During the reform process, "culture" referred, first and foremost, to older Osage ways, which were perceived as less polluted than their current, colonial, forms. The Osage Language Program mission statement, which was written during the same time period as the Osage reform process, reads, "Our Mission is to revitalize the Osage Language to its purest form and to teach our people to speak Osage within the realm of our unique ways and in daily conversation—our endeavors will be unwavering; our future depends on it."[19] For Mogri Lookout, the director of the Osage Language Department, this purity refers to the Osage language prior to contact with European languages, which he argues have changed the way Osage was spoken in terms of its grammar, pronunciation, and vocabulary.[20]

This goal of bringing the Osage language back to its purest form derives from a desire to maintain a difference in relation to mainstream American society. The mission statement of the Language Program and the work of its director fit the theoretical beliefs of many informal Osage leaders, such as the roadmen of local Native American Church meetings and the headmen from the yearly *In-Lon-Schka* dances.[21] These practices are believed to provide islands from which to resist the continued encroachment of dominant ideologies. The Osage language in particular was frequently discussed during the reform process in terms of a window into alternative ways of knowing and being, as an experience distinctly different than the ways of knowing and being enabled by the English language.

Whether it is through the act of dancing or eating at *In-Lon-Schka* or through learning the Osage language, "Osage culture" is more than an abstraction. In the act of incorporating these practices into our lives, a sense of ourselves as Osage is configured and reconfigured. This sense of Osage self is fundamentally different from, but not necessarily at odds with, the biological, resource, and sovereignty-based understandings that were deployed as part of the reform process.

While the Osage language has been carried forward from precolonial times, most other "cultural" practices are more recent. The *In-Lon-Schka* dances, for example, developed in the 1880s out of a trade network among Northern Plains nations, including the Osage, Kaw, and Ponca. Over time, however, the Osage added their own songs and adapted the dance, making it their own.[22] According to Osage historian Alice Callahan, *In-Lon-Schka* has become "a manifestation of tribal loyalty and continues to be a strong means of uniting the tribe and giving it a sense of identity."[23] Even though *In-Lon-Schka* cannot be tied to ancient Osage history, since it developed during the colonial era, it still represents a space separate from, and thus outside, mainstream America. Unlike pow-wows and other public Indian dances, the *In-Lon-Schka* is primarily a dance for and by Osage. The non-Osage who attend, and even dance, do so by invitation only. It is within the space of the *In-Lon-Schka* dances that some Osage descendants first develop a sense of an Osage self, distinct from an identity as Americans.

During the reform process, I occasionally asked people when they first understood themselves as Osage, with several answering that it was through their participation in the *In-Lon-Schka* dances. Commissioner Tony Daniels, for example, said, "My first recollection would have to be dancing under the arbor at Grayhorse and getting dressed and just the fun of that."[24] As Daniels described these experiences, he focused less on the dancing and more on the sense of community shared with his family and friends and on the meals they shared. *In-Lon-Schka* is certainly a foundational component of Osage community today, but it is significantly positioned as a space outside of Osage politics. This fact becomes most obvious in election years, when campaigning is specifically prohibited in or around the arbor, the covered pavilion area where the dances take place. *In-Lon-Schka* is in this way understood as uniting the Osage, unlike politics, which are more often viewed by Osage as divisive.

While attending Osage language classes in 2005 and 2006, I was frequently struck by the difference between the tensions and anxieties of OTC and OGRC meetings and the enthusiasm generated by the biweekly language classes. There was a feeling during the language classes that we were all working toward a common goal—to revitalize our language—in many ways similar to the feeling of helping the cooks during *In-Lon-Schka*. This contrasted sharply with the far more contentious and disjointed efforts surrounding governance and national reform.

After Maker finished his address to the Tulsa crowd requesting input on how to make the constitution reflect Osage culture, Billy Sam Fletcher introduced the commissioners, and then the floor was opened to the public. As the first speaker immediately began discussing his problems with the process, the commissioners shifted anxiously in their seats. As soon as the speaker finished, Fletcher quickly attempted to explain what he saw as the purpose of the day's meeting. Using the example of whether blood quantum was culturally appropriate, he explained, "Our job as this commission is to hear your input."[25] As the meeting progressed, it was clear that those in attendance had indeed come with opinions about the future of Osage governance, but it was not until the end of the meeting that this slippery issue of culture resurfaced.

With about ten minutes left in the meeting, a middle-aged man, who was very active on the national pow-wow scene, though not known for his high quantum of Osage blood, said that he wanted to share his opinion. "I have an opinion and it's blood quantum, but it is on the other end. It's a cap on the end. I don't know what that is, but I have seen this happen in other tribes where you get people who are 1/1000s da, da, da, da, da, and their tribe becomes an association. And that is where you lose your culture. Their tribe becomes an organization or association and their goal and their drive is for something else other than the retention of the people."[26] The language of depletion locates culture within the blood, mirroring racial ideologies.[27] The emphasis here, however, is not on biology so much as shared sense of culture. As with similar discourses surrounding

U.S. immigration debates, such a use of culture contains anxieties about difference.[28] For some American Indians, a biocultural difference from the settler population is seen as needed in order to stave off settler colonial threats of absorption. These desires stem from both the repeated threats of termination and the intended and unintended settler colonial processes of assimilation, which have had lasting impacts on Osage life. The danger with such desires comes when they are used to limit what "the retention of the people" actually involves.

Far more often, however, "Osage culture" was used to discredit, rather than support, a minimum blood quantum requirement. After he voted in the referendum, Mogri Lookout, who was the director of the Osage Language Program, a roadman for the Native American Church, and the headman at the Pawhuska *In-Lon-Schka* dances, discussed in an interview his problem with blood quantum: "I don't understand it. My idea of what is an Osage is somebody that goes to the [Native American] church, helps out at the *In-Lon-Schka* and wants to learn the [Osage] language. . . . Then you look at all these people that say they're Osage, but they never help out drum keepers [during *In-Lon-Schka*], and then you never see them in a [Native American] church, you hardly ever see them at a hand game, but yet they're wanting blood quantum, and if they want a blood quantum, they ought to practice what we do."[29] For Lookout, and for many other informal Osage leaders, the Osage are, most importantly, a group of people who share a particular set of embodied practices. While the primary goal of his statement was to discredit blood quantum, this elder highlights specific practices as fundamental for determining who is an Osage. This call to "practice what we do" is a particularly potent means of establishing the authority of culture in defining the Osage.

Mogri Lookout was hardly the only person to define the Osage culturally rather than racially. At a community meeting in Hominy, an older Osage woman, well known for her cooking abilities during *In-Lon-Schka*, argued: "I don't believe in the blood quantum because we're down now so low that one day there won't be an Osage and that's what we're fighting for, we're fighting to keep that Osage alive and for people's lives and their way of life alive. And if it's 1/132nd Osage and they can act Osage and be Osage and dance and take part I think they ought to be recognized whether they are a year old or 100 years old."[30] This speaker's primary goal is to discredit blood quantum as a means of determining Osage citizenship. In the process, however, she inserts her own understanding of who the Osage are. In stating that "we're fighting to keep that Osage . . . way of life alive," she positions past cultural practices as a fundamental part of ensuring an Osage future.

In these discussions, there was a general sense that the Osage were, above all, a group of people who shared a unique set of practices. More fundamental than the categories of race, annuitant, or centralized government, these participants saw culture as the most important component of being Osage. Frequently built into this assertion was the argument that without "Osage culture" the Osage would cease to be Osage and would therefore no longer be able to have a government. It was in such discussions that "Osage culture" took on its most static and problematic connotations. One informal leader expressed this idea in the following way: "What gives us sovereignty is our language, our dances, our names, our ways, our customs, our dress; that's our sovereignty."[31] He went on to elaborate: "It is the opinion of the traditional people[32] that it is because of them that this [the right to self-govern] exists. Because we do certain things—our language, our ways, our burials, our marriages, our celebrations, dance—because we do that, this occurs. If we did not do that then why would the [U.S.] government even recognize our government? It's those things we do that make us Osage that gives the power to create a constitution."[33] According to this informal leader, Osage practices are not only outside of the continuing colonial process but are also the fundamental component to ensuring an Osage future. The term "sovereignty" was a particularly loaded term in the context of the 2004–6 reform process because it was viewed as a central component of the 2006 Osage Constitution. In the interviewee's configuration, sovereignty stems from cultural difference, not historical political authority. For these informal Osage leaders, it is only through the creation and maintenance of these uniquely Osage practices that the Osage can maintain sovereignty.

Perhaps an even more important element of this statement, however, is the recurrence of the threats of federal termination that are used to make a particular argument for the future of the Osage. It becomes clear that culture works as a hazardous entanglement for some Osage, in that they fear that without this "culture" the U.S. government will cease to recognize the Osage Nation. While federal recognition is in fact based on treaties, and more recently on criteria having nothing to do with practices such as language or dance, Osage colonial experiences have created a sense of anxiety around what federal recognition really rests upon.[34] Regardless of whether this speaker genuinely thinks that the U.S. government would cease recognition if the Osage did not maintain "Osage tradition," he saw this threat as powerful enough to support his argument for the centrality of Osage culture. Through such a perceived threat of termination, the category of Osage culture is bounded, not only leaving all who fall outside of it suspect but also limiting what an Osage future can entail.

In these and similar arguments throughout the reform process, some people identified the Osage primarily as a group of people who did or should share a particular set of practices, frequently referred to as Osage culture. Some of these calls for "taking part," like the one quoted above by the Hominy Osage elder, were open-ended, allowing for multiple ways of inhabiting this space. Even when used as a potent means of attempting to create an outside to colonialized space, however, "culture" runs the risk of acting as problematic entanglement, limiting the possibility for a twenty-first-century Osage Nation. Such moments of community connection, when believed to represent the entirety of Osage experience, are problematic. Claims about the foundational nature of particular Osage cultural practices not only disguise the ways all aspects of Osage life, including the governing structure, are Osage, but also lend certain practices more authenticity than others.

When Osage culture is deployed as a tool for recognition it risks becoming static and having to live up to other peoples' standards of what counts as American Indian practice. It is through such limitations that it becomes harder, especially with the passage of time, to be deemed an authentic Indian "worthy" of a political status separate from mainstream America. It is in this way that culture becomes a problematic colonial entanglement, ensnaring American Indians in idealized notions of a primitive past. Almost no Osage, however, could imagine how these expressions of Osage culture could translate into a constitutional document, and many Osage went so far as to argue that such a translation was completely undesirable.

Keep It Separate

In May 2005, the OGRC gathered at Tulsa University for a training session, titled Indian Governance and Law, sponsored by the Indian Law program at the university. I met the commissioners on the Tulsa campus, arriving early to ensure I could find the room and set up the equipment before the start of the meeting. Following the winding corridors of the law school, I finally came to the classroom where the day's event would take place. A few of the commissioners had already perched themselves on the stadium seats and were swiveled around talking with one another in quiet voices. The tiered classroom had long lines of tables, a blackboard at the front of the room, and strong fluorescent lighting above. Glancing at the schedule, it appeared that we were in for a series of lectures from Tulsa University law professors on topics ranging from a general overview of Indian law to the specifics of personnel and employment law.

As the day progressed, it was hard to imagine how this material was going to help the OGRC with the task at hand. It was not going to be responsible for writing employment codes, and while the overview of American Indian law was fascinating, it was far too complex a topic to be covered effectively in a short lecture. Additionally, the Osage Nation has been exempted from much general American Indian policy, rendering most broad overviews unproductive. By the time Professor William Rice, an enrolled citizen of the United Keetoowah Band of Cherokee Indians in Oklahoma and a professor of law at the university, gave his lecture, "Tribal Constitutions: Skeletons, Beads, and Feathers," the commissioners were clearly ready for some concrete advice that they could implement.

Focusing on the need to keep constitutions as basic as possible, Rice suggested that the commissioners include in the constitution only those things they could not imagine living without. He then discussed what he knew of ancient Osage governance and core values, asking, "How important are these things to who the Osage are? Should they have a place in this constitution?"[35] As discussed above, this was not the first time that the commissioners had been faced with this question.

William Rice is one of many American Indian constitutional scholars who place a strong emphasis on the inclusion of "culture." The Native Nations Institute (NNI), a University of Arizona organization that grew out of the Harvard Project on American Indian Economic Development and whose mission is to assist with "capacity building" among American Indian nations, also highlights the importance of "culture." The central tenets of NNI's research on American Indian governmental reform greatly influenced the reform's acceptance among the OTC, Maker's planning, the commissioners' approach to the process, and, ultimately, the writing of the 2006 Osage Constitution. In March 2005, shortly after the OGRC was created, Leonard Maker, the head of planning for the OTC, paid NNI $60,000 to host a training session for the commissioners.[36] Maker had previously employed NNI consultants, using the promise of enhanced economic development to further persuade the OTC that wholesale governmental reform was needed, in part because the imposed OTC structure was not seen as a "cultural match for the Osage."[37]

Joseph P. Kalt, director of the Udall Center, which houses NNI at the University of Arizona, and co-founder of the Harvard Project on American Indian Economic Development, opened his OGRC training session with a lecture in which he presented the five elements essential to building economically successful nations. These elements included sovereignty, effective governing institutions, cultural matching, strategic thinking, and leadership. In his lecture on cultural matching, Kalt stressed the need to design governmental structures that "fit your society." He went on to say, "Without a cultural match, people turn their governments into tools of destruction."[38] Kalt illustrated his points with examples from various American Indian nations, tying their economic indicators to the ways their current governments matched, integrated, and supported "their culture."[39]

"Culture" here is a collective term for the core beliefs of a nation. Eric D. Lemont, an author concerned with American Indian constitutional reform, states, "A constitution must reflect a society's fundamental values if it is truly to serve as its highest law."[40] This process is difficult since most American Indian nations have had these values "systematically attacked and weakened by U.S. policies of termination, relocation, and assimilation."[41] "Reform leaders," he concludes, "must first reaffirm (and in some cases rediscover) these core beliefs and then develop strategies for having them serve as the foundation of their governments."[42]

Culture in this context becomes a burden; American Indian peoples are forced to overturn a destructive legacy of U.S. policies and reconnect to a culture damaged by the colonial process. As a colonial entanglement, American Indian culture is made to stand for all that is fundamental, pure, and noncolonized.[43] American Indian culture is also, however, fundamentally elusive, generally evades description, and only known through experience. The commissioners were faced with the daunting task of incorporating such indefinable phenomena into the constitution.

Mary Jo Webb, the commissioner who served on the Tulsa Catholic Diocese Synod Commission, surprised everyone at the Tulsa University legal training with her ready answer to the question of how to incorporate culture into the constitution. As it was still early in the process, Webb began by explaining to the other commissioners and the law professors present that she had studied the traditional government of the Osage Nation through the writings of Francis La Flesche as well as through members of her own family for twenty-five years.[44] Making her way carefully down to the blackboard at the head of the room, she drew two half circles on the board, with the one on top representing the Sky people and the one below representing the Earth people. Each, she explained, had their own high chief and lesser chiefs. Webb continued by saying that part of the governance structure involved a large gathering in the fall. "So they gather; they begin to fast and pray. And they come out of this lodge here [pointing to the blackboard] and they begin to dance on this side [Sky] like this and on this side [Earth] they dance like this. They meet in the middle. They do that for four days from sun up to sun down. They never sing the same song twice. They've got four days of memorized songs and each clan would have their own."[45] According to La Flesche, Osage governance in the early nineteenth century was modeled after the cosmos, with twenty-four *u-dsé-the*/fireplaces, or clans, representing the spectrum of life symbols, which included animals, plants, celestial bodies, and other occurrences such as storms and thunder. Each of these clans was divided into smaller bands as well as into the two larger groups, the Earth people (*Hun-kah*) and the Sky people (*Tzi-zho*): "Collectively all twenty-four clans, through their life symbols, symbolically represented the cosmos in all its diversity."[46]

Webb went on to explain that it was only possible for this event to take place if all the clans were present and each sang its own songs, which each clan alone knew. If there was any disharmony within the group, the members of the group had to settle their differences beforehand. She concluded by saying, "You had to forgive and have restitution all the time. This translates to me into two houses, government houses. It would bring in custom and tradition if we had a new government that had both the sky and the earth people involved and in the villages. That was the band people. So we know enough of our traditional customs to know how maybe to put this together. I don't know that anybody would want it like that or not, but each one could have representatives from these two sides."[47] As Webb took her seat, the room grew quiet, with many of the members of the OGRC looking uncomfortable. The silence that filled the room following Webb's proposal, and again when she reintroduced this idea in July as part of a discussion on governmental restructuring, indicated the commissioners' and, in their view, the majority of Osage members' disconnect from these older practices. The commissioners were active in many aspects of Osage life, but Webb was describing practices that had long ago been abandoned and almost entirely forgotten.

During the reform process, and particularly in dialogue with non-Osage, the OGRC was repeatedly faced with the question of how the new constitution was going to reflect "Osage culture." In addition to the reasons discussed above, such a use of culture was problematic since, like all peoples, the Osage do not share, and never have shared, a singular or static "culture."[48] Furthermore, the location of culture in a distant past with only vague resonance seems particularly impractical and can be a dangerous colonial tool for erasing indigenous presence today. By insisting that Osage culture is located in the remote past rather than in current practices, Osage are not only made to feel inauthentic but also are denied the ability to determine the shape of their own future.

Even more important, however, was the strong reaction against the calls for cultural inclusion by the people most active in the realm of "culture." Superficially, this response seems incongruous, since it was these same Osage who frequently stressed culture as an essential ingredient in establishing and maintaining the Osage. Such a contradiction, however, points to the way constitutional writing frequently involves the coalescing of authority, which is rarely unanimously supported. By insisting that the Osage government should have no part to play in "Osage culture," these elders were ensuring a continued space for their own authorities and practices outside of this centralized governing structure.

Of the over 1,300 Osage who returned the questionnaire, about 500 offered suggestions to the question, "How could the new governing document incorporate Osage culture?" Many of the responses focused on how the new government structure needed to ensure that language and cultural practices were "preserved" and "supported" by the new government, but few responses suggested any practical inclusion of these practices within the constitution.

The concept of an elders' council was one of the more pragmatic ideas proposed for the inclusion of culture within the constitution. The 1994 Osage Constitution had included a Council of Elders, which was to "serve in an advisory capacity to the Osage National Council on matters pertaining to cultural, historical, and traditional activities of the Osage people" (see appendix 3).[49] This Council of Elders had been partially modeled after the "Little Old Men," which Bailey argues was a group of tribal advisers who gathered together to observe and analyze the structure of the cosmos during and immediately before the time Francis La Flesche studied with the Osage.[50] This Council of Elders was referred to eight times within the questionnaire and approximately the same number of times during community meetings. However, while some supported the concept of an elders' council, there was a much stronger appeal to keep "Osage culture" entirely separate from governance.

Even those arguing for an elders' council expressed a desire for creating a clear distinction between these advisers and government affairs. One questionnaire response, for example, stated, "The government should not have anything to do with the preservation of the culture. It should be preserved by a Council of Elders, who direct the government on cultural issues. Anyone on the culture commission would not serve in government." While this instance demonstrates how culture became a generic term applied to complex and varied practices, it is also a telling example of the hesitancy many people felt about the authority of the new government, particularly over affairs understood as cultural. Such statements also reflect how the current Osage structure had been operating for the last hundred years, with the OTC functioning separately from operations such as the Native American Church and the *In-Lon-Schka* dances. The U.S. government originally set up the OTC with the sole purpose of managing the Mineral Estate, which had only over time begun to take on other governmental functions and had only recently begun funding activities such as language preservation.

Since political control had been decentralized for so long, the resistance to incorporation of other Osage activities was also a resistance to centralizing various local and informal governing institutions under a singular governing structure. This desire for separation appeared even more strongly in other questionnaire responses, with statements such as "Osage culture has done well without being incorporated into a governing document. Keep it separated, independent." Other Osage respondents voiced similar opinions, arguing that the new Osage governing document should be entirely separate from Osage culture, especially from the informal power structures that have governed these institutions over the last hundred years. It is evident from these responses that some Osage did not want to see these institutions affected by the consolidation of power under the new constitution.

Throughout the reform process, many participants expressed similar concerns regarding the consolidation of these "cultural" systems into the new governing system. One stated reason behind these concerns was to keep politics outside cultural events such as naming ceremonies and the yearly dances, which had their own means of determining authority. Most of the informal leaders I talked with or who spoke during the 2004–6 reform process wanted to make sure the new government was not able to meddle in their affairs. They each had their own recognizable sphere of control, whether it was the *In-Lon-Schka* dances or the Native American Church, and the government reform raised the possibility that the formal government was going to include and thus eclipse the authorities already existing within this space. Several tribal elders argued adamantly against the inclusion of anything from the old ways. As one elder stated: "If you don't know what you are doing, you could do a great deal of damage. We have an order to everything we do."[51] This statement reveals the perception of a threat from the overextension of the new constitutional government.

Calls for keeping "Osage culture" separate, however, also revealed a fluid understanding of what this concept entailed. In fact, at least part of the desire for keeping Osage practices outside of the new government was that the incorporation would render them static. Informal leaders are well aware of the ways these institutions, including the yearly *In-Lon-Schka* dances and the Native American Church, vary in character, depending on where they are performed and by whom, and of the fact that, like all practices, they have changed over time. To incorporate any aspect of them into the constitution, or to require participation in them as part of the citizenship requirements, was seen as detrimental to the living quality of these practices. As another respondent to the question of the government's role in promulgating culture stated: "It shouldn't [have a role]. Osage culture should be maintained and transferred by the people themselves. If you need a governing document to tell you how to be Osage, you've waited too late to take care of your culture." To constitutionalize was to freeze fluid activities that were constantly given new form. Such culturally labeled activities were considered to be outside formal governance, and certainly outside a constitutional structure, which had to be written and was therefore fixed.

While change is a fundamental part of all groups, oral and written history has positioned "moving to a new country" as a fundamental component of Osage society. One of the primary origin narratives of the Osage, recounted by John Joseph Mathews, involves not a singular lineage but unification of four groups through a shared change in lifestyle.[52] In his recounting of the origin story, Mathews argues that this was only the first of many moves to "a new country": "The Little Old Men spoke of these moves as one might speak of changing camping places, and each organizational step was a step away from the old, just as they walked away from the disorder of the old campsites."[53] As others have noted, these moves were more than geographical changes in location, but they also included changes in governing style, community structure, and spiritual practices.[54]

Drawing from extensive ethnohistory and archival research, Garrick Bailey writes, "Contrary to popular conceptions about American Indians, the traditional Osage were, and the contemporary Osage continue to be, strongly future oriented."[55] Bailey continues that, based on observations of the universe, Osage felt that only through change could they maintain order. In these ways, many Osage make sense of even drastic change as a necessity that is inherently part of what it means to be Osage, rather than a negative phenomenon that destroys Osage identity. In discussing the authority of the 1881 Constitution, for example, Osage academic Robert Warrior states: "I would like to suggest . . . that a major part of the answer lies not with the cultural practices the Osage were learning from outside their culture, but with the continuation of traditions they had developed over the course of centuries. In adopting their constitution, in other words, they were 'moving to a new country.'"[56] While the 1861 and 1881 Osage Constitutions were significantly different from the governing structures in existence prior to and in the time between these documents, the ability to thrive during change marks, rather than denies, Osage authority. Instead of creating an identity based on the maintenance of a certain way of life, many Osage have built an identity on a willingness to embrace change.

Throughout the 2004–6 Osage reform process, participants argued that older Osage practices, such as the system described by Mary Jo Webb, no longer made sense within the colonial context and that they should therefore not employ a fragmented and somewhat arbitrary cultural conception. Additionally, there was a strong sense among some Osage that these older cultural practices, which formed the basis of governance prior to the colonial period, should not be included because they no longer had significant cultural meaning to the majority of the Osage people. One elder who had extensively studied Osage history explained to me that these old ways were heavily integrated with a religion that was no longer practiced. "We have had to change with the flow of time and the old people knew that. They insisted that we not try to bring these things we could not understand forward."[57] Another elder expressed similar concerns about the use of older Osage words and ideas within the new governing document: "These words are not understood anymore. These are ideas that were supposed to be left behind."[58]

While colonial policies of removal, assimilation, and reorganization have had devastating impacts on American Indian lifeways,[59] Osage discussions of change are about more than "loss." These conversations signal the ways in which Osage people made choices about what they would bring forward and what they would leave behind. In particular, the discussions about not understanding the past powerfully signal both the trauma of settlement and the decision of Osage to embrace new ways of understanding the world around them. Viewed as neither wholly liberating nor constraining, such a colonial entanglement limits choices but does not negate them.

Lyons also notes this negotiation, referring to "modern" American Indian practice as "x-marks." He defines the x-mark as "a contaminated and coerced sign of consent made under conditions that are not of one's making. It signifies power and lack of power, agency and a lack of agency. It is a decision one makes when something has already been decided for you, but it is still a decision."[60] The classic example of an x-mark is the literal marking of an "x" on treaties, where an uncoerced assent was not possible but assent was given nonetheless. Lyons expands this notion of x-marks to incorporate such institutions as current American Indian nations. While, for Lyons, today's nations are not based on the same sort of organizing principles that were at work in most American Indian communities prior to colonization, they have become powerful means for these communities to assert themselves in the present. For Lyons, what matters today is how these x-marks are used, rather than where they came from.

At an OTC meeting in August 2005, it was brought to the council's attention that an Osage war bundle had been found for sale on eBay. Carrie Wilson, the Osage employee in charge of repatriation at the time, had immediately contacted the Native American Graves Protection and Repatriation Department as well as the FBI. The FBI gained possession of the bundle and wanted to know what should be done next. The Gilcrease Museum had offered to keep it. One of the people on the OTC suggested that since there had been a ceremony 100 years ago to "put the bundles away" by burying them, perhaps there should be some sort of ceremony to welcome this bundle back. Another person on the OTC, however, immediately protested, saying, "I want to go on the record at this point that we should not have any new ceremonies. We just need to put that stuff away. We don't know anything about it."[61] The rest of the OTC agreed to have the bundle buried immediately, without any new ceremonies.

On one hand, this decision to have no new ceremonies associated with bundles can be read as a colonial rupture, marking the violence of loss. For many Osage, however, this decision to "put the bundles away" is read as part of the tradition of change that was inevitable. A fundamental aspect of the "moving to a new country" concept was not only that objects like the war bundle could not be understood anymore and thus needed to be put away but also that cultural practices had to change in order to have meaning in peoples' lives. Kathryn Red Corn, the director of the Osage Tribal Museum, often spoke with me about her frustration with static notions of Osage and American Indian culture more generally. In her office one afternoon, she noted that American Indian culture was too often assumed to have some larger spiritual meaning. She gave the example of a visitor who had asked her the purpose of the fans during the yearly *In-Lon-Schka* dance. Her response was, "Have you noticed it is a hundred degrees out here?"[62] Through her sarcasm, Red Corn illustrates the absurdity of some of the beliefs about American Indian culture.

Most things, Red Corn went on to explain, were not done because they had some deeper spiritual meaning, but because they made sense at the time. She argued that if spiritual meaning does exist, it could rarely be separated in such neat ways from the functionality of the practice. As an example, she told me a story about her cousin, who had always cut turkeys in half before cooking them. The cousin was convinced that she was using an Osage recipe for cooking a turkey. One day, in talking with her mother, the cousin discovered that the only reason this had been done for generations was because the grandmother did not have an oven big enough for a full turkey. As in this instance, Red Corn concluded, all Osage practices changed over time to meet the needs of the people. Older Osage practices "had to be left behind. We can't go back, those things are gone. We have to go forward."[63]

It did not make sense to many Osage to imagine older governing structures as a possibility for the future because of the long colonial history that separated the majority of Osage from these practices. This was stated most articulately during an OGRC business meeting after one attendee had expressed concern that the Osage constitution had been patterned after the colonizer rather than "their own heritage." In response, one of the reform commissioners said:

> I think we all honor and reflect our heritage from before we were moved from Missouri and Kansas. . . . But what we discovered in our process,

which has been about 11 months talking to Osage people everywhere, is that the majority of Osage we talked to can't understand how those structures worked. Fortunately or unfortunately, they can understand the federal government system. So when we've asked this question in surveys, "would you like a three-part government or would you like something else," an overwhelming majority said they'd like a three-part government; it's one they're familiar with.[64]

The act of taking on the shape of the colonizer could, like other aspects of the Osage constitution, be described as a contradiction. For most of the participants within the reform process, however, the act of adopting the three-part government made sense in the same way that adopting any new tool or technology makes sense once it is proven to be effective. Embracing these new practices was generally not understood in any way as endangering the Osage as a people. Instead, such changes were fundamental to reforming an Osage Nation in the twenty-first century and ensuring that the Osage continue to exist as a people.

During another of the weekly OGRC business meetings, the discussion again turned to culture. While Mary Jo Webb had been arguing for the incorporation of some kind of cultural practice into the new governing document, she now took a different approach: "I think we all know culture changes . . . and for us as Osage, we changed. We had to adapt and we were good at it. That's another custom. We're good at adaptation. And we don't mind giving up whatever in order to gain the better. That's a part of our history too."[65] Osage practices, even within the tight space of "Osage culture," were understood as a fluid entity and were therefore unable to be solidified into a constitution. To write "Osage culture" into a governing structure would be to limit its ability to change, thereby destroying the ability to live and develop.

During the government reform writing retreat in early January 2006, one of the primary issues was whether cultural aspects, including an elders' council, should be incorporated into the constitution. Included in the constitutional draft assembled by Hepsi Barnett, the coordinator for the OGRC, was a Council of Elders similar to that of the 1994 Constitution (see appendix 3). Seeing the inclusion of the Council of Elders, one of the informal leaders in attendance stated that when his father had been on the OTC in the 1950s, he had gone to one of the districts to try to help with problems they were having with the *In-Lon-Schka* dances. "Dad went down there and said, is there any way the council can help you? And he was immediately told, in Osage, to get his rear end back to the hill and stay there. We'll take care of this, they said."[66] In sending the Osage government official back to the "hill," the area in Pawhuska where both the OTC and the Bureau of Indian Affairs have their offices, the OTC member was specifically told that his authority did not extend to the dances. In concluding his argument about the 2006 Osage Constitution, this informal leader said, "We already have that [order] in our cultural ways. You can't bring that into this [new governing structure]; it's oil and water."[67]

As is evident throughout this chapter, culture is a slippery concept, especially as it is being expressed by American Indians in the twenty-first century. On one hand, culture too often signals static practices from the distant past that mark American Indians as different from their Western colonizers. Yet the Osage in particular, and American Indians more generally, understand perhaps better than most other populations the importance of change as part of survival. Change was built into American Indian societies long before the colonial process and has enabled these nations to create a future for themselves. In debating the contents of the 2006 Osage Constitution, Osage citizens understood politics and culture to be like "oil and water," not just because they respected preexisting authorities in cultural matters but also because they understood the importance of allowing practices to maintain their fluidity. "Culture" could not be constituted because it had to be lived and debated.

One of the Osage lawyers in attendance at the writing retreat agreed with the characterization of politics and culture as "oil and water," saying that his father had taught him similar notions. He went on to suggest that it would be a major problem if the headmen from the yearly dances wanted to use the Council of Elders to become part of the government: "Then you have an added incentive for that position; people will try to get into that position to get into government."[68] He instead proposed a solution: "What if we just said in Section 1 that the government has a duty to promote language and culture. . . . That's something the government does better than interfering with traditional structures in place."[69] This Osage lawyer argued that the Osage government should not coalesce authorities within the Osage Nation but should instead allow other informal forms of authority to exist outside of the constitution.

The OGRC ended up incorporating these suggestions in Article XVI of the 2006 Osage Nation Constitution: "The Osage People have the inherent right to preserve and foster their historic linguistic and cultural lifeways. The Osage Nation shall protect and promote the language, culture, and traditional ways of the Osage people."[70] Additionally, the 2006 Constitution says, "The first regular congressional session of each year shall be titled the *Hun-kah* Session and the second regular congressional session of the year shall be titled the *Tzi-zho* Session. This schedule shall be in honor of the ancient moiety division of Earth and Sky and serves to remind all Osage of the responsibility to bring balance and harmony to the nation."[71] In 2006, the Osage voters approved a constitution that "honored" the ancient divisions and worked to "protect and promote the language, culture, and traditional ways" but that specifically did not solidify cultural practices within the governing document.[72]

Throughout the 2004–6 Osage reform process, practice-based understandings of community belonging were understood as incompatible with the bureaucratic process necessary in constituting citizenship and governance. This failure to coalesce, a primary function of constitution writing, had to do with the rise of informal authorities during the era of the OTC, skepticism about the consolidation of authority within centralized governments, and the desire for fluidity in these particular arenas. In fact, no participants in the 2004–6 reform process advocated using any "cultural practices" to define the Osage body politic in the twenty-first century. Such practices are inappropriately limiting when imagined as citizenship requirements or aspects of national structure, though they are frequently a central aspect of what constitutes internal notions of belonging. It is likely only because "culture" has acted as an entanglement in American Indian communities that it could ever be imagined as a necessary part of the constitutions.

Given that the 1861, 1881, and 1994 Osage Constitutions had tripartite governments with a very similar structure to the 2006 Osage Nation Constitution, the OGRC can indeed be thought to have created a cultural match, in the sense that it succeeded in matching the new institutions to older forms of governance. This fact, however, does not account for the strong reactions some Osage had to the question about the incorporation of Osage culture into the governing structure. For Kalt and others associated with the Harvard Project on American Indian Economic Development, effective self-rule necessarily involves the consolidation of power. As Miriam Jorgensen argues, effective self-governance involves achieving "substantive decision-making control over lands, resources, civic affairs, and community life."[73] Such control, particularly over community life, did not make sense in the case of the Osage Nation. Few Osage were interested in seeing the reconstituted Osage Nation take on such authority, since informal authorities had thrived for so long. Ultimately, the need to have a cultural match, as described by Kalt, meant that the Osage Nation refused to centralize authority.

Making sense of the desire for separation was just one of the obstacles the OGRC had to negotiate in the creation of a new governing structure. It was also charged with handling the politically sensitive issues relating to the Osage Mineral Estate. During an OGRC business meeting in September 2005, one of the commissioners, frustrated with the progress of the community meetings, stated that the real cultural match for the government had a lot less to do with cultural practices and a lot more to do with the Osage headright system, which had been in place for the last hundred years. Few reform topics received full community attention because the discussion would almost inevitably return to the Mineral Estate. Fundamental to these discussions, much like those concerning Osage culture, was a disdain for the consolidation of power. I will turn next to the Osage Mineral Estate and the ways some Osage annuitants worked to limit the authorities and possibilities of the newly reconstituted Osage Nation through their focus on the Mineral Estate.

Chapter 4 **Minerals**

We were all apprehensive as several of the reform commissioners, their lawyer, and I made the trek out to Grayhorse, the most remote Osage community. The Grayhorse Indian camp has always been known not just for its isolation but also for its inhabitants' fierce independence and skepticism, especially concerning issues of Osage governance. They were the last of the three Osage districts to settle on the Osage reservation, making the migration from the Kansas lands only with great trepidation.[1] Additionally, this was the first community meeting to be held after the 2005 referendum vote, where all but one issue was decided by a large margin (see appendix 6). The one remaining issue dealt with how the Osage Mineral Estate was going to be incorporated into the new government. For the Osage annuitants, who made up the majority of participants in the 2004–6 Osage reform process, this was a very serious and contentious matter.

When we walked into the aluminum-sided community building in the center of Grayhorse, we were greeted by the stares of two dozen citizens, who were already waiting for the meeting to begin. The long and narrow room was filled with tables and folding chairs facing the single table reserved for the commissioners at the front of the room. Behind the audience, the kitchen sat dark and empty, evidence of the meeting's lack of advance notice. Unlike the earlier meetings, when the commissioners went to great lengths to encourage participation, including elaborately catered meals by well-known Osage cooks, this round of meetings had few such attractions and was solely intended to address the vocal minority of annuitants who had concerns about the new constitution.

From the beginning of the meeting in Grayhorse, it was clear that the apprehension felt on the long drive across the reservation was well founded. This issue of how the Osage Mineral Estate should be incorporated into the new governing structure resulted in a great deal of anxiety for some Osage annuitants, who were deeply skeptical of any change to the original 1906 Osage Allotment Act (34 Stat. 539). If there was one constant theme throughout the community meetings, it was that the Osage Mineral Estate should be left alone. At Grayhorse, this sentiment took on even more force, with tensions reaching a peak. One middle-aged annuitant from Fairfax, the nearest town to Grayhorse, grew visibly upset, repeatedly pounding his fist on the table and yelling, "It's ours!," asserting that all of the natural resources on the Osage Reservation, and even the gaming proceeds, belonged to the Osage annuitants alone.

Even though all of the commissioners were annuitants, he continued yelling: "You all need to stay out of the Mineral Estate. You all stay out of it. You have no business in there." Later in the meeting, when he had calmed down, he explained: "What you need is to look at the Minerals Council as a corporation. You have no control over the corporation; only the shareholders do. You cannot as an elected official in Osage County go over and tell Conoco you have to give us money. Conoco is controlled by shareholders. The Minerals fund is controlled by the shareholders and the 1906 [Osage Allotment] Act, which has not been reformed, [and] remains the same. Only shareholders can decide how it should be done."[2] The tension between the authority of a new constitutional government and the hundred-year-old Osage Mineral Estate was a constant roadblock throughout the 2004–6 Osage reform process, as well as the most contentious issue, as evidenced in tense interactions like this one. The language of annuitants as shareholders in a corporation, however, both belies and obscures the deep history of colonial entanglement behind the Osage Mineral Estate.

The story of Osage oil, a tale of wealth and prosperity, is also a classic tale of colonization. Oil production on Osage land began at the end of the nineteenth century, with a blanket lease to the entire reservation going to Kansas railroad man Henry Foster and his brother Edwin in 1896. The Osage agent, H. B. Freeman, the Office of Indian Affairs (OIA), and Foster negotiated the deal, and only after the fact did the 1881 Osage Constitution's governing body, the Osage National Council, put it to a vote. The initial lease passed by the narrow margin of seven to six, but a little over a year later the National Council voted to annul the contract. William Pollock, Freeman's successor as Osage agent, however, overrode the National Council seven months later, reinstating the contract.[3] Given the competitive advantage lost with the blanket lease, it is hard to understand the OIA motivation here as anything but an example of early corporate lobbying, not unlike what happened later across Indian Country.[4]

The 1906 Osage Allotment Act created the Osage Mineral Estate as part of the unique deal struck between the Osage and the OIA, who wanted to open up Indian Country for white settlement and statehood. The surface of the Osage reservation was allotted, but the subsurface, including rights to oil, natural gas, and other minerals, was left under national control, to be distributed to those listed on the 1906 Osage roll. While the most common narrative about the Osage allotment is that Chief Bigheart was able to negotiate a better allotment because the Osage had purchased their reservation land and understood the importance of collective ownership, it is likely that the oil lobby played a key role in keeping the subsurface from being allotted.[5] In the congressional hearings concerning allotment, there was discussion about the unique arrangement, which included reference to both keeping costs low for the oil company and sharing the wealth equally among all Osage.[6]

As Alexandra Harmon points out, the argument of equity does not make sense given the strict cut-off date for the 1906 roll.[7] In the last hundred years, the Mineral Estate has created a deep divide between Osage "haves" and "have-nots." Osage descendants born after July 1, 1907, were not only landless and denied any voice in national politics but were also excluded from the proceeds of the communally owned Mineral Estate, which was distributed equally among all those listed on the 1906 roll. Tying Osage citizenship to the Mineral Estate created high tensions among Osage descendants, thwarted earlier attempts at reorganization, and created many obstacles during the 2004–6 reform process. This history also worked to instill in some Osage a sense that their headrights were personal property rather than an asset of the Nation, from which they received annuity checks.

My grandfather, George Orville Dennison, was born eighteen months before the July 1, 1907, cut-off date, and so he received three 160-acre parcels of land within the Osage reservation, a 1/2,230th share of all monies produced from the Mineral Estate, and, when he turned twenty-one, a vote in Osage elections.[8] His two brothers, who were born after the 1907 cut-off date, received nothing and had no voice in the government. This led my great-grandmother to distribute my grandfather's money among the three boys, until my grandfather married and his wife put an end to the redistribution. These Mineral Estate proceeds divided the family, leading my great-grandmother to favor the brothers' children at gift-giving occasions, rather than my grandfather's children. This further estranged my father from the larger family, who as a young boy did not understand the unfairness. This money also divided the Osage Nation, as a growing percentage of Osage descendants were disenfranchised and began fighting for equal voting rights through organizations such as the Osage Nation Organization. My grandfather—and more frequently my grandmother—often voiced disapproval of non-headright-owning Osage, who were "just trying to get our money."

The fear that the non–headright holders were going to find a way of accessing the Mineral Estate funds was only further reinforced by the troubles of the roaring 1920s. After the discovery of oil in 1897, the market for Osage oil grew dramatically, bringing much wealth to Osage headright holders. At its peak in 1925, when each annuitant earned $13,200 a quarter, many people came onto the Osage reservation as legal guardians, merchants, suitors, swindlers, and murderers in search of access to or an advantage in acquiring this wealth.[9] The Osage eventually paid the FBI to investigate the murders of sixty Osage, which ended in several convictions.[10] This did not, however, bring to a halt the loss of millions of dollars to price-gauging shop owners and legal guardians, who, as Harmon states, "could skim money from their charges' account with an ease too tempting for many to resist."[11]

Rather than buying freedom, Osage wealth led to deep entanglements. In addition to the introduction of the oil lobby into Osage Nation affairs and the arrival of many non-Osage in search of Osage wealth, the Mineral Estate also increased the role of the U.S. government in Osage affairs. From the beginning of the oil production on the reservation, the OIA overrode Osage decisions and created policies that went against Osage desires and interests. In 1921, the U.S. Congress went so far as to pass a law that "non-competent" Osage, generally those listed as having over one-half Indian blood, could have access to only $4,000 of their annuitant payments per year. This was justified as an attempt to obstruct Osage consumption patterns and the flagrant fraud occurring throughout the reservation. Both of these justifications were themselves deeply colonial. As Harmon points out, Osage consumption was on par with the spending habits of others in this income bracket during this time, but it was disconcerting because it challenged stereotypes of the poor Indian. As for the outright fraud happening across the reservation, this would have more appropriately been dealt with by punishing the perpetrators rather than the victims.[12]

While many Osage did fight the rigid caps imposed on their funds, many did have an ambivalent relationship with U.S. guardianship. Given the murder and fraud brought on by the Mineral Estate, it is easy to understand why any protection would be desirable. But there is a good deal of evidence suggesting that U.S. officials were not ideal guardians. In 1917, the Osage Tribal Council (OTC) complained that Superintendent George Wright was "more greatly concerned about and . . . favorable to the interests of big oil companies and men of large financial means and political influence than . . . to the interests of the Osage people."[13] The OTC went on to argue that Wright's agency was spending Osage money needlessly and without their consent.[14] This mismanagement is sadly not limited to the early twentieth century. After twelve years of U.S. Court of Federal Claims trust accounting and trust management lawsuits, a U.S. District Court for the District of Columbia trust accounting case, and extensive discovery, motions, and rulings, the Osage Nation and the U.S. government negotiated an agreement on October 14, 2011, for $380 million to compensate for mismanagement of tribal trust funds that occurred between 1972 and 2000.[15] This and other evidence illustrates the continuing failure of the United States to act as a responsible manager of Osage affairs.

Through these intertwined forces, the colonial process has made the Mineral Estate into another hazardous entanglement. The hidden ties to oil corporations, the fostering of divisive internal politics, privilege, status, U.S. guardianship, and the fear of losing the Mineral Estate were all still very much present during the 2004–6 Osage reform process. In light of this history, along with the money and authority at stake, it is little wonder that some Osage focus their energy and concern on the Mineral Estate, arguing against other visions of an Osage future. This way of understanding the Osage, as a group of shareholders focused solely on the protection and extraction of resources, had, like other definitions of the Osage, to be reconciled in the writing of the 2006 constitution.

The fact remained that, unlike what some annuitants claimed, the 1906 Osage Allotment Act had been reformed by the 2004 legislation. It was only the distribution of the shares that remained unassailable. The legislation created by the OTC and passed by the U.S. Congress, which enabled the reform, stated, "Notwithstanding section 9 of the Act entitled, 'An Act for the division of lands and funds of the Osage Indians in Oklahoma Territory, and for other purposes,' approved June 28, 1906 (34 Stat. 539), Congress hereby reaffirms the inherent sovereign right of the Osage Tribe to determine its own form of government provided that the rights of any person to Osage Mineral Estate shares are not diminished thereby" (see appendix 5).[16] This 2004 act was, however, just the beginning. Simply because the Osage Nation had the right to change its government structure did not mean that change had to happen, and some vocal Osage annuitants were wary of any reform.

As the Grayhorse community meeting continued, the lawyer for the reform process attempted to explain the importance of having a larger, non-headright-based government to protect important concerns such as the environment, which a corporate-style structure, focused solely on profit, could never be expected to take seriously. He also drove home the need for rebuilding a strong Osage nation "for your children and grandchildren" and highlighted benefits such as "improved health care, improved housing, roads, highways, and public school." Concluding, he said, "There are lots of ways as a member of the Osage Nation that you can expect to benefit from this government."[17] In instances such as this community meeting, it was however the Mineral Estate, not the structure of the national government, that consumed the time and energy of the Osage Government Reform Commission (OGRC).

The Osage annuitants in attendance at this Grayhorse community meeting were deeply skeptical of this transformation from a resource-based structure, which was focused on their perceived property interest, to a larger constitutional structure serving all Osage descendants. Responding to the lawyer's impassioned speech about the benefits that could come from a constitutional government, another annuitant from the Grayhorse area argued: "But what you're saying is that the Osage Tribal Council won't have authority to exercise any autonomy over the Mineral Estate? You're going to say that the new government can dictate laws and regulations for producers and this Minerals Council to follow. That won't mix."[18] It was clear from these interactions that these Osage subjectivities were first and foremost framed by interest in the Osage Mineral Estate.

The meeting at Grayhorse was hardly the first time during the 2004–6 reform process that an OGRC community meeting had been derailed over issues relating to the Osage Mineral Estate. A majority of the community meetings were spent on the topic of the Mineral Estate, with the commissioners repeatedly assuring those in attendance that their headrights were protected by the legislation itself. These declarations could never quite calm these vocal annuitants, however, making it clear that these tensions were not just about the right to profit from the Mineral Estate. After almost a hundred years of controlling Osage affairs, not all Osage annuitants were willing to give up their monopoly on Osage authority so easily, nor were they sure that such a change would be beneficial to themselves or the Osage Mineral Estate in the long run.

This chapter will investigate the tensions surrounding the Osage Mineral Estate, including fears instilled by the ongoing colonial process and the doubts about the expansion of Osage governance, which lay behind desires to leave the Osage Mineral Estate alone. In order to understand how these intertwined motivations operated, it will be necessary to look closely at the various debates during and after the 2004–6 Osage reform process, with a particular focus on how change was situated. In this chapter, we will see how the Osage Mineral Estate operated as a colonial entanglement for some Osage. These Osage annuitants understood the Mineral Estate as the most fundamental component of the Osage Nation, an understanding that had very real consequences not only on the reform process but also on the implementation of the 2006 Osage Constitution.

Debating Change

My first in-person encounter with the Osage Shareholders Association (OSA) was an eye-opening experience. The August 2005 OSA meeting was held in the airy Dave Landrum Community Center in Pawhuska, Oklahoma, a neutral space outside the control of the Osage Nation. The brick structure, with its steep red metal roof and copula, was built in 2003 with money donated by Pawhuska philanthropists Carl and Virginia Short. The large open space that dominated the community center was used primarily as a meeting space for Osage County governance affairs but was also available for other community events.

I had been documenting the progress of the OGRC for almost four months and had heard a great deal about the fabled OSA but had yet to attend a meeting. The OSA was founded in September 1994 in Pawhuska, Oklahoma, and its charter reads that the purpose of the organization is to promote "efficient administration," a "streamlining" and "strict enforcement" of federal laws and regulations, and the preservation of "the federal trust status" of the Osage Mineral Estate.[19] The OSA was organized as a watchdog group over the Mineral Estate shortly after the passage of the 1994 Constitution. It is little wonder then that it would play an active role in the 2004–6 Osage reform process, when the authority of the Osage headright holders over all aspects of Osage governance was again challenged.

Beginning with a large potluck buffet, the meeting was off to an amiable start. Most of those in attendance were females over the age of sixty, and they sat at the round tables that filled the room, some joking and laughing while others were engaged in more serious conversation. After dinner, I cautiously approached Billy Sam Fletcher, who had arrived shortly after the potluck began. In addition to his position as chairman of the OGRC, he had also recently been elected chairman of the OSA, a situation that, over the course of the next year, would stretch both allegiances thin. Fletcher was a formidable Osage man. Standing at least six and a half feet tall, he was often referred to as one of the last Osage full-bloods.

Best known for his role as lead litigant in the lawsuit that set the 1994 government reform effort in motion, Fletcher, now in his sixties, had a commanding presence. Shaking his hand in proper Osage fashion, I asked if he thought anyone would mind if I recorded the OSA's meeting.

Jim Gray, chief of the Osage Nation, was scheduled to give a talk on compacting the Mineral Estate later in the meeting. In addition to his efforts in reforming Osage citizenship and governance, Chief Gray was spearheading an effort to enter into self-government compacts with the federal government. In 1975, the U.S. Congress passed the Indian Self-Determination and Education Assistance Act, which transferred resources from the Bureau of Indian Affairs (BIA) to the nations themselves. Rather than having the BIA oversee all the programs, services, functions, and activities of each nation, interested American Indian nations negotiated with the BIA to establish the roles and responsibilities each government would have in running various programs. This transference allowed nations to have a far greater representation in how programs, ranging from health care to Mineral Estate leasing, would serve national needs as well as how federal funds would be used. Chief Gray, hoping to build a stronger and larger Osage Nation, argued that the compacting process would lead to greater Osage authority.

Gray's vision was not likely to receive a warm reception from the members of the OSA, however, who seemed wary of any changes that might unsettle their authority. I was eager to gain a better understanding of their viewpoint, which was, paradoxically, familiar yet alien to me. My grandfather and grandmother, though long deceased, had shared the mind-set of the people who filled the sunlit room on that hot August day. They had vocally disparaged early reform efforts, convinced that change was motivated by greed for their annuity checks. As a young woman attending graduate school removed in both time and distance from the reservation on which my grandfather grew up, I failed to understand the intensity of their fears and agreed with Chief Gray that having Osage take control over our own affairs would surely be better than the many years of mismanagement we had suffered under full BIA control.

Fletcher considered my question briefly and, smiling warmly, assured me that the meeting was open to the public and that I was free to document it. He always seemed content to be in the limelight and never shied away from the camera. He also said he was glad that the OSA would be included in my research. I happily returned to my table on the far side of the room and set up my camera, relieved that I did not have to rely on notes alone to capture the events of the meeting. Upon Chief Gray's arrival, the afternoon's friendly tone changed dramatically. Quiet whispers filled the room, and I caught several of the older women rolling their eyes as he began talking.

Chief Gray opened with a discussion about the responsibilities of getting ready for the new governing structure and the excitement of this moment in Osage history. He talked about how self-governance would improve Osage lives and the economy of the area and cited the Harvard Project on American Indian Economic Development to argue that everyone would benefit from the Osage taking over more control from the BIA. Focusing much of his attention on the Mineral Estate, he argued that compacting would increase accountability and allow the Osage to better monitor the oil at every stage, putting an end to the theft and mismanagement that had plagued the Osage for a hundred years. After talking for approximately thirty minutes about the benefits of self-governance, he opened the floor for questions.

I found Chief Gray's oration persuasive, but it soon became clear that I was one of the few in the room, other than the chief's mother, who did. Without batting an eyelash, those in attendance eagerly asked pointed questions for the next forty minutes. One of the first to speak asked: "According to the article that came out in the Tulsa paper, the Osage Tribe is not really in compliance with [the National Indian Gaming Commission] on some things. If they're not capable of handling this and getting all their ducks in a row, why should we trust the Council now to manage the Minerals?"[20] Chief Gray responded that the arguments by the National Indian Gaming Commission were "just part of the process" and that the Osage were doing exactly what needed to be done, but fears that the Osage were unprepared for increased authority could not be assuaged.

Others at the meeting continued this line of argument by saying that the Nation was losing money on many of its enterprises, most notably the Palace Grocery store, and should not yet be expanding its authority. The doubts about the Osage Nation overextending itself did have some legitimacy. Over the last hundred years, the United States and the State of Oklahoma had limited the scope of the Osage Nation so that it did not have the complete infrastructure in place that would be necessary for immediate expansion. In the case of the grocery store, although it did temporarily turn a profit, the Nation was ultimately forced to sell it.

These interrogations signal the tenuous position the Osage Nation was in at this moment, but they must also be read in their political context.

The act of creating a larger constitution-style government would inevitably shrink the authority of headright holders. The Osage that filled this room had the most to lose with the upcoming reform process, and the timing of compacting, along with Chief Gray's speech linking the two efforts, did little to garner their support for the process. They had battled the federal government for the last hundred years to extend the life of the Osage Mineral Estate, and it is little wonder that these Osage annuitants now decided that the safest road was to maintain the status quo, especially when it was their status that was at stake. In this way, it is possible to see the two primary things at stake for annuitants: the right to profit from their shares in the Mineral Estate and the right to exclusive governance of Osage national affairs.

There was, however, another aspect to their resistance to the constitutional process, which quickly surfaced when a woman asked: "If you take the contract from the BIA, what protection do we still have that it is still in restricted funds? Because, once you take it out of the BIA, it loses all restrictions."[21] Worried that the process of governmental reform was going to remove federal protection of the minerals or in some other way bring an end to the Osage Mineral Estate as a cooperatively owned Osage resource, this woman expressed a common concern about what compacting actually involved. Chief Gray quickly responded:

> The law of self-governance has been on the books for decades. . . . Part of the critical elements of this bill ever getting passed to begin with and a significant issue for all the tribes who have compacted over half of the BIA budget now, is the trust relationship has not changed. This is a negotiated management agreement between the tribe and the federal government. . . . The benefits of self-governance are not fear, but hope. You have to have faith in yourself and faith in your other tribal members to assume that we can bring the tools and resources together.

Throughout his tenure as chief of the Osage, Gray argued adamantly for building a powerful Osage Nation. Drawing on the tools and tactics of other successful American Indian nations, Gray hoped to strengthen Osage authority through federal policies of self-governance. Members of the OSA, however, did everything in their power to block these efforts, ultimately convincing the OTC that compacting the Mineral Estate was not a good political strategy. For these Osage annuitants, the federal government's self-determination policy appeared to threaten the trust relationship and was therefore subject to intense scrutiny.

The trust relationship to which Chief Gray referred is arguably the original colonial entanglement, built as it is out of settler colonial mentalities such as manifest destiny. The U.S. government in its earliest treaties established itself as "protector" of American Indian nations,[22] and the 1808 and subsequent Osage treaties are riddled with such phrases. For example, Article 10 of the 1808 Osage treaty reads: "The United States receives the Great and Little Osage nations into their friendship and under their protection; and the said nations, on their part, declare that they will consider themselves under the protection of no other power whatsoever."[23] The Supreme Court first suggested the existence of a trust relationship in 1831 in *Cherokee Nation v. Georgia*. Chief Justice John Marshall's majority opinion characterized the Cherokee Nation as "a domestic dependent nation . . . in a state of pupilage. . . . Their relation to the United States resembles that of a ward to his guardian."[24]

In 1942, the Supreme Court held that this promised protection created a unique bond between the United States and each recognized American Indian nation, imposing on the federal government "moral obligations of the highest responsibility and trust."[25] Although treaty making ended in 1871, another Supreme Court case held that laws could also create a trust responsibility since they would be used to fulfill treaty obligations and stipulate further fiduciary responsibility.[26] Since the Congress has plenary power, allowing it to change or negate any of its trust responsibilities, these are moral obligations rather than any genuine guarantee of protection.[27]

The Osage Nation has long used its relationship with other nations, including the U.S. government, to establish its authority. As Kathleen DuVal writes, the Osage historically placed great value on their relations with European nations: "The Osage took advantage of French exchange to build their own trading empire, expanding onto new lands, and casting out native rivals. . . . Rather than weakness, interdependence was a form of power. A people with no links of interdependence could be in trouble, as Europeans quickly discovered."[28] American paternalism, in the form of the management of Osage funds from oil proceeds, is likewise perceived by many Osage annuitants as part of this legacy of responsibility, and it is seen as one of the obligations the federal government owes the Osage people in exchange for all of the lands and resources that have been extorted from them. While all nations strive to form alliances with other nations, this relationship with the United States has been more paternalistic than mutually interdependent. The trust relationship thus functions as a hazardous entanglement for some Osage, situating the Osage Mineral Estate as part of the federal government's responsibilities rather than as an asset of the Osage Nation.

I had learned a great deal about the entanglement of the Mineral Estate from the OSA meeting. In combination with the concerns that the federal government was using "self-determination" as the latest tactic to terminate the Osage Mineral Estate, those in attendance at this OSA meeting used these notions of trust responsibility to make a compelling case against Chief Gray's efforts to transfer more authority to an enlarged Osage government. Based on the historical relationship of the Osage with the U.S. government, these concerns are hardly unfounded. These concerns, however, were not impartial to the interests of the annuitants and must also be understood as a powerful strategy for maintaining control. By denying the need for a larger Osage government, these Osage annuitants privileged minerals as the defining component of the Osage Nation in the twenty-first century. As a result of this meeting, I viewed the tensions surrounding the Osage Mineral Estate as a more complex phenomenon, clearly seeing the snares created by the continuing colonial process.

This discussion of compacting and trust sheds light on the obstacles that disrupted early OGRC community meetings, limiting the discussions that should have been taking place on the crucial aspects of the proposed constitution. The intersecting desire for continued control and the fear of change repeatedly centered conversation around the Mineral Estate and drew much-needed attention from the other issues of national reform. The Code of Federal Regulations (CFR) (24 C.F.R. Part 91) that was in place to support the operation of the OTC and the distribution of the Osage Mineral Estate proceeds surfaced repeatedly at these community meetings as something that could not possibly be changed without impacting the Mineral Estate: "You're not going to change—you're not going to. . . . Like she said, 'your Mineral Estates are protected.' It's ruled by CFR Regulations. . . . This referendum thing here has no dealings with that. You can't say anything about that so I want everyone to know that you can't change that part of it. Is it true that just what you are here to do is to form a new government?"[29] The contradictory assertions in this statement are evident: The OGRC is told to form a new government but also to leave the Mineral Estate alone.

The Mineral Estate had been operating as the primary government for the last hundred years, so some change in authority would be inevitable in the process of creating a new government. During the reform process, the CFR were repeatedly referenced, usually ending conversations about alternative government structures and refocusing the discussion around the laws already in place. These regulations were originally written to support the 1906 congressional act and have been amended many times by the federal government in the last hundred years. The commissioners themselves spent many hours mired in discussions about the CFR and how they could work around them if changing them was not an option.

Finally, the OGRC turned to the BIA for guidance to determine how the federal government would react to any changes in the CFR. When Osage superintendent Melissa Currey was approached about this subject, she told the commissioners that the federal government would change the CFR to meet the new Osage constitution. While many Osage active in the reform process were relieved that they did have this freedom, members of the OSA continued to argue that such change was dangerous. The threats of termination had created potent fears of change. These fears were often introduced during community meetings, where it was argued that during colonial history change had led to a loss of Osage authority. Whereas many Osage viewed change as a fundamental part of their history, some feared that the U.S. government would use this change to terminate the Mineral Estate and even the Nation.

During the question-and-answer period at the beginning of one government reform meeting, Cora Jean Jech, an annuitant who would in 2009 be the first plaintiff in a court case challenging the authority of the 2006 Osage Constitution over the Osage Mineral Estate, drew a strong connection between these past colonial encroachments and the current reform effort by arguing: "There are several Osage that think that there is a plot going on to try to get the Minerals from underneath the trust; that the [new Osage] government will actually end up with the Minerals and they'll no longer be ours; that they'll be turned over to somebody else because it goes back to greed. When you look at this land all around us and think at one time we owned every inch of this ground—and now we have hardly nothing."[30] Due to the long history of colonial encroachment, Osage annuitants certainly have good reason to fear further losses. The U.S. government continually made promises that the Osage lands would remain intact, only to later renege on its agreements. Playing Osage political parties against each other in an effort to gain support for the treaties and later for the laws, these tactics shrunk Osage territory and ultimately led to allotment. In particular, it is still a fresh insult for many Osage that in the twentieth century whites appropriated Osage reservation lands through fraud and even murder of Osage annuitants. These Osage annuitants used the history of colonial encroachment to reinforce the dangers associated with all change to the headright system, particularly efforts to build a centralized Osage Nation serving all descendants.

Not all Osage, however, agreed that change was dangerous. By 2004, it was clear to most Osage that the OTC had done a great deal of damage to the Osage as a nation. Only those Osage who had inherited a share in the Mineral Estate had the right to vote for elected officials, and many voters had only a fraction of a vote. While in 2004 all lineal descendants of the 1906 roll were eligible for membership cards and for many tribal services such as health care and partial college scholarships, they could not elect tribal officials or run for office unless they held a headright. Nonshareholding Osage were counted in order to gain access to more federal grant dollars, but these same individuals had no say in how those funds were spent.[31] Furthermore, all informal institutions, from Osage naming to the five-person committees in the districts, were open to and included all Osage descendants, not just headright holders. It was less clear who the BIA recognized as the Osage Nation, with some evidence pointing only to the original annuitants (see appendix 4).

Because of these factors, and especially the fear that with the death of the last original allottee the relationship with the federal government would end, there were few during the reform process who argued for continued limitations on citizenship. One of the debates specifically treating this subject occurred during a Pawhuska community meeting. In response to the impassioned plea of an older Osage annuitant to leave the Mineral Estate voting system in place, one middle-aged annuitant responded: "We've been dealing with this for years and years. Like he said, the 1906 [act] has been very good to us. But our people have always been moving forward and we always change, and change is needed. We have to make some changes because there are Osage that are totally estranged from their own nation."[32] While the OTC is presented here as a beneficial entity, this speaker also highlights the need for change because of the disenfranchisement of Osage descendants who, holding no headright, are disqualified from participating in the official Osage political structure. Contrary to the members of the OSA, who were deeply skeptical of change, the majority of Osage embraced change as part of who the Osage are.

When the OGRC asked all lineal descendants of the original allottees who had addresses listed with the Nation whether government reform was needed, 77.3 percent of the 1,379 respondents answered in the

affirmative. Only 38.5 percent of the total respondents were non-annuitants, likely because this population had long been alienated from tribal
politics. This meant that while members of the OSA were vocal throughout and following the reform, they did not represent the majority even
of those Osage who held headrights. Change was ultimately embraced as
a central part of the Osage story, something that not even colonial insistence on the static Indian could erode.

The issue remained, however, of deciding exactly what this change was
going to involve. Throughout the reform process, many Osage argued that
the change most needed was the implementation of a system of checks
and balances to keep elected officials under control. The 1861, 1881, and
1994 Osage Constitutions all contained executive, legislative, and judicial branches, which now gave historical legitimacy to a tripartite division
of authority. As one Osage descendant from Pawhuska, who had yet to
inherit a headright, told me during the Sovereignty Day Independence
celebration interview:

> I would like it to have a three-branch system of government like the
> United States has, with a judicial, a legislative, and an executive. That
> way they can have checks and balances; no individual's power running
> things. Even in the old Osage ways they used to have leadership from
> the different groups, the earth people and the sky people. . . . I would
> like to see an executive carrying out the laws of the nation and [a]
> legislative that is not micromanaging but is looking at the laws and
> policies of a nation. Of course, [I would like] an independent court sys-
> tem, independent of politics, that has review over both of the other
> branches to see if they're acting constitutionally.[33]

Many Osage vote in local and federal U.S. elections and are familiar with
the U.S. form of government, lending this structure of governance additional authority. While Osage are often quite critical of state and federal
assertions of authority over Osage lands, they also feel that the best
tool for change within a democratic system is political engagement. This
is not, however, the sole justification in arguing for a tripartite government. Older Osage practices are also cited to validate a move away from
the council-style structure, where power was concentrated in the hands
of a few.

As Osage tribal councilman Mark Freeman told me in an interview,
the OTC structure that had been imposed by the U.S. government had
several problems: "As far as a form of government, this resolution form of

government is good for one thing; you can pass a resolution one day and then do away with it the next. That's not too good a way of running a business, so there's where I've come to a constitutional form of government with better checks and balances. And when you pass laws that are trouble to do away with, hopefully people will take a little more time before they pass it, hopefully."[34] Here the OTC's lack of a constitution, which made it reliant on easily overridden resolutions, is cited as a major obstacle. Such complaints against the current government structure were commonly cited throughout the reform process and were clearly a major motivation for change. Checks and balances, oversight, and accountability were seen as crucial to a twenty-first-century Osage constitution.

Even while polls suggested that a majority of the Osage wanted to see government reform, there was no way to make the desired changes without affecting the structure of the Osage Mineral Estate as it had been created in 1906. One solution was to create a bicameral system of governance. During an early community meeting, my father Gene Dennison, a local lawyer and Osage annuitant from Skiatook, gave voice to this desire for continued authority while also maintaining unity:

> I don't particularly want to see a nation [new government] and a tribe [minerals council]. I want to see us all together. One way to do that would be to have a bicameral form of government where you have the Council that is elected by the shareholders. It's going to happen no matter what because that's part of the law. . . . But also have a House that would be elected by all of the Osage. . . . I think if we put it all together in one unit, one government, we could do something that would be effective as far as all of us working together.[35]

While there were several suggested variations on the bicameral system during the reform process, such as the version put forward by commissioner Mary Jo Webb, the general agreement was that the Osage annuitants would elect one body and the general Osage population, including the annuitants, would elect another. It was hoped that this voting structure would have the effect of uniting the Nation and also appeasing the annuitants, who were afraid that, once outside of their full control, the new government would in some way harm the Mineral Estate. Such a system would continue to privilege the annuitants, by giving them a branch of their own within the newly structured Nation.

Two months later, during one of the OGRC's business meetings, Webb again referenced the potential behind a bicameral system, arguing that "the Osage were sent from the stars to create order. So why can't we have two equal chiefs to promote such order?"[36] Webb's point was that the two groups would have to meet in the middle to talk about their problems and find compromises. This idea had enough support from the commissioners that it made its way onto the November 2005 referendum. The primary competing idea was that a minerals council should be created as an independent body, stripped of all governmental authorities, and should be focused solely on overseeing minerals leasing. This approach was drawn from the many comments that stressed the necessity of leaving the Osage Mineral Estate entirely alone. During a Bartlesville community meeting, an annuitant who was a supporter of reform suggested: "It's one government, the way I see it. . . . When the constitution is done, we have a president or chief, and the Mineral Estate becomes a board. . . . It's no longer a government because they're not dealing with my health care anymore, my education, my housing. . . . The Mineral Estate now becomes a true economic developing board."[37] The OGRC addressed these different ideas with the following referendum question:

> Option A. The newly reformed Osage government is reorganized under one governing constitution of the Osage Nation with one governing body organized into a 3 branch system that does not include the Osage Tribal Council as part of that system. The Osage Tribal Council functions as an independent body with no governmental authority, yet retaining all its present fundamental organization, authority, and responsibilities over the Osage Mineral Estate in accordance with the Osage Allotment Act of June 28, 1906 (sec. 9, 34 Stat. 539).

> Or

> Option B: The newly reformed Osage government is reorganized under one governing constitution of the Osage nation with one governing body organized into a 3 branch system that does include the Osage Tribal Council as part of that system. The Osage Tribal Council is established as a second chamber of a bicameral, or two house system, within the legislative branch of the newly reformed Osage government. Elected by Osage shareholders, the Osage Tribal Council retains all its present fundamental organization, authority, and responsibilities over the Osage Mineral Estate in accordance with the Osage Allotment Act of June 28, 1906 (sec. 9, 34 Stat. 539). All legislative authority, other than that specified to manage the Mineral Estate, is delegated to

a house of representatives elected at large by all adult members of the Osage Nation. A bright line must be drawn between the two houses to clearly delineate duties and responsibilities [see appendix 6].

Osage voters were almost exactly split down the middle, with 51.6 percent voting for option A and 48.40 percent voting for option B. It was clear from these results that the Osage were not united around a bicameral system of governance. Option A had officially won the referendum election, meaning that a minerals council could not be part of the three-branch system in the form of one-half of the legislature.

The decision to create a separate minerals council outside the legislative structure still left the problem of how the Mineral Estate could be included in the government and be subject to the laws of the Nation while at the same time maintaining the greatest possible independence as desired by vocal Osage annuitants. The members of the OGRC developed a solution after discussing the matter with various Osage lawyers through a law symposium, as well as through many discussions with their own lawyers. They then took the proposed solution back to the Osage people through a series of community meetings. One of the commissioners offered this description of their findings at a Hominy community meeting:

> It's well understood that the tribal Council or Minerals Council would not have the same role that they've always played. They will no longer be the governing body of the Osage people. But it's our feeling and the feelings of the Osage people that we've visited with that they certainly want that Council to exist and they want them to handle strictly the Minerals shares for the shareholders. The problem remains, how do we keep a government-to-government relationship existing? We don't want to go back to two governments and we will not. We'll have one governing body and then the Minerals Council will be a separate part, still elected by the shareholders. . . . The way we feel it will be tied to the government is that a clause could be written in there that within five days of a lease, the chief would have a right to decline it if it violates Osage law set by the constitution. He can't decline just because he doesn't like it. But if it violates Osage law he can then decline it. That is the tie that brings it into the new government to keep its sovereign immunity powers under the government. Without it we were afraid, and we've had attorneys advise us, that the Bureau of Indian Affairs could say we're no longer going to deal with this because that's not the governing body any more.[38]

In 2006, this approach to incorporating the Osage Mineral Estate as a minerals council with limited authority under a larger Osage Nation was accepted by a two-thirds majority of the Osage voters. Even though some Osage annuitants were wary of any change in the authority of the Mineral Estate, the constitution passed, placing the Minerals squarely under the authority of a larger Osage government.

Article XV, section 4, of the 2006 Osage Nation Constitution created a minerals management agency, which was named the Osage Minerals Council. This agency was, as the 2006 Constitution reads, "established for the sole purpose of continuing its previous duties to administer and develop the Osage Mineral Estate in accordance with the Osage Allotment Act of June 28, 1906, as amended, with no legislative authority for the Osage Nation government." To assure that the Osage Minerals Council did not violate Osage law, the same section of the 2006 Constitution includes this stipulation: "Minerals leases approved and executed by the Council shall be deemed approved by the Osage Nation unless, within five (5) working days, written objection is received from the Office of the Principal Chief that the executed lease or other development activity violates Osage law or regulation. Any dispute that arises through this process may be heard before the Supreme Court of the Osage Nation Judiciary." Particularly important here is the fact that those annuitants voting for the new system, including the members of the current OTC, voted for a system in which they were going to lose their monopoly over general Osage affairs. When asked about the annuitants' partial loss of power, Fletcher, who had multiple headrights, responded, "That is power I should never have had to begin with."[39]

The 2006 Osage Constitution also further safeguarded payment of royalties to annuitants. Article XV, section 4, states, "The government shall further ensure that the rights of members of the Osage Nation to income derived from that mineral estate are protected." In this way, the Mineral Estate funds were protected from redistribution or taxation. This action, however, was not enough to ease the concerns of some Osage annuitants.

Fighting for "The Way It Was"

I had followed online discussions during the reform process, but it was not until I was away from the reservation that I truly appreciated the Osage territory that existed on the World Wide Web. No Osage group was more active on the web than the members of the OSA, whose membership consisted primarily of off-reservation Osage annuitants. Shortly after I attended my first OSA meeting, they created a webpage with an online discussion forum. This forum was and continues to be the home of the most aggressive criticisms of the 2006 Osage Constitution. Like the views expressed in the OSA meetings, the postings generally focus on finding a way to undo the changes made by the passage of the 2006 Osage Constitution. While certainly not representative of a majority of Osage, the group is made up of the most vocal and politically active of the Osage citizens and therefore continues to play a formidable role in Osage politics.

Postings to OSA's discussion page included discussion about potential and actual lawsuits, all of which expressed concern with the idea that the Osage Mineral Estate had been diminished by its new placement within the larger Osage Nation. Contributors to the forum expressed their concerns that this new system gave the Nation and the chief too much authority over the Mineral Estate, especially since it was not required that the chief be an annuitant. Other concerns included that the Minerals Council no longer had a chief or assistant chief, leaving it with just eight council members, and that there had never been a vote by just the Osage annuitants that reform should even take place. Fears similar to those expressed during the reform process were expressed with the growing certainty that the Osage annuitants had been wronged by the 2006 Constitution. The OSA webpage became the primary space in which these assertions gained traction.

Galen Crum, an annuitant who, after unsuccessfully running for the Osage Congress in 2006, was elected to the Osage Minerals Council in 2010, took an early role in fighting against the changes that he felt had been imposed by the successful passage of the 2006 Constitution. Crum was from California and had made his name known among a wider Osage population through his presence on the OSA discussion board. He argued in a post to the OSA's webpage in October 2006 that change might cause problems for the minerals trust held by the U.S. government:

It's all about the legal concept of a trust and about keeping the Osage Trust intact, so that the special relationship the 1906 Act gives all the Osage people with the federal government, will not be destroyed. A trust can be thought of as a box in which something of value is kept safe for the owners. It is usually meant to keep the valuables safe not only from outside forces, but also from unauthorized use from the owners. So there are special rules as to its use and a trustee is placed in charge of both protecting the valuables and regulating their use. As long as the box is kept intact and all the rules are followed the trust itself can be thought of as being intact and unassailable. . . . I want agreements made that are consistent with the CFR.[40]

Crum's main point here is that changes made during the reform process, which would require a change in the CFR, might be used against the Osage and might provide justification for the federal government to dissolve the Mineral Estate and perhaps even the Nation. Because of the effort to extend the Mineral Estate in perpetuity, there were historical reasons to fear that the U.S. government might use any excuse to destroy the Osage Mineral Estate. Maintaining this relationship with the United States was therefore a central motivator behind many of the concerns found on the OSA webpage about the changes the 2006 Osage Constitution had implemented.

This focus on the minerals trust, however, must also be seen as a political strategy. Crum had only four months previously lost his bid for the Osage Nation Congress. By posting on the OSA's webpage, he hoped to bolster his campaign prospects for 2010. Later, on his 2010 campaign webpage, he argued: "Politically, my goal will be to return Minerals Trust control to the annuitants. I firmly believe the Minerals Council, as the body elected by Osage Shareholders to conduct Trust business, should do so without interference from the Chief or Congress." He went on to explain the benevolence of the Osage annuitants in allowing themselves to become minority voters in the Osage Nation and "only asking for one thing in return, that the Minerals Trust be left in their control." He concluded by asking for the return of control over Minerals Council funds and lawsuits to the annuitants alone.[41] The goal for Crum, and most of the growing membership of the OSA, was not to wholly disrupt the new Osage Nation but instead to create a minerals council that was entirely separate from the new government and that had authority over its own affairs.

A month after Crum's posting on the OSA webpage, a member of the Osage Minerals Council, Talee Redcorn, wrote a posting entitled, "White Hair Stills the Wind," which employed Osage history to support the author's vision of the current state of the Osage. The posting tells a story about the Grand Village and the Little Osage Village. According to Redcorn, the Little Osage Village had asked and received permission to secede, but after being surrounded by enemies, the Little Osage asked the larger group if they could return. The Little Osage ended up settling about six miles away. Redcorn went on to say that in 1806, when U.S. Army lieutenant Zebulon Montgomery Pike visited the Osage, he could not convince White Hair, the chief leader of the Grand Village, to help him establish a route to the Colorado area. The Little Osage, however, were willing to help him. Due to his "reckless temperament," however, Pike ended up abandoning all his men, who lacked sufficient food and protection from the elements. Pike was eventually captured by the Spanish. The posting concludes with this moral:

> In modern day Osage politics, there seems to be a willingness by the US government to remove their responsibility to the Osage. Is this the same reckless temperament White Hair saw in the folly of the Americans in 1806? Also, are Shareholder Osage (also known as "1906 Osage") equivalent to Grand Village Osage of 1806 when they demonstrate their willingness to grant a group of Osage permission to pursue their own political endeavor? I am sure that the temperament of the 1906 Osage will once more be demonstrated if the efforts of the new government fall short of expectation. There seems to be a substantial effort displayed by the new Osage government as they tend toward the betterment of our Osage people. But cautious concern, as demonstrated by White Hair in 1806, to protect the Osage Trust should be our greater calling as the electorate. Let's not forget that the 1906 Act was probably second only to the life ways and ancient rule of the Grand Village of the Osage, on the Osage River in Missouri.[42]

This posting, like many that fill the OSA discussion page, clearly illustrates the power the Osage Mineral Estate continues to hold for many Osage annuitants, as well as the entanglement the trust relationship in general and the Mineral Estate in particular have created for the Osage. Desires to keep settlers from securing the Osage Mineral Estate, like they did with much of the surface reservation land, have led to a deep-rooted distrust of change. Rather than investing their energies into building a stronger Osage Nation, these annuitants focused their efforts on questioning its potential as a threat to the Mineral Estate.

Redcorn's posting may also be seen as an argument against the expansion of the Osage Nation. By focusing on the importance of the 1906 act and the authority of the Osage Minerals Council, many OSA posters emphasized the need to keep the Mineral Estate completely outside of the reconstituted Osage Nation, thus limiting the new constitution's authority over the minerals in areas ranging from environmental laws to control over lawsuits. As these Osage annuitants turned to the BIA to protect them from the newly reconstituted Osage Nation, they were hoping to use their relationship with the U.S. government as a tool to establish their authority and diminish that of the newly reconstituted Nation. For these individuals, it was through this relationship with the U.S. government that the future of the Mineral Estate could be ensured.

OSA fears of change were so powerful that they led to a 2009 lawsuit, *Jech v. U.S.*, by eight Osage annuitants against the U.S. Department of the Interior, who alleged that the Interior "unlawfully failed to hold the election for the Osage Nation Constitution as it applied to the Mineral Estate; have further unlawfully failed to hold elections for Minerals Council in accordance with the 1906 Act and 25 C.F.R. Part 90, and are unlawfully recognizing the Osage Nation Constitution as applicable to the Mineral Estate."[43] By turning to the federal government to settle the internal power struggle that they had lost during the 2006 election, these annuitants hoped to reinstate the Mineral Estate's authority, which had been usurped by the Osage Constitution.

Perhaps the most provocative aspect of the annuitants' argument was that prior to allowing all Osage descendants to vote during the 2004–6 Osage reform process, the OGRC should have held a vote of only the annuitants. They based this argument on the elections that had taken place since 1906, which excluded all but headright holders from taking part. They also cited Public Law 108-431, stating: "Congress hereby clarifies that the term 'legal membership' in section 1 of the [1906 act], means the persons eligible for allotments of Osage Reservation lands and a *pro rata* share of the Osage Mineral Estate as provided in that Act, not membership in the Osage Tribe for all purposes. Congress hereby reaffirms the inherent sovereign right of the Osage Tribe to determine its own membership, provided that the rights of any person to the Osage Mineral Estate shares are not diminished thereby [see appendix 5]."[44] The citizens of the Osage Nation who were to be granted the authority to determine citizenship in the newly reformed Osage Nation became a crucial question. While the plaintiffs argued that only the annuitants had the legal right to vote, various pieces of Osage legislation, as well as BIA opinions, outlined other understandings of Osage citizenship.

Nonshareholding Osage were eligible for Osage membership cards prior to the 2004–6 reform process. In fact, according to OTC resolutions, all Osage descendants had long been considered part of the Osage Nation, even if voting rights extended only to headright holders. In 1990, the OTC passed resolution number 28-31, which defined members of the Osage Nation as "descendants of Osage Indian blood" who were listed on the 1906 roll. The significant point here is that it was not just headright holders who were considered Osage members. This resolution stated as part of its justification that "the Osage Tribal Council has consistently declared the membership of the Osage Nation to be all 'allottees, their heirs, and descendants.'"

In the fall of 2002, the 31st Osage Tribal Council again passed a resolution granting membership to all lineal descendants. Prior to this decision, federal programs, those administered by the BIA and those administered by the Osage Nation, had served all Osage lineal descendants and had used these individuals as part of Osage grant applications. While federal court cases have made clear that the OTC was the recognized government of the Osage, legal critics such as Alex Skibine have argued that Osage membership was never as clear-cut. Skibine outlines "many references in the legislative history of all the acts that have amended the 1906 Act, as well as a Solicitor's Opinion, [which] indicate that children born of Osage parents were considered members of the Tribe before inheriting a headright."[45] Skibine also discusses *Akers v. Hodel*, which complicates this picture of Osage citizenship with its statement that to be an Osage you had to have more than just Osage blood, implying, but never spelling out, that a headright interest was required.[46] The participants in the 31st Osage Tribal Council themselves argued that they had been elected with the mandate of granting citizenship to all Osage descendants and thus had the right to establish the reform process and determine who would participate.

Additionally, if the *Jech* plaintiffs truly wanted to go back to who the BIA considered an Osage citizen prior to 2004 legislation, they would end up excluding even themselves. As Terrance L. Virden, the director of the BIA, explained in a letter to Leonard Marker in 2003, "The Osage Allotment Act of June 28, 1906 (34 Stat. 539), as amended, authorized the establishment and *closing* of the Osage Tribe's membership roll. This legislation has not been repealed and remains in effect [see appendix 4]."[47] In other words, in 2003 there was only one person whom the BIA officially recognized as an Osage citizen, the sole surviving original allottee. All other Osage were considered descendants, without U.S. recognition as Osage citizens. The letter resolved: "In order to extend membership, Congressional action will be needed." This is exactly what the 2004 legislation did, giving the right to determine Osage citizenship to the "Osage Tribe."

The complex legal situation of Osage citizenship is typical of Osage affairs and is part of the reason Osage so frequently turn to the courts to sort such matters out. As Mogri Lookout stated early in the reform process, it was inevitable that the future of the Osage Nation would be taken to the courts:

> If they decide to allow all Osage into the system, then the headright holders have a right to sue because the Osage Tribal Council has not protected the headrights by bringing in all these voters. If they create a two part system, with one group over the Mineral Estate, then the other group will sue because they are not having full say in their government. Either way they should just do it and get the lawsuit out of the way, because it will decide what kind of government we are going to have.[48]

By 2010 it was clear that the 2006 Constitution had created enough turmoil and derision to mobilize some Osage annuitants into seeking an external remedy to what they saw as an injustice against their authority as annuitants.

Not all annuitants, however, felt comfortable with this solution. Crum, now on the Osage Minerals Council, used the OSA discussion board to express his frustration with the *Jech* case, especially the vote, which was later overturned, by the Minerals Council to support the case with a $50,000 donation.[49] He said that he did not support the case and instead suggested using internal Osage Nation processes to amend the 2006 Osage Constitution. Crum was quickly criticized on the OSA discussion board for being more concerned about the well-being of the Nation than the Mineral Estate, with posters to the forum questioning his loyalty to the headright holders. This discussion then turned into a debate about what the *Jech* case could or could not accomplish, with many posters arguing that the goal was not to overturn the Osage Nation as much as to ensure the separation of the Mineral Estate from the government. Those arguing against the value of the case, several of whom were Osage lawyers, pointed out that the way the case was worded could result in the overturning of the entire Osage Nation Constitution, thus allowing a U.S. court system to again determine Osage governance.

Whether or not this was the full intent of the *Jech* plaintiffs, the more general attitude on the OSA's blog was perhaps best summarized by one anonymous respondent: "The [Osage constitutional] election will not be overturned, if it is, so what? We as shareholders vote again and carefully elect people who will protect the shareholders from this happening again."[50] Others, meanwhile, particularly Crum and elected officials of the Osage Nation, expressed fear that the lawsuit was going to do more to upset the Nation than it would ever do to benefit the Mineral Estate. They pointed out that the BIA had been a poor manager of the Osage trust, leading to multiple legal cases of its own, and that the current elected officials of the Osage Nation, almost all of whom were annuitants, were far more likely to take better care of the Osage Mineral Estate.

Such statements only increased the fervor of the posters. The same anonymous poster further argued:

> Shareholders need the protection of the trust. Do I believe the BIA has been our friend through the years? Absolutely not, however, the trust gives us needed protection and also keeps us from being out voted by non-shareholders. Shareholders have been put in a little box with a neatly tied bow along with the Council and set aside in the corner, told to be quiet and do as we are told. Accept the crumbs given and be happy. In many ways, we have handed them our rights and our checkbook. No other business in America would conduct business in this manner.[51]

As in many of the discussions leading up to, contemporaneous with, and following the writing of the 2006 Constitution, this posting makes clear that for members of the OSA, the primary concern was for the safety of the Osage Mineral Estate, which they perceived as a business interest operating outside the jurisdiction of the Osage Nation. Focusing their attention on the protection of the Mineral Estate, they hoped to ensure not only their property interests but also their own authority.

The problem remained, however, that such a focus on the Mineral Estate is at the cost of the Osage Nation. As another OSA poster, whose online name was Southside Osage, put it: "I for one do not want to risk a good part of my income on ideology. I love the idea of Osage government taking care of Osage but I have seen nothing in my lifetime, from nearly all governments, not just the Osage, to suggest that would be the case."[52] Given the hundred-year colonial legacy that had created an inadequate structure and denied the Osage valuable time in maturing their structures, it is no wonder that many Osage are skeptical of the new constitution. This skepticism was deep-rooted, extending to all forms of governance that, as Southside Osage went on to explain, "reward people that have a self interest."[53] From these discussions, it is clear that for these OSA members governments simply could not be trusted, Osage or otherwise.

In addition to limiting the infrastructure necessary to develop a flourishing Osage Nation, continued colonialism has created an entrenched distrust of government more generally.

In 2004, when the OGRC set out to reform the Osage Nation government, its members knew they had a complex job ahead of them. A majority of Osage, annuitants and non-annuitants alike, wanted to change citizenship, and even to create a constitutional government, but there was no clear answer for how to deal with the Mineral Estate. Many of those active in the reform process felt that the Mineral Estate needed the protection of the Osage Nation, particularly the sovereign immunity a direct connection would allow, leading the writers of the 2006 Constitution to subsume the Mineral Estate under the Osage Nation. It was hoped that this approach would limit the disputes between the Osage Minerals Council and the Nation, creating a clear pathway for their interaction. This system instead continued to promote fear and animosity, leading to legal challenges against the 2006 Constitution.

In the debates during the 2004–6 reform process, it was obvious that there were many competing hopes and fears for the future of the Osage Nation. While economic development and increased services were potent motivators, the fears surrounding the reform process often spoke louder than these hopes. Most discussions about the Nation returned to the Mineral Estate, focusing on the impossibilities of, rather than the possibilities for, change. Constitutions attempt to coalesce authority and resources within a singular national structure.[54] In the case of the Mineral Estate, as with "Osage culture," this consolidation was undesirable for some. The *Jech* case was dismissed before it proceeded very far in the judicial circuit, and it is not yet clear whether the future Osage officials will be able to find ways of bridging this divide.

These tensions, whether racial-, cultural-, or mineral-based, could not, however, prevent the passage of the 2006 Osage Nation Constitution. In the last chapter, I will focus on the arguments for greater Osage Nation authority, on who the major actors were in this process, and on how their arguments for sovereign authority were written into the 2006 Osage Nation Constitution. In addition to these internal disputes, the newly reformed Osage Nation also has to contend with the authority asserted by the State of Oklahoma, which attempts to deny Osage sovereignty. In further discussing the internal and external negotiations around authority, this book will conclude with a discussion of the possibilities for and limitations of constitutionalism within this continuing colonial moment.

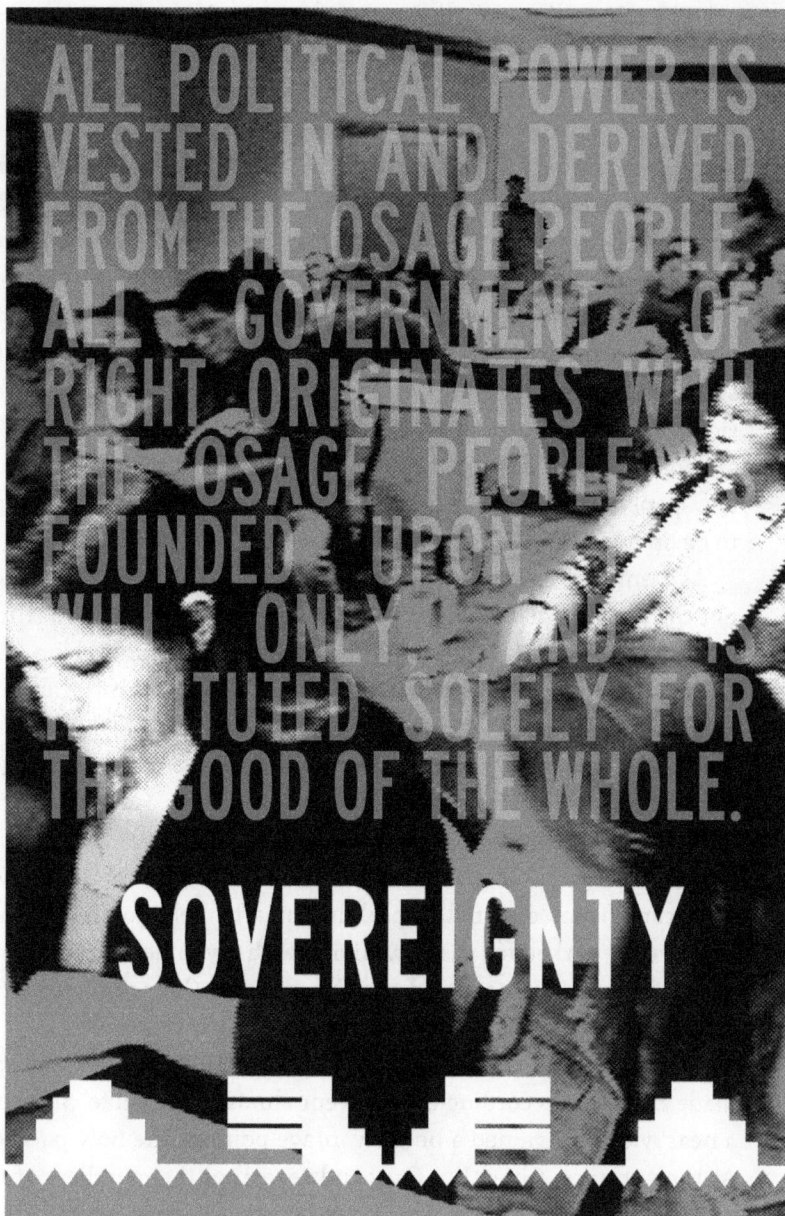

Chapter 5 **Sovereignty**

ALL POLITICAL POWER IS VESTED IN AND DERIVED FROM THE OSAGE PEOPLE. ALL GOVERNMENT OF RIGHT ORIGINATES WITH THE OSAGE PEOPLE, IS FOUNDED UPON WILL ONLY AND IS INSTITUTED SOLELY FOR THE GOOD OF THE WHOLE.

SOVEREIGNTY

arly in the morning on an unseasonably warm February day in 2005, I made the forty-minute drive northwest from Skiatook to Pawhuska, the capital of the Osage Nation. While this drive would later become routine with my almost daily travel, for now its scenery still captured my attention. The wildflowers that would cover the rolling prairie were not yet sprouts in the hard earth, leaving only the tall brown grass and scrub oaks to mark the rolling hills. Given the recent spike in the cost of gasoline, almost all the rusty oil wells lining the horizon were once again slowly tottering up and down. The power lines and barbwire fences raced alongside the road, connecting the scattered houses along the winding hills. Fields for grazing and the occasional crop of soybeans lay dormant for the winter. Except for the inhabitants of Barnsdall, a town of around 1,300, with its own grocery store and newspaper, most of the residents of this part of the reservation appeared to be on four legs, with cattle and horses the most visible.

As I entered Pawhuska, however, the scene changed; it was certainly not the thriving metropolis it had been during the oil boom of the 1920s, but Pawhuska's many office buildings had begun to fill back up, primarily due to the recent expansion of the Osage Nation. Chain restaurants such as Sonic and Pizza Hut were accompanied by the local favorites, including Bad Brad's BBQ, Sally's Sandwich Shop, The Greek's, and the Osage Country Club, which had its own nine-hole golf course. Turning up the steep hill in the center of town, I entered the Osage campus, with its old stone and concrete structures. Although I arrived well ahead of the 9 A.M. event start time, I was directed to park in a nearby field, joining about thirty cars already parked for the day. Hiking with my camera equipment across the Osage campus, I entered the Osage Tribal Council (OTC) chambers, where the day's events were set to begin.

By five minutes to nine, the room was so full that the press of people made any video recording of the event almost impossible. Stepping onto a nearby chair, I gained a better vantage point of the now-packed room. At the entrance, Chief Jim Gray and several of the members of the OTC glanced approvingly over the large crowd. As they entered, the room respectfully quieted as a path was cleared to the front table. The event began with a prayer before quickly moving to a choreographed signing of the Declaration of Sovereignty and Independence by the People of the Osage Nation. Once the members of the OTC had all signed, I joined the long line, adding my name to the one-page document.

Despite its brevity, the document speaks volumes. Perhaps most importantly, it states: "We declare that our inherent rights as a sovereign nation predate the Constitution of the United States. . . . Further, that we have never relinquished any of those rights and we strongly assert that the Osage Reservation has never been disestablished." Osage Sovereignty Day, as the daylong event was designated, was intended to commemorate the passage of the 2004 federal law 108-431, "To reaffirm the inherent sovereign rights of the Osage Tribe to determine its membership and form of government." The Sovereignty Day's larger goal, however, was to declare the independence of the Osage people from almost a hundred years of direct colonial control and to begin the process of building a stronger Osage Nation.

Within this context, sovereignty signals a centralized system of governmental authority that allows for the assertion of independence within and control over a territory. This vision of an independent and centralized nation, able to manage its own affairs and create an economic renaissance on the reservation, was the primary aim of the 2004–6 reform as envisioned by those most actively involved in the process. This was not, however, the only vision of an Osage future. Notions of the Osage as a "unique race," as a people united by particular "practices that are located outside the realm of governance," or as "shareholders in a Mineral Estate corporation" each had to be managed, often distracting attention from this effort to build the infrastructure necessary for operating a sovereign nation. Constitution writing is always such a realm of contestation, marking tensions around how much authority the people are willing to give to a centralized governing body.

This chapter will explore how sovereignty was articulated during the reform process and in the 2006 Constitution, as well as how these ideas conflicted with the sovereign assertions of the State of Oklahoma. Tracing sovereignty, however, is a complicated endeavor. The academic compulsion to deconstruct sovereignty threatens to aid settler colonial efforts to discredit indigenous authority. These debates over sovereignty take place within larger colonial struggles over authority and power, where there is a lot at stake in claiming, denying, or even dissecting sovereignty. The academic debate over sovereign power too often limits sovereignty to an attribute of statehood and statehood to European styles of governance.[1] While the term "sovereignty" is certainly mired in Western and colonial histories,[2] the desires behind the word, primarily for political autonomy, cannot so easily be dismissed.[3] These can never simply be academic arguments. As with "blood," "culture," and "minerals," Osage are redefining "sovereignty" and attempting to use it to build a better Osage future.

Sovereignty, like many of the forces discussed throughout this book, is clearly entangled in the continuing colonial process. How could one ever really reconcile the assertion of Osage sovereignty through its "reaffirmation" by U.S. law, without viewing it as the ultimate entanglement of the 2004–6 Osage reform process? How sovereignty operates today is caught up with the desires of Oklahoma governing officials to claim the Osage reservation as just another county in the middle of their state. Sovereignty is also caught up with the unique U.S. relationship with American Indian nations, which at once recognizes American Indian national sovereignty while it claims plenary authority over their citizens, territory, and authority.[4]

In seeking to simultaneously take seriously the potential of sovereignty and acknowledge the limitations of the ongoing colonial moment, this chapter must walk a nearly impossible line. This means placing Osage desires for control above, without downplaying, the forces obstructing it. It also means allowing sovereignty to be at once more and less than its most common legal definitions often permit. Sovereignty has a wide variety of meanings, ranging from a "personalized monarch" to a "symbol of basic governance competencies" and everything in between.[5] While certainly rooted in a European tradition, sovereignty has become common across the globe and today is most explicitly tied to the nation-state system, which was originally created to combat religion-based empires.[6] This global system continues to be marked by tensions among empires, international organizations, and sovereign nations, particularly over how boundaries are drawn and where authority is located.

Building on anthropologists Valerie Lambert's and Jessica Cattelino's ethnographic descriptions and analysis of sovereignty as a process of negotiation, this chapter will seek to capture both the ideals and the hurdles of twenty-first-century enactments of Osage sovereignty. In her book on the Choctaw Nation, Lambert writes: "The Choctaws and other Indian tribes in the United States are not alone in having to negotiate certain aspects of their sovereignty. All nations must (and do)."[7] Lambert goes on to explain that in the American Indian context, sovereignty is a set of inherent rights. These include the ability to "elect their own leaders, determine their own membership, maintain tribal police forces, levy taxes, regulate property under tribal jurisdiction, control the conduct of their members by tribal ordinances, regulate the domestic relations of their members, and administer justice."[8] These inherent rights, however, are not without contestation by the State of Oklahoma and the U.S. government, which have "overlapping and competing sovereignties."[9]

In trying to make sense of these competing sovereignties, Kevin Bruyneel argues for a "third space of sovereignty that resides neither simply inside nor outside the American political system but rather exists on these very boundaries, exposing both the practices and the contingencies of American colonial rule."[10] This means that while the United States acknowledges American Indian national sovereignty, this sovereignty is not limited to these acknowledgments. While American Indian national sovereignty might come under attack, it can also be used to fight back, in turn challenging the authorities of the United States or the State of Oklahoma. In order to do this, it is necessary to see American Indian national sovereignty as no different from any other sovereignty throughout the world and as part of the shifting politics of power that mark unequal power dynamics also at work in those sovereignties. Above all, it is essential that academic writing opens up, rather than forecloses, future possibilities for American Indian national sovereignty.

Sovereignty marks a dissonance for the Osage and other indigenous nations who have never assented to colonial rule. The Declaration's use of Osage sovereignty, and particularly its assertion that it predates the U.S. Constitution, is one of the most powerful ways to state that might does not make right. Osage sovereignty is deployed as a mechanism to deny U.S. claims to authority over the Osage reservation, insisting instead on an alternative imagining of this territory. This sovereignty refuses to take the U.S. political space too seriously and labors to enable other polities within this space. Sovereignty is thus used to deny the authority of empire and assert self-control. In defining the Osage as a sovereign nation, the Declaration takes a stand against the ongoing colonial process and attempts to change the course of the Osage people.

Enacting Sovereignty

After signing the Declaration, I joined the even larger crowd gathering outside in an enormous white pavilion tent erected for the day's events. I was lucky enough to have staked out a place on the aisle early in the day near the front, where I was sure to have a good view of the processional and the speeches to follow. I was also within earshot of the singers, who had gathered around a large drum and were preparing for a full day of playing. Before the processional began, the lead singer stood up, thanked his fellow singers for joining him at the drum, and said, "Today is a big day for our people here. All of our ancestors were up on this hill just like we are doing now. We want these people to get that feeling today. When you are singing today bring that feeling in here." Sitting back down, he nodded and the drumming began.

While not referencing sovereignty directly, the singer's comments reflected the theme as much as the many longer formal speeches to follow. Because the Osage existed as a political body prior to the American Constitution, Osage sovereignty is understood here as simply needing to be brought forward. The authority of the past can be enacted to enable a strong future. As this singer's comments signal, sovereignty is also about feeling that you have the authority to control your own affairs.

As stated in the Declaration, Osage Nation sovereignty "predate[s] the Constitution of the United States." The document goes on to say that "these rights have been affirmed through the Constitution of the United States, various treaties and agreements between our Nation and the United States of America, legal precedents and the principles of human rights, and rights of indigenous peoples recognized throughout the world." Not only is the Osage Nation located historically prior to the birth of its colonizer, but also its sovereign authority has been reaffirmed by both the United States itself and international sources such as the United Nations. By drawing from multiple sources, the Declaration illustrates how Osage sovereignty is not limited to the rights recognized by the U.S. government. It existed not only before the United States but also outside of the United States.

Throughout Osage Sovereignty Day, I collected interviews from various people in attendance, asking them what they thought about the possibility of government reform, what sort of citizenship requirements they would like to see implemented, and how the new government should be structured. After a long day of interviews, I began packing up my bags, hoping to catch the fireworks show scheduled for shortly after dark. As I was taking my camera from its tripod, a middle-aged woman in grease-stained clothes hurried into the office I was using as a recording studio, asking if she was too late to participate. She had been cooking all day long to feed the people in attendance but wanted to comment on the importance of the day.

After answering my questions about the reform process, she responded to a question about "what it meant to be Osage today" by saying:

I am really happy that we have chosen to designate this day as our day of sovereignty and independence. I believe that we Osage have been sovereigns over our dominion from our first forefathers, our right from God, and nobody has the right to take that away from us. And anybody that wants to argue our sovereignty—I say, go to God. . . . We must work together and be patriotic for our Osage Nation and work out what is best for us and work out a great future for our children and our grandchildren so they may enjoy the blessings and freedoms of the Osage Nation as it goes into the twenty-first century.[11]

In addition to anchoring Osage nationhood in the past, these words illustrate the desire to work together to rebuild a strong Osage Nation for a sovereign future.

As we have seen, the 2004–6 Osage reform process was an internally negotiated debate about the definition of the Osage. In addition to race, culture, and minerals-based concerns, there were also sovereignty-based motivations. In order to understand what rebuilding a stronger nation meant, it is important to look at how it was articulated by key players throughout the reform process. These included Jim Gray, Leonard Maker, Hepsi Barnett, Billy Sam Fletcher, and Mark Freeman. Each of these officials gave priority to sovereignty throughout the reform process, asserting that the Osage Nation should begin taking more control of its own affairs.

As both chief of the 31st Osage Tribal Council and as the first chief of the newly reconstituted Osage Nation, Jim Gray was an unremitting advocate for Osage sovereignty. His speech during the Osage Sovereignty Day celebration, perhaps better than any other single statement, reflected this commitment to strengthening the authority of the Osage Nation. When it was his turn to address the crowd gathered for the celebration, Gray started by arguing that the Osage people must embrace this change in order to move forward as a people. He then went on to say: "Over 100 years ago, a man named Wah-ti-an-kah, my forefather, was sent to this land, and he said, 'There is something in the land that will ensure that our children will never starve.' Many of us thought that to be oil. . . . Today, I know what he meant—the sovereignty of the Osage Nation—and that is what will sustain us."[12] In asserting this need for change, he argued that the path forward was not through the Mineral Estate, as so many had argued in the past and continued to argue, but through the sovereignty of the Osage Nation.

Gray also addressed the effects of the colonial process that had limited the possibilities for an Osage Nation in the past, saying that the most devastating aspect was that it "has limited our own people's ability to see in themselves the confidence to overcome these problems."[13] This single statement of regret, that paternalism had whittled away at not only the governance authority of the Osage people but also their ability to unite against the ongoing colonial process, speaks pointedly to this twenty-first-century moment of colonial entanglement. Through a variety of strategies, including racial-, cultural-, and resource-based divisions, paternalism, and the erosion of Osage governing authority, many Osage had lost faith in their own ability to manage their affairs.

Toward the close of his speech, Gray outlined what he hoped to see in this newly reformed Nation: "For after today the Osage themselves must move back and take their sovereignty. . . . We must create a democracy that contains checks and balances, a strong independent judiciary, and [a] common set of laws that protects the interests of Osage and non-Osage alike."[14] For Gray, this moment was one of recognizing and acting upon the inherent sovereignty of the Osage, a sovereignty that was impotent if it did not have a powerful and well-crafted nation to actualize it. Gray employed sovereignty as a call to action.

Gray was hardly alone in his hope that the 2004–6 Osage reform process would lead to the creation of a national structure more capable of realizing the full sovereignty of the Osage. Maker, who was primarily responsible for convincing the OTC that government reform was needed and who planned the reform in addition to acting as a liaison between the Osage Government Reform Commission (OGRC) and the OTC, was another advocate for Osage sovereignty. In an interview I conducted with Maker, he defined sovereignty as "the ability of our tribe to meet the needs of our people in a way that is special to us."[15] Throughout the reform process, he stressed the importance of using this particular moment to assert full sovereign authority, saying that sovereignty "means we can do whatever we want. We don't need the Secretary [of the Interior] to approve it. . . . It is up to us not to have other people telling us what to do."[16] The understanding that the Osage have not just the right but also the obligation to take this moment and make something out of it was central to Maker's impetus for the reform process. He continually asked what the current OTC was doing for the Osage people and wanted to build a nation that would better provide for Osage needs through services and economic development.

Shortly after the commissioners had been appointed, Leonard Maker addressed them and highlighted the OGRC's job in educating the public about sovereignty: "Most of our people don't understand sovereignty; it's not part of their daily life. They say, 'it's a nice phrase but what does it mean to me?' . . . I think that's one of the tasks of the commission, to make sure that people are aware of what sovereignty is and why it's important."[17] Through the Osage Sovereignty Day and the OGRC community meetings, Osage officials and employees inserted this idea of sovereignty into Osage discussions of the reform process. In emphasizing sovereignty, they hoped to shift authority away from the federal government and also to illustrate the positive outcomes the Osage Nation could create for the Osage people.

Maker then went on to describe the tangible results of sovereignty, such as increased employment on the reservation through casinos and other Osage economic development projects and the improved funding of programs such as education and housing. Through these hopes for national advancement, Maker and others during the reform were attempting to sell the idea of sovereignty to the Osage people. Such unmet needs were also understood, however, to require a national structure, which could meet current Osage necessities in areas such as health care, education, and economic development. For these Osage leaders, there was a strong connection between sovereignty, a constitutional government, and the increased ability to serve Osage needs. The material results of sovereignty, such as the creation of jobs or the increase of services, were understood as the primary goal of the reform, requiring a centralized national structure to bring them into being.

As the project coordinator for the OGRC, Hepsi Barnett was the single most active person in the 2004–6 reform process. Although her primary role was as a facilitator for the commissioners, she was the person most responsible for making reform happen. Unlike the commissioners, Barnett was paid for her work, and thus she could devote herself full time to the completion of the reform process and the writing of the 2006 Constitution. Barnett had earned a master's degree in public administration from the Kennedy School of Government, working as part of the Harvard Project on American Indian Economic Development. Since its founding in 1987, the Harvard Project has conducted extensive research with American Indian nations across the continent, seeking to ascertain why some economic development projects in Indian Country succeed while others fail. The Harvard Project is a vocal advocate for increased American Indian control over their own affairs, claiming that "when Native nations make their own decisions about what development approaches to take, they consistently out-perform external decision makers."[18] Throughout the reform process, Barnett used her education and experience to argue that a strong Osage Nation government had to be created if economic development was to be successful.

At an OGRC community meeting in Dallas, Texas, Barnett was particularly vocal about the importance of asserting sovereign control: "The research out there regarding Indian nations prospering under their own self-determined government far outweighs the research out there where the Bureau is in control. Indian nations who organize their own governments and control their own affairs out-perform by 400 percent the Indian nations who continue to be primarily under the BIA [Bureau of Indian Affairs]."[19] By drawing on the Harvard Project's research, sovereignty was turned from an abstract concept into a concrete tool that could be used to improve individual Osage lives. As demonstrated here, sovereignty was positioned during the reform process as a means to ensure a prosperous future for the Osage people. Through rebuilding a strong Osage Nation, the Osage people could realize their sovereign potential, which would in turn further economic opportunities in the region. In this way, Barnett positioned sovereignty as more important than blood, culture, or minerals to ensuring the future of the Osage people.

Billy Sam Fletcher, who was chairman of the OGRC, also frequently spoke to the importance of sovereignty. Fletcher had been a vocal advocate for revitalizing the Osage Nation for over twenty years and had been the primary party to the lawsuit in the 1990s, which declared that the 1881 Osage Constitution had been illegally abolished by the Office of Indian Affairs and was thus still in effect. During his interview with me on Sovereignty Day, he said: "I am here today to celebrate the return of our sovereignty. It was always there, it was just inoperative."[20] Fletcher's simple but direct statement reveals much of the complexity surrounding this term. While always existing, sovereignty is here understood as something that must be enacted, with no value as an inert entity.

Throughout the reform process, Fletcher continued to advocate for Osage sovereignty, telling others about its historical connections and future possibilities. During an early OGRC meeting, soon after its formation, Fletcher discussed the need for a constitutional form of government that amended the 1881 Constitution because he felt that it created the strongest link with the historically located Osage sovereignty. "So that [the 1881 Constitution] keeps sovereignty flowing from the past to the future."[21] At the same time that Fletcher is historically locating Osage sovereignty within the 1881 Constitution, he is making a larger case for national reform. He argues that the colonial process cannot disrupt Osage sovereignty so long as it is brought into the present through a revised constitutional government.

Mark Freeman was the councilman most active in the passage of Public Law 108-431 because of his desire to see that full citizenship in the Osage Nation was permanently opened to all lineal descendants of the 1906 roll. He worked with the lawyers, traveled to Washington, and established the necessary relationship with Congressman Frank Lucas of Oklahoma, convincing him that this bill was worthwhile. He was also an advocate for Osage control in general, saying that we needed to be in a position where we could stop sitting idly by, blaming others for our problems, and finally take matters into our own hands.[22] In his State of the Nation address on Osage Sovereignty Day, he said, "Now we are a sovereign Nation. . . . Now we face the formidable task of developing an Osage Nation governing body that will lead us successfully into the future."[23] For Freeman, this meant the establishment of a strong government that could manage Osage authority in an efficient way. It also meant asserting control in areas that had long been neglected.

One of these areas of control was over water rights and other resources in the reservation territory. Freeman was interested in regaining control over the entire reservation area. In an interview with me he said: "We need to get started working on getting a determination of our sovereignty in the water on the Osage reservation. We need to step up to the plate on our reservation status. By not fighting for it in the past we've allowed the State [of Oklahoma] to take over some things; we're going to have to take them back."[24] Here we begin to see the ways sovereignty was also a space of contention, a battle continually fought over control and authority within a territory. As was clear in the Declaration, the assertion of control over Osage territory, most frequently called the Osage reservation, is the primary space in which discussions about Osage sovereignty took shape. This space, the reservation, is a key link to how Osage authority was asserted through the writing of the 2006 Constitution.

Within the 2006 Constitution, Osage sovereignty is clearly deployed to define the Osage Nation against both internal and external definitions of authority. Whether it was against the Osage annuitants, who saw themselves, rather than the Nation, as owners of the Osage Mineral Estate, or against the State of Oklahoma, which—as we will see—insisted it had jurisdiction over reservation lands, the writers of the 2006 Constitution took a strong stand. The act of writing an Osage constitution worked against these forces to establish the Osage Nation as the premier political entity in the territory.

The primary section in which sovereignty is discussed is Article II, which lays out the territory and jurisdiction of the Osage Nation:

> Territory is defined as the Osage reservation and all other lands under federally-restricted status title which is held by the Nation or the People, or by the United States in trust on behalf of the Nation or the People, and any such additional lands as are hereafter acquired and similarly held by the Nation or the People or by the United States on behalf of the Nation or the People. Territory is defined as, but is not limited to, air, water, surface, sub-surface, natural resources and any interest therein, notwithstanding the issuance of any patent or right of way in fee or otherwise, by the governments of the United States or the Osage Nation, existing and/or in the future.[25]

Osage territory is specifically defined against other existing claims. The 2006 Osage Constitution asserts ultimate authority by claiming that both the subsurface rights, which some Osage annuitants assert their own authority over, and the water rights, which the State of Oklahoma has attempted to control, ultimately belong to the Osage Nation.

The 2006 Constitution then goes on to describe the Osage Nation's jurisdiction as extending "over all persons, subjects, property, and over all activities that occur within the territory of the Osage Nation and over all Osage citizens, subjects, property and activities outside such territory affecting the rights and laws of the Osage Nation."[26] Not only does this statement give the Osage Nation authority over all Osage citizens, regardless of their location within or outside Osage territory, but it also asserts control over all people and activities in the territory. This statement is clearly written against the colonial moment, where federal laws at times deny the rights of Indian nations not only over non-Indians but also over some matters relating to their own Indian citizens.[27] Article II of the 2006 Osage Constitution concludes by saying: "Nothing in this Article shall be construed to limit or impair the ability of the Osage Nation to exercise its jurisdiction within or without its territory based upon its inherent sovereign authority as a nation of Osage People."[28]

The writers of the 2006 Constitution clearly saw the process as a moment to assert full Osage sovereignty. By denying all other authorities, both internal and external, the right to "limit or impair" the Nation's jurisdiction, this document makes a clear statement about the sovereignty of the newly reconstituted Osage Nation. These statements are working against the belief that the Osage reservation only exists underground, a belief born out of the fact that when the surface land was allotted in 1906, the subsurface oil interests remained in trust, with the OTC managing leases and distributing the income among Osage annuitants.[29] As more of the reservation surface land has left Osage control, the Osage, like many other American Indian nations, have a patchwork of Osage, Indian, and non-Indian controlled land on the reservation.[30] This situation makes jurisdictional control, particularly in the case of police enforcement, very complicated, resulting in negotiated solutions like the cross-deputizing of Osage County and Osage Nation police forces and the establishment of intergovernmental agreements. In the face of such arguments, however, the 2006 Osage Constitution puts forward an all-encompassing understanding of Osage territory and jurisdictional control.

In addition to defining jurisdiction, Article IV, the Declaration of Rights, also makes sovereignty a fundamental component of the newly constituted Osage Nation. It states, in part: "The Osage People have the exclusive right of governing themselves as a free, sovereign, and independent nation as done from time immemorial."[31] The inclusion of the "exclusive right" of the Osage is potent not just because it has been located in time immemorial but also because of the stance it is taking against the ongoing colonial process and other definitions of the Osage. From these excerpts, it is clear that the Osage Constitution is less a statement of where the Osage Nation is today than a statement about the possibilities for the Nation in the future.

Encounters with the State

When I returned to the Dave Landrum Community Center in Pawhuska, Oklahoma, on March 21, 2006, skeptics of the Osage Nation's authority once again surrounded me. This time, however, there were only a few Osage annuitants present. Unlike the Osage Shareholders Association (OSA) meetings, there was no potluck meal, and the people filling the many tables were almost all wearing blue jeans and cowboy hats. They talked in frustrated but hushed tones and ignored me as I set up my camera. They were ready to take a stand, and they wanted it witnessed by as many people as possible.

The night before, as I was leaving one of the biweekly Osage language classes, I had been told about a growing movement against the recently passed 2006 Osage Constitution. A stand was going to be taken at the community meeting with Oklahoma state representative Frank Lucas, which was scheduled for the following afternoon. Members of the Osage Cattlemen's Association had written a letter in which they denied the authority asserted by the Osage Nation over their land, air, water, and person, and they wanted protection from county, state, and federal officials in case the Osage attempted to enforce sovereign authority over the settler population—97 percent of the reservation's population were settlers, usually second or third generation, so it was understandable that the 2006 Constitution's assertions would be a cause for concern.

Lucas began the community meeting like he must have begun other meetings in his jurisdiction, with a discussion of how federal monies were primarily going to the war in Iraq and to rebuilding areas hit by hurricanes in the United States. He explained that he was failing to get much traction on his farm subsidy bills, given the weight of these other concerns. He also said that he had not voted for the extension of the Patriot Act because he saw it as an overextension of the government, but he did vote for a bill that increased border control.

Even though Lucas was only in the middle of his speech, a member of the audience raised his hand and interjected the primary issue the audience was there to have addressed: "Here in Osage County we have a unique situation. This is the Osage mineral reservation underground. We're worried about possible conflict of interest with the Constitution asserting sovereignty over the area of the reservation. We'd like to know exactly where the reservation is or isn't."[32] Lucas responded that the bill he had sponsored only gave the Osage what the other nations in Oklahoma had, but that he was not sure about the reservation question. He explained that the status of the reservation was currently a matter of debate in the federal courts and that they would have to wait until a decision was reached. With much grumbling, the ranchers left the meeting, still worried about the future.

For a little over a year, these concerns remained below the surface, but in late May 2007, the Osage Nation Congress began reviewing a natural resource bill, quickly stirring up fresh controversy among some Osage County residents. The bill proposed the creation of an environmental commission that would propose legislation for the Osage Nation and enable higher environmental standards. The *Bartlesville Examiner-Enterprise* newspaper reported that Dick Surber, representing the Osage County Cattlemen's Association, saw the bill as an attempt by the Osage Nation to assert control over the entire county. Surber was quoted as saying: "We landowners, both Osage and non-Osage, reject blatant attempts by the executive branch of the Osage tribe to exert jurisdiction over our land, air and water."[33] The environmental bill was quickly tabled, but it had already unleashed "vitriolic and deafening objections" throughout Osage County.[34] These strong reactions are part and parcel of the contestations that mark assertions of sovereignty, particularly in settler colonial spaces.[35]

In 1907, at the time of Oklahoma statehood, Osage County had been established directly on top of and mirroring the jurisdiction of the Osage reservation. While the Osage reservation was only allotted to those people listed on the 1906 Osage allotment roll, land was eventually sold, stolen, or seized, enabling non-Indians to greatly outnumber Osage within the territory, with only 3 percent of the population enrolled as Osage citizens in 2006. Additionally, as a result of the limitations the federal government created for Osage governance, particularly with its insistence on a council focused on the Mineral Estate, there has been a shared jurisdiction between Osage County and the reservation, marked by cross-deputizing, intergovernmental agreements, state and tribal compacts, payments in lieu of taxes, and simple contracts for services.

By the twenty-first century, and particularly after the passage of Public Law 108-431, there was a growing effort by the OTC and then the newly reconstituted Osage Nation to take over as many of the state services as possible. This included a series of efforts by the Osage to assert control over a wide range of areas, from Osage child support services to local emergency services, with the State of Oklahoma frequently giving up control, and therefore the costs, happily. The passage of the 2006 Constitution, however, with its insistence on full authority over the territory, increased conflicts over whether or not the 2,296 square miles of land in northeastern Oklahoma known as the Osage reservation is legally a reservation or merely the largest county in the state.

Much of the anger over reservation status was based on misunderstandings about what it would mean for Osage County to be officially treated like a reservation. In addition to the fears about stringent environmental laws, there were a host of concerns ranging from land loss to taxation to complete lawlessness. These apprehensions quickly swelled and affected interactions between the Osage Nation and non-Osage residents, including the denial of the authority of the Osage Nation's police officers to issue state traffic tickets, even though cross-deputization had been in place for eleven years. These anxieties, while certainly based on misunderstandings, were also marked by the discord between how different people understood and defined what the twenty-first-century Osage sovereignty should entail.

Osage County ranchers were unlikely to easily accept assertions of Osage Nation sovereignty, since this would mean their own loss of authority. This reaction results from the power struggle that plays out between a sovereign nation and those who inhabit the same territory but are excluded from participation in its governance. American Indian law expert Joseph Flies-Away acknowledges this larger problem: "On a practical level, tribal constitutional limitation of nonmember participation in tribal government provides anti-Indian interests with arguments for further circumscribing the scope of the sovereignty exercised by tribes."[36] While no nation-state anywhere in the world has a citizenship body that entirely matches the inhabitants of its territorial base,[37] this disparity is particularly problematic for colonized nations that have had their territories taken over by a settler population. If non-Osage are unable to participate or have a say in Osage governance, then there need to be powerful reasons for agreeing to Osage authority, such as an increase in economic development, assurance their lands will not be taken away, and services to the population of the territory as a whole.

The fear of a diminished authority led some non-Osage landowners to do everything in their power to discredit the Osage Nation, including writing editorials in newspapers such as the conservative *Daily Oklahoman*, which criticized the firm stance Chief Jim Gray and the newly reconstituted Osage Nation took toward asserting Osage sovereignty. One such editorial focused on the environmental bill and Gray's effort to prevent State of Oklahoma inspectors from entering any Osage business on the reservation. Such a stance was basic protocol on most reservations, simply because the state does not have jurisdiction on reservation, trust, or other lands considered to be part of Indian Country. The anonymous writer states: "Guess . . . Gray won't mind if the Highway Patrol stops enforcing the speed limits on the winding highways that run through Osage County. Or if the Department of Transportation removes from its maintenance list any roads and bridges in the County that need repair. . . .

Gray wants the tribe to stand-alone. It seems to us he ought to be careful what he wishes for."[38]

This comment signals several important aspects of the entanglement of Osage sovereignty at the beginning of the twenty-first century. First, because the State of Oklahoma has encroached on Osage reservation affairs, Osage County has a much larger infrastructure in place for operations such as law enforcement, transportation, and other public works. The Osage Nation has begun to develop these areas but does not have the necessary infrastructure to immediately take over their full operation across the reservation. Asserting full sovereignty will take time and will require resources from gaming and other economic development. Secondly, non-Osage landowners, like the Osage annuitants, are going to try to use these weaknesses to discredit Osage Nation sovereignty, despite the Osage administration's efforts to build up the necessary infrastructure over time. Their reasons for discrediting the Nation are obvious but, as stated above, not inevitable.

When the *Daily Oklahoman* editorial was posted on the OSA discussion board, there was an involved debate about whether the assertion of sovereignty was worth the potential backlash that might come from upsetting the majority settler population on the reservation and from the U.S. government. To these concerns, one Osage responded:

How sad it is that you perceive yourself, and all Osage, in such a sad pathetic light! Seriously, I really feel bad for you. It can't be comfortable to live such a diminished, marginalized existence. Did you go to a government boarding school? Did they, the U.S. government, do this to you? It doesn't have to be this way. God isn't white and the whites aren't gods. They're no better than we Osage. . . . Formerly oppressed native peoples can and do move beyond the mental artifacts which make them prisoners in their own skins. You can as well. Kick that hateful little white-man right out of your head![39]

For this writer, embracing Osage sovereignty is central to the process of decolonization. Rather than feeling oppressed by the limitations that others are attempting to place on Osage sovereignty today, this contributor to the forum looks forward to a sovereign Osage future beyond settler colonial narratives.

The concerns expressed in the *Daily Oklahoman* editorial mark the tensions involved with any deployment of sovereignty across the globe. In the U.S. federalist system, there exists a tension between federal, state, county, and local governments over the jurisdiction of any given location. In this system, the authority of these governments, including jurisdictional control, is still quite dynamic, as is the case with the legalization of medical marijuana in California or with gay marriage laws across the United States. Similar tensions also exist between Osage County and the Osage reservation. Each polity clearly has its own definition of how authority should be determined within the Osage context.

The importance of reservation status is most pronounced in the case of Osage casinos, some of which were not located on Osage trust land until August 2011. Before opening a casino in north Tulsa, the National Indian Gaming Commission (NIGC) had to be convinced that the area was still part of a recognized reservation and thus in Indian Country.[40] In her opinion for the NIGC, Osage attorney Elizabeth Lohah Homer used Department of the Interior documents to argue for the continued recognition of the Osage reservation by the federal government. Among the documents supporting her opinion were the act of June 5, 1872, CH. 310, 17 Stat. 228 (An Act to Confirm to the Great and Little Osage Indians a Reservation in the Indian Territory), the 1906 Osage Allotment Act (34 Stat. 539), which allotted the reservation but repeatedly refers to the reservation's continuation, and a 2004 lease agreement approved by the BIA, all of which illustrated the continued existence of the Osage reservation.

Another of the documents cited in her NIGC opinion is a report of the solicitor general, Nathan R. Margold, written on December 17, 1935. Concerning this document she says: "The Solicitor determined that the lands are 'Tribal lands within the reservation boundaries' and further noted that 'So far as I am advised no act of Congress has severed these lands from the reservation. In the absence of such Congressional action they not only remain within the reservation but also qualify as "Indian country" under the rule that "Indian country" remains such until the Indian title is extinguished unless other wise [sic] provided by Congress.'"[41] In addition to Margold's report, the NIGC opinion cited a 1997 Oklahoma gubernatorial proclamation, which stated that "the Osage reservation covering all of Osage County is the only federally recognized reservation remaining in Oklahoma,"[42] as well as a 1992 map of Indian land published by the U.S. Department of the Interior. The NIGC opinion concludes: "Based on the above documents, we understand that at least some offices within the Department of the Interior have concluded that the Osage Nation reservation has not been disestablished. . . . Please advise us immediately if your office disagrees with our understandings of the status of the Indian nation's reservation."[43] The Department of the Interior did not issue a response, and the casino opened in north Tulsa, on nontrust Osage reservation land.

Throughout this opinion, we see not only how Homer demonstrated Osage authority over the entire land base but also how various people and federal departments have acknowledged the Osage reservation over the last hundred years. The evidence and findings cited in her opinion work to authorize Osage sovereignty over the territory. Even if the Osage Nation still must contend with the federal government's claims to plenary authority over the entire territory of the United States, this opinion and its evidence devalue the State of Oklahoma's assertions to authority over nontrust Osage-owned lands.

American Indian nations have often run into direct conflict with state and local governments as they have increasingly asserted their sovereignty over their territories. These disputes have often been settled in federal court, but the decisions were both costly and unequal. To address these issues, particularly as they related to Indian gaming, the U.S. Congress passed the Indian Gaming and Regulatory Act in 1988, forcing Indian nations and states to enter into consensual agreements.[44] Central to compacting with the state, as this practice came to be known in Oklahoma, is an understanding that neither group can claim complete authority over the territory but must work with the other to reach a compromise. Gaming created a path for Indian nations and states to follow in order to avoid litigation while allowing for the negotiation of other issues such as taxation. However, it also further entangled American Indian national sovereignty with state governments.

The path to compacting in Oklahoma has been particularly fraught with difficulty. As Indian nations began to be competitors with other tobacco retailers in the state, Oklahoma responded with more regulations. Oklahoma's legislature passed a law that forbade wholesalers from selling to Indian smoke shops without the proper Oklahoma tax stamp. This came as a result of lower state tax revenues from tobacco sales and increased lobbying from the QuikTrip corporation and other retailers, who were losing profits to Indian smoke shops. In response, Indian smoke shops began purchasing from out-of-state wholesalers. The state could do little to enforce its tax collection in Indian Country because sovereign immunity prevented it from taking legal action.[45] Without the ability to take Indian nations to court, the state had to find other ways to exercise authority over cigarette taxation.

The state was "losing" millions of dollars in tax revenue, and it turned to compacting as a possible model for accessing some of these funds. To support this process and protect its own interests and the interests of corporate smoke shops, the Oklahoma legislature in 1992 passed a tax law that stopped the taxation of retailers and instead placed the burden on wholesalers. Any untaxed cigarettes acquired from wholesalers were then considered contraband and were subject to seizure. This law also recognized the right of Indian Country smoke shops to import tobacco from out of state and gave the smoke shops a 75 percent break from the state tax rate.[46] Pressure for Indian nations to sign these compacts came primarily from Indian smoke shop owners, who were hesitant to act outside state law and eager to take advantage of the new tax breaks.[47]

American Indian nations also benefited from these agreements through taxation of their shops, which created a new revenue source. Through these compacts, Indian nations were able to establish more authority over their territory and gain further recognition from the state. In response to criticism that the nations were "selling out to the state," Bill Anoatubby, governor of the Chickasaw, replied: "This government-to-government compact is the most reasonable method of settling disputes. This is a true exercise of Tribal sovereignty."[48] Wilma Mankiller, principal chief of the Cherokee Nation, argued for compacting in just these terms: "Some may say the Indians would be giving up something, but I say we are dealing from a position of strength. I think it would be a nice legacy to lead the first step toward collaboration."[49] For many Indian leaders, compacting became a way to assert sovereignty.[50]

When these compacts began to expire in 2003, Chief Gray worked with other American Indian nations to negotiate a single new compact with the state and all nations. Oklahoma's director of finance, Scott Meacham, ignored these requests and refused to meet with all nations together.[51] The Indian nations were outraged. Not only were state officials refusing to meet with American Indian nations as a whole group, but they were also supplanting the negotiated compact process with a single take-it-or-leave-it offer. After the Choctaw and Chickasaw nations negotiated their own compacts, other Indian nations, including the Osage, began to vie for the best position. The Osage were able to extend the exception rule for nations residing near the border to fit twelve of their fifteen smoke shops.[52] This meant that these shops were only paying the state at a rate of six cents per pack of cigarettes, compared to the eighty-six-cent non-exemption rate. Complicating these agreements was State Question 713, which raised tobacco taxes to $1.03 per pack but also eliminated sales tax from all tobacco sales. This not only cut the margin of the Indian smoke shops but also violated existing compacts.[53]

Meanwhile, Meacham was unable to live up to his promise to the Oklahoma legislature that his changes in tobacco tax regulations would lead to a large financial increase for the state. Bowing to pressure to do away with sales between Indian smoke shops, which it argued was the cause of the missing revenue, the Oklahoma Tax Commission adopted emergency rules late in 2005 that allowed wholesalers to sell only 10 percent more cigarettes to smoke shops than they did in 2004. This procedure was cumbersome, though there were some exceptions for expanding businesses. The result was that many tribal smoke shops lost business or had to shut down.[54] Early in 2006, twenty-six leaders from the Osage, Muscogee Creek, Cherokee, and other Indian nations met and attempted to unify in opposition to the state. Chief Gray presented his case on the failure of the compacting process, referring to it as "Meacham's Mess." Gray continued: "This has created a full-fledged political mess. . . . It's a clear indicator that this isn't about cigarettes; it's about compacts and sovereignty."[55]

In several letters to Oklahoma governor Brad Henry, Chief Gray requested that the governor refuse to sign the emergency tax laws because they violated the existing compact and imposed unilateral legislation.[56] When this request was denied, the Osage took the Oklahoma Tax Commission to federal court on charges that the new rules broke the compact as well as the "United States Constitution through the restriction of the commerce, and breaking of the contracts clause of the constitution."[57] The U.S. district court ruled that Governor Henry had to engage in arbitration with the Osage to settle the dispute. The state managed to stall this process until November 2008, during which time Osage smoke shops continued retail-to-retail sales and other creative maneuvers to work around state regulations. By December 2008, the Osage Nation finally succeeded in renegotiating its tobacco compact with the state and in the process agreed to stop selling to other Indian nations. In return for the Osage Nation's agreement to these stipulations, various investigations of the Nation by the state were dropped.[58]

The complicated entanglement of Oklahoma and American Indian national sovereignties is clearly evident from this condensed history of tobacco compacting. While American Indian nations were working toward a relationship built on negotiation and mutual recognition, the State of Oklahoma's actions reveal a determined resistance to coequal negotiations. Playing to interest groups like the QuikTrip lobby, the state has shown a brazen disregard for the sovereignty of the Indian nations, painting them instead as renegades who refuse to follow "the law." By presenting Indian nations in this light, the State of Oklahoma is trying to limit the possibilities of American Indian national sovereignty. In the meantime, due to the creative response to the State of Oklahoma's lack of jurisdiction, American Indian tobacco shops gained almost half of the cigarette market but, according to state records, were only paying 12 percent of collected taxes.[59] While this disparity finally led the state back to the negotiation table, it is clear that the State of Oklahoma is still far from recognizing the sovereignty of Indian nations.

Tobacco taxes are not the only space in which the Oklahoma Tax Commission has attempted to deny indigenous sovereignty. Between 1985 and 1995, four different Oklahoma Indian nations took the Tax Commission to court for attempting to collect income taxes in Indian Country. In each case, the courts told the commission that it had to recognize the sovereignty of Indian land within the state.[60] In 2001, the Osage Nation filed a similar suit against the Oklahoma Tax Commission, seeking "an injunction restraining the State of Oklahoma from levying and collecting income taxes upon the income of the nation's members who are employed, earn income, and reside within the nation's reservation."[61] While this appeared to be a clear-cut case like the others, it has instead served to bolster the sovereignty of the State of Oklahoma. Before hearing the merits of the case, which was scheduled to begin several months later, U.S. District Judge James Payne ruled in January 2009 that Osage tribal members who lived and worked on nonrestricted Osage County land were not exempt from state income taxes because the full reservation no longer existed. A three-judge 10th Circuit Board of Appeals agreed with this decision in March 2010.

In the opinions offered by these judges, it is clear that they are seeking to deny the existence of a continued Osage territorial authority. Payne writes: "Oklahoma has governed Osage County as a County for over 100 years. The County is predominately non-Indian and non-Osage. The Osage have not sought to reestablish their claimed reservation or to challenge the state's taxation until recently. Recognizing Osage County as a reservation and ousting Oklahoma income taxation over Osage members would have significant practical consequences not only for income taxation but potentially for civil, criminal and regulatory jurisdiction in Osage County."[62] The illegal abolishment of the 1881 Osage Constitution, coerced allotment, fraudulent white enrollment, the murder of Osage for land and money, and opportunistic white settlement are here disregarded, leaving only the predominance of non-Indians and the authority of the State of Oklahoma as dispositive. It is as a result of this colonial context, however, that the Osage had little choice but to allow whites to live within Osage territory. Furthermore, the resulting jurisdictional authority of the state is cited as a motivation in itself, as if the settler colonial process justifies its own continuation. Finally, it is inaccurate to say that the Osage have not asserted authority until recently; the reality of jurisdiction over this territory is far more complicated. There has been a whole host of shared relationships since the imposition of statehood in 1907. Judge Payne hoped to make the case for Oklahoma State authority incontrovertible through selective evidence, when the facts present a far more complex picture.

Similarly, the findings of the 10th Circuit judges also told a limited story, one that fortified the authority of the State of Oklahoma at the expense of Osage sovereignty. These judges argued that the precedent of *Solem v. Bartlett* (465 U.S. 463) led to ambiguous results in the case of the Osage. *Solem* set up a test for determining whether or not a reservation still existed, looking for the transfer of surplus lands to non-Indians, compensation issued for lost lands, and the language of termination, all of which the courts agreed were missing in the Osage case. While they do not make clear what led to their determination that the findings were ambiguous, they used this conclusion to focus on what they saw as "contemporaneous understandings." Through this approach, these judges were able to use the precedent of *Solem* and deploy their own evidence of dissolution.

In the sources they cite, it is apparent that these three judges, one of whom had previously worked for the Oklahoma Tax Commission, are only interested in including evidence that sustains the dissolution of the reservation, citing none of the same sources mentioned in the NIGC report, except to say that these sources did not reflect contemporaneous understandings. For example, they include reference to a 1984 book written by Francis Paul Prucha, in which he writes that the federal government's general goal during allotment was to do away with Indian nations, even though Prucha is in no way referring to the unique Osage case. They also include reference to dubious sources such as the *Chronicles of Oklahoma*, the journal of the Oklahoma Historical Society, and other sources that would naturally argue against Osage authority over the newly formed colonial territory. In utilizing evidence that solely supports their case, these judges are providing legitimacy for Oklahoma State authority, hoping such evidence can be used to dismantle the Osage reservation.

Anthropologist John Moore has written about the continued existence of the Osage reservation, citing its specific absence from the 1887 Dawes General Allotment Act, the 1890 Oklahoma Organic Act, the 1897 Curtis Act, and the 1906 Oklahoma Enabling Act.[63] Moore is hardly alone in arguing for the continuance of the Osage reservation.[64] These discussions were, however, entirely absent from the court's findings. Also absent were the Supreme Court decisions that found that Indian Country existed in Osage County, including *Pickett v. United States* (1910), *Kennedy v. United States* (1924), and *United States v. Ramsey* (1926). By selecting the evidence that supported their case and by focusing on aspects outside of existing law, such as demography, these judges relate a biased narrative, one that attempts to deny the possibilities for a twenty-first-century Osage reservation.

In considering American Indian policy in the United States, Rennard Strickland finds that similar tactics are rampant throughout Indian law. Actual legal considerations are infrequently what drive these court cases. Strickland writes: "One of the problems today is that Indians are not behaving in the forms that white society has historically defined as the appropriate Indian form. . . . Indian lawyers are behaving in a way which the white inventor of the Indian image did not imagine; therefore, such conduct is intolerable."[65] Choctaw lawyer Gary Pitchlynn argues that the legal facts, which clearly substantiate the Osage reservation case, could do little to dispel the white judges' opinions that the Osage reservation does not look the way an Indian reservation should.[66]

As anthropologist Garrick Bailey explained when discussing the judges' use of demography to argue against the existence of the Osage reservation, "This is only one step removed from saying 'they don't look like a tribe.' Given the demographic changes in the U.S. population and increasing national economic problems, I think that Indian national sovereignty is going to be increasingly challenged in the coming decades. Indian status cannot be maintained by legal arguments alone."[67] Indian nations today, like many nations fighting to assert themselves against colonial and neocolonial forces, are not contesting on a level playing field. Given such constraints, however, the growing authority and prosperity of these nations is a testament to the power of local desires for self-control.

The case was appealed to the Supreme Court, but the Court refused to hear it, perhaps because of the May 27, 2011, opinion of the acting U.S. solicitor general. In this opinion, the solicitor general argued that some evidence, including the unique allotment of the Osage and "the present tense references to the Reservation in the Osage Allotment Act and the Oklahoma Enabling Act," could "imply a continuing reservation."[68] According to the solicitor general, however, this did not mean that the state had been excluded from authority within this territory, particularly over income taxation. The inclusion of the Osage in the Oklahoma Constitutional Convention, the layering of Osage County directly over the reservation territory, and various federal laws stipulating state authority over the territory, all signaled to the solicitor general that the state authority "includes the assessment of the personal income taxes at issue."[69] Finally, the solicitor general argued that the Osage case was too unique to impact the status of any other American Indian territory and was thus a "poor vehicle for addressing disestablishment and diminishment questions."[70] In other words, the solicitor general argued that the Osage reservation was a deeply entangled space.

Responding to this opinion and the following decision of the Supreme Court not to hear the Osage reservation case, Osage Chief John Red Eagle said: "I am disappointed with the Supreme Court's decision to allow a clearly wrong decision to stand, but this does not end the Osage Nation's efforts to protect our homelands. . . . We will continue to exercise our inherent rights as a sovereign nation."[71] In the Osage response to the Oklahoma Tax Commission, it was clear that Osage leaders would continue to believe in and fight for their right to control Osage territory. Of course, Osage sovereignty is not dependent on the status of the reservation. Osage sovereignty, as for all American Indian nations, will continue to be recognized on trust lands. Furthermore, the Osage will continue to work to gain ground in the battle over authority in their refusal to submit to the assertions of the settler state.

From the conflicting evidence regarding the existence of the Osage reservation, we can clearly see how authority over Osage territory is under debate. By using territory as an analytical tool for investigating how authority is constructed, it becomes clear that while both the State of Oklahoma and the Osage Nation have competing sovereignty claims, the evidence of this case weighs in favor of the continuance of the Osage reservation. Such evidence, however, is not enough to ensure that the reservation will be recognized by the settler state. As demonstrated by the Supreme Court's refusal to hear the case, Osage sovereignty is not given the same legal weight as Oklahoma's claims. It is, after all, the settler state itself that is being asked to make this decision about where sovereignty lies.

Such circumstances do not mean, however, that we should think of indigenous sovereignty as somehow inherently limited but must instead find or make other spaces in which these sovereignties can be realized. In 2006, Osage voters enacted a government in which sovereignty could be realized. Debates about whether the Osage are primarily a race of people sharing particular biological fluids, a culture made up of particular practices, or annuitants in a Mineral Estate all commanded the attention of the writers of the 2006 Constitution. It was, however, sovereignty that took center stage in the document. The key question remains, however, whether the Osage Nation will be able to fully realize this sovereignty and serve the needs of the Osage people or whether it will continue to be challenged on all sides (by Osage and non-Osage alike), with the result that authority is ceded to the colonial state.

In February 2011, as the Egyptian people were demonstrating for an end to the repressive regime of their president, Hosni Mubarak, Jim Gray, former chief of the Osage Nation, posted on Facebook a long discussion entitled, "Nation Building in Native America and in Egypt?" in which he argued that at this moment, when many Americans were distrustful of the revolution in Egypt, it was of fundamental importance to unite behind the "struggle for self-determination, whether it's in the Americas or a plaza in Cairo, Egypt. That is what Nation-Building is all about. How can an American Indian watch the courage of the people protesting in the streets of Cairo and not feel deep down inside, a sense of kinship to their struggle for freedom?"[72] Gray's statement illustrates the power of self-determination at this early moment in the twenty-first century. This is not just an issue for the Osage, or for American Indians, but a growing movement toward increased worldwide self-governance. It is also not just about the centralization of authority over a particular location, but it is also about forming a government that is responsive to the needs of all its citizens.

Gray goes on to note that the term "sovereignty" is "more than just a matter for academic study and philosophical debate among the elite; it is real, it works, and it sets the stage for people to find ways to work and succeed together."[73] As this chapter has shown, strong nations are built through the exercise of sovereignty, which works not as an abstract and comprehensive legal term but as a contested node of authority in lived realities. In following contestations of Osage sovereignty, I have sought to move past the limited legal constraints of this word to better understand the authority and limitation it contains. Gray concludes his posting: "Today, our neighbors are beginning to understand that when the tribes are strong, everyone benefits, a rising tide lifts all boats. This has been done, not on the white man's terms, but on our own. It's not revenge, it's rebirth[,] and as our elders say, it is good."[74]

This too is my desire for our nation, and it is nothing short of a revolution in our ways of thinking and being. As with the silk ribbon acquired in trade with the French in the eighteenth century, we must cut, fold, and stitch together these strips to form our own unique patterns. Ultimately, we must do what is needed to make the Osage Nation work for us. It is only by uniting behind Osage sovereignty that we have any hope of ensuring an Osage future.

Appendix 1 **1861 Constitution of the Osage Nation**

Therefore we the people of the Osage Nation in convention assembled at the Council Village on the North Side of the Neosho River in the Osage Nation, on the 21st day of August, A.D. 1861 in pursuance of a previous agreement do hereby ordain and establish this Constitution for the Osage Nation of Indians.

Article 1

Section 1. The Legislative and Judicial power of this Nation shall be vested in a council of (14) fourteen members chosen annually by ballot from among the citizens of the Osage Nation. The members shall be residents of the Nation and twenty-five years of age.

Section 2. A majority of the members shall be a quorum. To do business the President of the Council and any one or more members shall constitute the monthly court.

Section 3. The Legislative Council shall provide by law the manner and place of holding elections of offices of the Nation.

Section 4. All officers before entering upon their duties shall take an oath in accordance with their religious belief to support the Constitution of the United States and of the Osage Nation and faithfully to discharge the duties of their office to the best of their ability.

Section 5. The Legislative Council shall be the judges of the qualification of its members and determine the rules of their proceedings and shall keep a journal of all their proceedings and have published all laws they may pass. They shall appoint a clerk door keeper and all necessary officers to attend their sitting.

Section 6. The Legislative Council shall fix the seat of government and cause to be executed all necessary buildings for the convenience of the Nation Officers.

Section 7. The Council will provide by-laws for a general system of education and district schools[;] they shall fix the salaries and compensation of all officers and employees. They shall provide by-laws for the protection of persons and property and for the punishment of all crimes know to the common law.

Section 8. Any person or persons in the Osage Nation whether citizen or not who shall by speaking, writing, act, or deed, try to subvert this constitution and overthrow the government shall be deemed guilty of treason and on conviction suffer death as shall be prescribed by the Legislative Council.

Section 9. The Legislative Council shall provide by law for the expenses of the government, and borrow money on the credit of the Nation. If necessary they shall provide for the support and protection of the poor, the helpless, the blind, the orphans and the property of descendants, deaf & dumb. They shall provide for the just and equitable distribution of national property and general funds of the Nation.

Section 10. The Legislative Council shall sit twice a year to enact laws, and shall receive, hear, and determine all petitions and memorials of the citizens. They shall meet and organize as soon as elected by the convention and fix by law the time of sitting.

Section 11. The Legislative Council shall sit once every month at a fixed time as a Judicial tribunal and shall hear and determine all cases of dispute regularly brought before them for adjudication, and shall have power to issue all necessary proceeds to enforce their orders and decrees while provisions are made by law for regular judges of courts.

Section 12. The presiding officer of the Legislative Council hereafter provided for in this Constitution shall be the Chief Justice of the Judicial tribunal. When sitting as a court of justice of both tribunals he shall keep strict order and decorum in the settings of both tribunals. He shall sign the journals of the court and of the Legislature.

Section 13. The Council shall designate the districts of each chief and hold him responsible for the good conduct of the citizens of his district. They shall fix by law the qualifications of votes and of citizenship of the Nation, and fill all vacancies of members of the Legislature until the election.

Section 14. This Constitution may be altered or amended in the following manner but shall never be abolished. That on a petition of a majority of the people to the Legislature, or whenever two-thirds of the Legislative Council may desire amendment they shall pass a law calling a convention of the people by the delegates at a time and place to be fixed by law and if the delegates shall determine on certain amendments they shall report it to the next Legislative Council and if two-thirds concur it shall be part of the Constitution or two-thirds of the Council proposing amendments and two-thirds of the next council thereafter confirming said propositions shall be part of the Constitution.

Article 2

Section 1. The Executive power shall be vested in a Chief Magistrate of the Osage Nation. He shall hold his office for the term of two years and together with the president of the Council shall be elected bi-annually at the general election of Councilmen.

Section 2. The Chief Magistrate shall be designated by the governor of the Nation. He shall sign all laws he may approve and have a veto power and reprieve.

Section 3. The Chief Magistrate shall by and with the consent of the Council appoint all officers and see that all laws are faithfully executed. He shall with the consent of the Council adopt a seal of the Nation.

Section 4. The Chief Magistrate shall appoint a Secretary, a Treasurer, Auditor, Solicitor, and Chief Marshall whose duties shall be defined by law. And they shall be the legal advisors to the Governor. He shall advise the Legislature from time to time on the state of affairs.

Article 3

Section 1. The Governor and Council or any Delegate or Representative duly authorized by them under the Seal of the Nation shall have full power and authority to negotiate treaties, sell and dispose of the public domain in accordance with the Constitution of the United States and subject to the confirmation of two-thirds of the Council.

Section 2. In the case of vacancy of the Office of Governor the President of the Council shall act as governor and the Council shall then elect a pro-tem from their own body.

Section 3. The Legislative Council shall provide by law for the punishment of malfeasance in office and the dismissal of offenders.

Section 4. The Governor shall have power to convene the Legislature on extraordinary actions, either for Executive, Legislative, or Judicial purposes, and issue commissions for all officers properly appointed.

Section 5. The President of the Council elect shall be fully empowered with authority to administer the Oath of Office to the members and other officers until persons are duly authorized by law to administer Oaths and any member, after sworn, may administer the Oath to the President.

Section 6. The Secretary of State, and Governor may take the acknowledgement of deeds and conveyances.

Section 7. A copy of this constitution shall be sent to the Commissioner of Indian Affairs at Washington with request to lay the same before the

President of the United States, and one copy to the Governor of Kansas, and to the Cherokee Nation.

Luis Choctaw, Secretary
Joseph Swift, President of Convention
Executive Office, Osage Nation, October 5, 1861

Appendix 2 1881 Constitution of the Osage Nation

The Constitution of the Osage Nation, prepared by the authorized committee and adopted by the National Council.

The Great and Little Osages having united and become one body politic, under the style and title of the Osage Nation: therefore,

We, the people of the Osage Nation, in National Council assembled, in order to establish justice, insure tranquility, promote the common welfare, and to secure to ourselves and our posterity the blessing of freedom—acknowledging with humility and gratitude the goodness of the Sovereign Ruler of the universe in permitting us so to do, and imploring his aid and guidance in its accomplishment—do ordain and establish this Constitution for the government of the Osage Nation.

Article I.

Section 1. The boundary of the Osage Nation shall be that described in the treaty of 1876 between the United States and the Great and Little Osages, except that portion purchased by the Kaws.

Sec. 2. The lands of the Osage Nation shall remain common property, until the National Council shall request an allotment of the same, but the improvements made thereon and in possession of the citizens of this Nation are the exclusive and indefeasible property of the citizens respectively who made or may rightfully be in possession of them. PROVIDED, That the citizen of this Nation possessing exclusive and indefeasible right to their improvements, as expressed in this article, shall possess no right or power to dispose of their improvements, in any manner whatever, to the United States, individual States, or to individual citizens thereof: and that, whenever any citizen shall remove with his effects out of the limits of this Nation, and become a citizen of any other government, all his rights and privileges as a citizen of this Nation shall cease: PROVIDED, NEVERTHELESS, That the National Council shall have power to re-admit by law, to all the rights of citizenship any such persons who may at any time desire to return to the Nation, on memorializing the National Council for such re-admission.

Moreover, the National Council shall have power to adopt such laws and regulations as it may deem expedient and proper to prevent citizens from monopolizing improvements with the view of speculation.

Article II.

Section 1. The power of this government shall be divided into three distinct departments, the Legislative, the Executive, and the Judicial.

Sec. 2. No person or persons belonging to one of these departments shall exercise any of the powers properly belonging to either of the others, except in the cases hereinafter expressly directed or permitted.

Article III.

Section 1. The legislative power shall be vested in a National Council, and the style of their acts shall be: - BE IT ENACTED BY THE NATIONAL COUNCIL.

Sec. 2. The National Council shall make provision, by law, for laying off the Osage Nation into five districts, and, if subsequently it should be deemed expedient, one or two may be added thereto.

Sec. 3. The National Council shall consist of three members from each district, to be chosen by the qualified electors in their respective district, for two years, the elections to be held in the respective districts every two years, at such times and places as may be directed by law.

The National Council shall, after the present year, be held annually, to be convened on the first Monday in November, at such place as may be designated by the National Council, or, in case of emergency, by the Principal Chief.

Sec. 4. Before the districts shall be laid off, any election which may take place, shall be by general vote of the electors throughout the Nation, for all officers to be elected.

The first election for all officers of the government—Chiefs, Executive Council, members of the National Council, Judges and Sheriffs—shall be held at Pawhuska, before the rising of this council: and the term of service of all officers elected previous to the first Monday in November, 1882, shall be extended to embrace, in addition to the regular constitutional term, the time intervening from their election to the first Monday in November, 1882.

Sec. 5. No person shall be eligible to a seat in the National Council, but an Osage male citizen, who shall have attained to the age of twenty-five years.

Sec. 6. The members of the National Council shall in all cases, except those of felony or breach of the peace, be privileged from arrest, during their attendance at the National Council, in going to, and returning.

Sec. 7. In all elections by the people the electors shall vote viva voce. All male citizens, who shall have attained to the age of eighteen years, shall be equally entitled to vote at all public elections.

Sec. 8. The National Council shall judge of the qualifications and returns of its own members, determine the rules of its proceedings, punish a member for disorderly behavior, and with the concurrence of two-third, expel a member; but not a second time for the same offense.

Sec. 9. The National Council, when assembled, shall choose its own officers; a majority shall constitute a quorum to do business, but a smaller number may adjourn from day to day and compel the attendance of absent members, in such manner, and under such penalty as the council may prescribe.

Sec. 10. The members of the National Council shall each receive a compensation for their services, which shall be one hundred dollars per annum: PROVIDED, That the same may be increased or diminished by law; but no alteration shall take effect during the period of services of the members of the National Council by whom such alteration may have been made.

Sec. 11. The National Council shall regulate by law, by whom, and in what manner, writs of elections shall be issued to fill the vacancies which may happen in the Council thereof.

Sec. 12. Each member of the National Council, before he takes his seat, shall take the following oath of affirmation:

"I, A. B., do solemnly swear (or affirm, as the case may be) that I have not, obtained my election by bribery, treat, or any undue and unlawful means, used by myself, or others, by my desire or approbation for that purpose: that I consider myself constitutionally qualified as a member of _____, and that on all questions and measures which may come before me, I will so give my vote, and so conduct myself, as, in my judgment, shall appear most conducive to the interest and prosperity of this Nation, and that I will bear true faith and allegiance to the same, and to the utmost of my ability and power, observe, conform to, support, and defend the constitution thereof."

Sec. 13. No person who may be convicted of felony shall be eligible to any office or appointment of honor, profit or trust, within this Nation.

Sec. 14. The National Council shall have power to make all laws and regulations which they shall deem necessary and proper for the good of the Nation, which shall not be contrary to this constitution.

Sec. 15. It shall be the duty of the National Council to pass such laws as may be necessary and proper to decide differences by arbitration, to be appointed by the parties who may choose that summary mode of adjustment.

Sec. 16. No power of suspending the laws of this Nation shall be exercised, unless by the National Council or its authority.

Sec. 17. No retrospective law, nor any law impairing the obligations of contracts, shall be passed.

Sec. 18. The National Council shall have power to make laws for laying and collecting taxes for the purpose of raising a revenue.

Sec. 19. All acknowledged treaties shall be the supreme law of the land, and the National Council shall have the sole power of deciding on the constructions of all treaty stipulations.

Sec. 20. The Council shall have the sole power of impeaching. All impeachments shall be tried by the National Council, when sitting for that purpose; the members shall be upon oath or affirmation, and no person shall be convicted without the concurrence of two-thirds of the members present.

Sec. 21. The Principal Chief, Assistant Principal Chief, and all civil officers shall be liable to impeachment for misdemeanor in office; but judgment in such cases shall not extend further than removal from office, and disqualification to hold any office of honor, trust, or profit under the government of this Nation. The party, whether convicted or acquitted, shall, nevertheless, be liable to indictment, trial, judgment, and punishment according to law.

Article IV.

Section 1. The supreme executive power of this Nation shall be vested in a Principal Chief, who shall be styled "The Principal Chief of the Osage Nation." The Principal Chief shall hold his office for the term of two years, and shall be elected by the qualified electors on the same day: and at the place where they shall respectively vote for members to the National Council. The returns of the elections for Principal Chief shall be sealed up and directed to the President of the National Council, who shall open and publish them in the presence of the Council assembled. The person having the highest number of votes shall be Principal Chief, but if two or more shall be equal and highest in votes, one of them shall be chosen by vote of the National Council: the manner of determining contested elections shall be directed by law.

Sec. 2. No person, except a natural born citizen, shall be eligible to the office of Principal Chief; neither shall any person be eligible to that office who shall not have attained to the age of thirty-five years.

Sec. 3. There shall also be chosen, at the same time, by the qualified electors, in the same manner, for two years, an Assistant Principal Chief, who shall have attained to the age of thirty-five years.

Sec. 4. In case of the removal of the Principal Chief from office, or of his death, or resignation, or inability to discharge the powers and duties of the said office, the same shall devolve on the Assistant Principal Chief.

Sec. 5. The National Council may by law, provide for the case of removal, death, resignation, or disability of both the Principal and Assistant Principal Chief, declaring what officer shall then act as Principal Chief until the disability be removed or a Principal Chief shall be elected.

Sec. 6. The Principal Chief and the Assistant Principal Chief shall, at stated times, receive for their services a compensation which shall neither be increased nor diminished during the period for which they shall have been elected, and they shall not receive within that period any other emolument from the Osage Nation or any other government.

Sec. 7. Before the Principal Chief enters on the execution of his office, he shall take the following oath or affirmation: "I do solemnly swear (or affirm) that I will faithfully execute the duties of Principal Chief of the Osage Nation, and will, to the best of my ability, preserve, protect, and defend the Constitution of the Osage Nation."

Sec. 8. He may, on extraordinary occasions, convene the National Council at the seat of government.

Sec. 9. He shall, from time to time, give to the Council information of the state of the government, and recommend to their consideration, such measures as he may deem expedient.

Sec. 10. He shall take care that the laws be faithfully executed.

Sec. 11. It shall be his duty to visit the different districts at least once in two years, to inform himself of the general condition of the country.

Sec. 12. The Assistant Principal Chief shall by virtue of his office, aid and advise the Principal Chief in the administration of the government at all times during his continuance in office.

Sec. 13. Vacancies that may occur in offices, the appointment of which is vested in the National Council shall be filled by the Principal Chief during the recess of the National Council, by granting commissions, which shall expire at the end of the next session thereof.

Sec. 14. Every bill, which shall pass the National Council, shall, before it becomes a law, be presented to the Principal Chief: if he approves, he shall sign it, but if not, he shall return it with his objections to the Council, who shall enter the objections at large on their journals, and proceed to reconsider it.

If, after such consideration, two-thirds of the Council shall agree to pass the bill, it becomes a law, if any bill shall not be returned by the Principal Chief within five days (Sunday excepted) after the same has been presented to him, it shall become law, in like manner as if he had signed it; unless the National Council, by their adjournment, prevent its return, in which case it shall be a law, unless sent back within three days after their next meeting.

Sec. 15. Members of the National Council and all officers, executive and judicial, shall be bound by oath, to support the Constitution of their Nation: and to perform the duties of their respective offices with fidelity.

Sec. 16. The Principal Chief shall, during the session of the National Council, attend at the seat of government.

Sec. 17. The Principal Chief shall recommend three persons, to be appointed by the National Council, whom the Principal Chief shall have full power at his discretion to assemble: he, together with the Assistant Principal Chief and the Counsellors, or a majority of them, may, from time to time, hold and keep a Council for ordering and directing the affairs of the Nation according to law.

Sec. 18. The members of the Executive Council shall be chosen for the term of two years.

Sec. 19. The Treasurer of the Osage Nation shall be chosen by the National Council for the term of two years.

Sec. 20. The Treasurer shall, before entering on the duties of his office, give bond to the Nation with sureties to the satisfaction of the National Council, for the faithful discharge of his trust.

Sec. 21. No money shall be drawn from the treasury, but by warrant from the Principal Chief, and in consequence of appropriations made by law.

Sec. 22. It shall be the duty of the Treasurer to receive all public moneys, and to make a regular statement and account of the receipts and expenditures of all public moneys at the annual session of the National Council.

Sec. 23. The "Fiscal Year" of the Osage Nation shall begin on the 1st day of October, and close on the 30th day of September of each year; and all books and accounts of the Treasurer, shall be kept, and duties of his office performed with regard to the beginning and ending of the fiscal year. The National Treasurer shall receive for his services ten (10) per cent, of all moneys that may pass through his hands as provided by law.

Article V.

Section 1. The judicial powers shall be vested in a supreme court, and such circuits and inferior courts as the National Council may, from time to time, ordain and establish.

Sec. 2. The judges of the Supreme and Circuit courts shall hold their commission for the term of two years, but any of them may be removed from office on the address of two-thirds of the National Council to the Principal Chief, for that purpose.

Sec. 3. The judges of the Supreme court and Circuit courts, shall at stated times receive a compensation which shall not be diminished during their continuance in office but they shall receive no fees or perquisites of office, nor hold any other office of profit or trust under the government of this Nation or any other power.

Sec. 4. No person shall be appointed a judge of any of the courts, until he shall have attained the age of thirty years.

Sec. 5. The judges of the Supreme courts and Circuit courts shall be elected by the National Council.

Sec. 6. The judges of the Supreme courts and of the Circuit courts shall have complete criminal jurisdiction in such cases and in such manner as may be pointed out by law.

Sec. 7. No judge shall sit on trial of any cause when the parties are connected (with him) by affinity or consanguinity except by consent of the parties. In case all the judges of the Supreme court shall be interested in the issue of any court or related to all or either of the parties, the National Council may provide by law for the selection of a suitable number of persons of good character and knowledge for the determination thereof, and who shall be specially commissioned for the adjudication of such case by the Principal Chief.

Sec. 8. All writs and other process shall run "in the name of the Osage Nation" and bear test and be signed by the respective clerks.

Sec. 9. Indictments shall conclude against the peace and dignity of the Osage Nation.

Sec. 10. The supreme court shall, after the present year, hold its session three times a year, at the seat of government, to be convened on the first Monday in October, February and June of each year.

Sec. 11. In all criminal prosecutions the accused shall have the right of being heard: of demanding the nature of accusation: of meeting the witnesses face to face: of having compulsory process for obtaining witnesses in his or their favor, and in prosecutions by indictment or information a speedy public trial: nor shall the accused by compelled to give evidence against himself.

Sec. 12. All persons shall be bailable by sufficient securities, unless for capital offences when the proof is evident or presumption great.

Article VI.

Section 1. No person who denies the being of a God or a future state of reward and punishment, shall hold any office in the civil department in this Nation.

Sec. 2. When the National Council shall determine the expediency of appointing delegates, or other public agents for the purpose of transacting business with the Government of the United States, the Principal Chief shall recommend, and by the advice and consent of the National Council appoint and commission such delegates or public agents accordingly on all matters of interest touching the rights of the citizens of this Nation which may require the attention of the United States Government.

Sec. 3. All commissions shall be in the name and by the authority of the Osage Nation, and signed by the Principal Chief. The Principal Chief shall make use of his private seal until a national one shall be provided.

Sec. 4. A sheriff shall be elected in each district by the qualified electors thereof, who shall hold his office two years unless sooner removed. Should a vacancy occur subsequent to election, it shall be filled by the Principal Chief as in other cases, and the person so appointed shall continue in office until the next regular election.

Sec. 5. The appointment of all officers not otherwise directed by this constitution shall be elected by the National Council.

Sec. 6. The National Council may propose such amendments to this Constitution as two-thirds of the Council may deem expedient, and the Principal Chief shall issue a proclamation directing all officers of the several districts to promulgate the same as extensively as possible within their respective districts at least six months previous to the next general election, and if at the first session of Council after such general election, two-thirds of the Council shall by ayes and noes ratify such proposed amendments, they shall be valid to all extent and purposes as part of this constitution. Provided. That such proposed amendments shall be read on three several days in Council, as well as when the same are proposed as when they are ratified.

Done in convention at Pawhuska, Osage Nation, this thirty-first day of December. A.D., 1881.

JAMES BIGHEART
President of the National Convention

Ne-kah-ke-pon-ah.
Wah-ti-an-kah.
Saucy Chief.
Tah-wah-che-he.
William Penn.
Clamore.
Two-giver.
Tall Chief.
Sa-pah-ke-ah.
Black Dog.
Thomas Big-chief.
Ne-kah-wah-she-ton-kah.
Joseph Pawnee-no-pah-she.
White Hair.
Cyprian Tayrian.
Paul Akin,
    Interpreter.
E. M. Matthews,
    Secretary.

Preamble

The Great and Little Osages having united and become one body politic, under the style and title of the Osage Nation; therefore, We the people of the Osage Nation in order to establish justice, insure tranquility, promote the common welfare, and to secure to ourselves and our posterity the blessing of freedom, including the blessings of our ancestral heritage, culture, and tribal sovereignty, acknowledging with humility and gratitude the goodness of the Sovereign Ruler of the universe in permitting us so to do, and imploring aid and guidance in its accomplishment—do ordain and establish this Constitution for the government of the sovereign Osage Nation.

Article I.

JURISDICTION

SECTION 1. The boundary of the Osage Indian Reservation shall be that described in the Act of June 5, 1872, 17 Stat. 229, except that portion purchased by the Kaws. Provided, that any allotments of land and the improvements thereon, in possession of the citizens of this Nation, are vested in the citizens respectively who may rightfully be in possession of them, as provided by Federal law.

SECTION 2. The jurisdiction of the Osage Nation shall extend to the Gray Horse, Hominy, and Pawhuska Villages whose lands are within the exterior boundaries of the Osage Indian Reservation, and in addition may extend to that area included in Section 1 of this Article to all other trust or restricted land held now or later acquired by the Osage Nation or its members.

Article II.

PROTECTION OF THE MINERAL ESTATE

SECTION 1. Ownership of the mineral estate of the Osage Indian Reservation is to be determined by the Act of June 28, 1906, 34 Stat. 539, as amended. The right to receive income from the mineral estate is vested in those allottees and their successors in interest whose names and shares appear on the Osage Headright Quarterly Annuity Roll, maintained by the Secretary of the Interior, as amended from time to time, as provided by Federal law. No authority is granted to the Osage National Council or any department created by this Constitution over the Osage Tribal Council on matters of the mineral estate or to affect the right of individuals to receive income from this mineral estate so long as they are protected by Federal law.

SECTION 2. The mineral estate shall be administered by the Osage Tribal Council, who shall be elected and shall serve in accordance with the provisions of the Act of June 28, 1906, 34 Stat. 539; the Act of March 2, 1929, 45 Stat. 1481; and the Act of August 28, 1957, 71 Stat. 471; as may be amended from time to time; and the regulations found at Title 25 Code of Federal Regulations Part 90, as may be amended from time to time; Provided, that no elected official of the Osage Tribal Council shall be eligible to hold any other elected office in the Osage Nation; and Provided further, that all resolutions, laws, and ordinances of the Osage National Council that adversely impacts the mineral estate shall be reviewed by the Osage Tribal Council and the Secretary of the Interior, and shall require Secretarial approval for legal validity. Any resolution, law, or ordinance of the Osage National Council which adversely impacts the mineral estate, as determined by the Secretary of the Interior through his disapproval, shall be invalid as a matter of law.

Article III.

MEMBERSHIP

SECTION 1. The membership of the Osage Nation shall consist of those persons whose names appear on the final roll of the Osage Nation approved pursuant to the Act of June 28, 1906, 34 Stat. 539, and their lineal descendants by blood, within and without the State of Oklahoma, regardless of membership or affiliation with any other federally recognized tribe, band, or nation.

SECTION 2. The Osage National Council shall have the authority to enact rules and regulations regarding future enrollment of tribal members.

SECTION 3. Membership in the Osage Nation shall not confer any right on any individual to receive income from the Osage mineral estate as provided by federal law.

SECTION 4. A membership board comprised of five members shall be appointed by the President of the Osage Nation with the advice and consent of the Osage National Council and charged with the responsibility of the establishment and maintenance of a membership roll.

Article IV.

GOVERNMENTAL STRUCTURE

SECTION 1. The powers of the Osage Nation Government shall be divided into three distinct departments: the Legislative, the Executive, and the Judicial.

SECTION 2. No person or persons belonging to one of these departments shall exercise any of the powers properly belonging to either of the others, except in the cases hereinafter expressly directed or permitted.

Article V.

GENERAL COUNCIL

SECTION 1. The General Council shall mean a meeting of all members of the Osage Nation who assemble annually on the last Saturday of April at Pawhuska, Oklahoma, the seat of the government.

SECTION 2. Notice of the General Council Meeting shall be given by the President not less than 30 days preceding the meeting through the U.S. Postal Service and by public notice. Such notice shall include an agenda which provides for other business. During the conducting of the other business portion of the agenda, any member shall have the right to bring up relevant matters.

SECTION 3. The annual meeting shall be called and chaired by the President.

SECTION 4. The President shall present to the General Council his state of the Nation address.

Article VI.

LEGISLATIVE DEPARTMENT

SECTION 1. The legislative power shall be vested in the Osage National Council, and the style of their acts shall be:-Be it enacted by the Osage National Council. All such legislative acts shall be committed to writing and made available to the public at all reasonable times at the Osage Nation headquarters in Pawhuska, Oklahoma.

SECTION 2. The Osage National Council shall consist of nine members, chosen at large by the duly qualified electors for four year terms, the elections to be held every two years, at such time and place as may be directed by tribal law, except as provided in Section 4 of this Article.

SECTION 3. Any member of the Osage Nation shall be eligible to run for tribal office provided the member:

(A) has attained the age of 25 years on the date of the election; and

(B) has never been convicted of a felony.

SECTION 4. The first election for all members of the Osage National Council shall be June 6, 1994, and the terms of service for five members of the Osage National Council shall be four years and for four members shall be two years. The five candidates receiving the highest number of votes cast shall serve for four years, and the remaining four successful candidates elected to serve for two years. Thereafter an election shall be held every two years in accordance with Article XI, Section 1 to elect members of the Osage National Council for four year terms.

SECTION 5. The Osage National Council, at the first regular Osage National Council Meeting and thereafter as may be necessary, shall choose its officers from among its own members, consisting of a Speaker and Second Speaker. The Speaker or in the Speaker's absence, the Second Speaker, shall preside over all meetings, but shall have no vote unless the Osage National Council be equally divided.

SECTION 6. Robert's Rules of Order as revised shall be followed in conducting Osage National Council business unless in conflict with this Constitution. The Osage National Council may meet in executive session, wherein no minutes shall be taken, to discuss personnel matters, matters involving attorney client privilege, and business matters including consideration of bids or contracts which are privileged or confidential. Executive session requires an affirmative vote of two-thirds (2/3) of the members present; however, any official action taken upon any matter discussed in executive session shall be in accordance with Section 8 of this Article. Verbatim minutes of the meetings of the Osage National Council shall be maintained and available to the public at all reasonable times at the Osage Nation headquarters in Pawhuska, Oklahoma.

(A) Regular meetings of the Osage National Council shall be called at least twelve (12) times a year, at monthly intervals, at the Osage Council Chambers in Pawhuska, Oklahoma, or as otherwise designated by the Osage National Council. The first regular meeting after the July 18, 1994 installation shall be held on the following Monday, July 25, 1994, at 10 A.M. in the Osage Council Chambers and thereafter as prescribed by tribal law.

(B) Special meetings of the Osage National Council shall be called by the Speaker:

(1) at the discretion of the Speaker of the Osage National Council;

(2) upon the written request of any three (3) Osage National Council members;

(3) upon a written request made by the President of the Osage Nation to the Speaker of the Osage National Council; or

(4) upon the petition of ten percent (10%) of the eligible tribal voters, Provided, That at least seventy-two (72) hours written notice of such meeting shall be given by the Speaker of the Osage National Council to each Osage National Council Member. Notice of the special meeting shall also be posted at the Osage Council Chambers in Pawhuska, Oklahoma. If the Speaker of the Osage National Council fails to call a special meeting within ten (10) days of the request by three (3) Osage National Council Members, or the receipt of a petition, or the request of the President, any Osage National Council Member may call the meeting; Provided, that the seventy-two (72) hour written notice of such meeting is given by the party calling the meeting to each Osage National Council Member. No action taken at a special meeting shall be valid unless these notice requirements have been complied with.

SECTION 7. A quorum shall exist when five (5) or more members of the Osage National Council are present. A quorum is required at all meetings in order to conduct official business of the Osage National Council.

SECTION 8. The Osage National Council shall conduct official business of the Osage Nation by a majority vote of the members present at a duly called meeting in which a quorum exists, unless otherwise stated in the Constitution. All votes on any matter shall be in open session and shall be made viva voce by roll call. A written record of all roll call votes shall be maintained by the Osage National Council.

SECTION 9. Any Osage National Council Member who has a direct personal or financial interest in any matter before the Osage National Council shall not be permitted to vote on such matters. An Osage National Council Member shall reveal a direct personal or financial interest to the other members of the Osage National Council and failure to do so constitutes a violation of Article VII CD and Article X, Section 2(A).

SECTION 10. The Osage Nation may compensate members of the Osage National Council for their services, as prescribed by tribal law, except that no funds from the mineral estate held in trust shall be so expended.

SECTION 11. If an Osage National Council Member should die, resign, be removed, or be recalled from office, the Osage National Council shall declare the position vacant. The vacancy shall be filled by special election within sixty (60) days unless only ninety (90) days remain in the term, in which case the position shall remain vacant. The person who fills the vacant position shall serve out the term of the person whom he or she is replacing, and shall be sworn into office at the next Osage National Council meeting following the date on which the results of the special election are certified.

Article VII.
POWERS OF THE OSAGE NATIONAL COUNCIL

The Osage National Council of the Osage Nation shall be vested with all powers of its inherent sovereignty and Federal law and shall, in accordance with established customs, traditions and values of the Osage Nation and subject to the express limitations contained in this Constitution and the applicable laws of the United States, have the following powers:

(A) To make all laws and regulations which they shall deem necessary and proper for the good of the Nation, which shall not be contrary to Federal or tribal law or to this Constitution; except that this power does not extend to any action that the Secretary of the Interior determines to have an adverse impact on the mineral estate held in trust for the Osage Tribe and headright owners, as defined in the Act of June 28, 1906, 34 Stat. 539, as amended, or as may be amended from time to time;

(B) To negotiate and make contracts and grants with the Federal, State, and local governments;

(C) To make laws for the levy and collection of taxes for the purpose of raising revenue, except that this power does not extend nor grant any authority to tax or in any measure, burden the mineral estate which is held in trust including any Osage Indian headright interest, as defined in the Act of June 28, 1906, 34 Stat 539, as amended, or as may be amended from time to time; It is further provided that the Osage National Council shall have no authority to levy any tax, assessment, or fee on the purchasers and/or producers of oil, gas, coal, and other minerals underlying the Osage Indian Reservation.

(D) To purchase, lease, acquire by gift, take by devise or bequeath, acquire by eminent domain or otherwise acquire land, interests in land, personal property, or other assets which may be deemed beneficial to the Osage Nation;

(E) To regulate the sale, disposition, lease, or encumbrance of tribal lands, interest in lands, or other assets, excluding the mineral estate, as provided in the Act of June 28, 1906, 34 Stat. 539, as amended or as may be amended from time to time;

(F) To employ legal counsel, the choice of counsel and fixing of fees to be subject to the approval of the Secretary of the Interior, but only so long as such approval is required by Federal law;

(G) To manage all tribal economic affairs and enterprises;

(H) To make expenditures from available funds for tribal purposes subject to all regulations and applicable laws. All expenditures of tribal funds shall be a matter of public record open to all the citizens of the Osage Nation at all reasonable times at the Osage Nation headquarters in Pawhuska, Oklahoma.

(I) To adopt a Code of Ethics governing the conduct of tribal officials, which may include disciplinary procedures so long as due process is afforded.

(J) To take any and all actions necessary and proper in the exercise of the powers and duties of the Osage Nation, including any powers and duties not enumerated above, and all other powers and duties now or hereafter delegated to the Osage National Council, or vested in the Osage National Council by virtue of its inherent sovereignty; Provided that no such powers and duties shall be deemed to extend to the Osage mineral estate nor to any Osage headright interest, as defined in the Act of June 28, 1906, 34 Stat. 539, as amended, or as may be amended from time to time.

(K) It shall be the duty of the Osage National Council to pass such laws as may be necessary and proper to decide differences by arbitration or traditional form of dispute resolution, to be utilized by the parties who may choose that summary mode of adjustment.

Article VII.

EXECUTIVE DEPARTMENT

SECTION 1. The supreme executive power of the Osage Nation shall be vested in a President, who shall be known as "The President of the Osage Nation," and a Vice-President, who shall be known as "The Vice-President of the Osage Nation."

SECTION 2. The President and Vice-President shall hold office for the term of four years, and shall be elected by the qualified electors as prescribed by law.

SECTION 3. Any member of the Osage Nation shall be eligible to run for President or Vice-President provided the member:

(A) has attained the age of 35 years on the date of the election; and
(B) has never been convicted of a felony.

SECTION 4. In case of the removal of the President from office, or of death, resignation, or inability to discharge the powers and duties of the said office, the same shall devolve on the Vice-President. If vacancies should occur in both the President and Vice-President positions, the Speaker of the Osage National Council shall discharge the powers and duties of said offices.

SECTION 5. The Osage Nation may compensate the President and Vice-President for their services, as prescribed by law except that no funds from the mineral estate held in trust shall be so expended.

SECTION 6. Duties.

(A) The President or in the President's absence the Vice-President may on extraordinary occasions request in writing the Speaker of the Osage National Council to convene a meeting at the Osage Council Chambers in Pawhuska, Oklahoma.
(B) The President shall from time to time, however, not less than once a year, give the Osage National Council information on the state of the government including a financial statement and recommend for its consideration such measures as may be deemed necessary and expedient.
(C) The President shall faithfully execute the laws of the Osage Nation.
(D) The Vice-President shall by virtue of this office, aid and advise the President in the administration of the government.
(E) Every bill which shall pass the Osage National Council, shall before it becomes law, be forwarded to the President. If the President approves the bill, it shall be signed, but if not, it shall be returned with written objections to the Osage National Council who shall enter the objections in the journals of record and proceed to reconsider it. If any bill has not been acted upon by the President within

five business days of the receipt of the bill from the Osage National Council, as provided herein, it shall become law in like manner as if it had been signed. If, after such reconsideration, two-thirds of the Osage National Council shall agree to pass the bill, it becomes law.

(F) The President shall prepare an annual budget and administer funds pursuant to appropriations authorized by law. The "Fiscal Year" of the Osage Nation shall begin on the Last day of October, and close on the 30th day of September of each year. All books and accounts of the Treasurer, shall be kept, and duties of this office performed with regard to the beginning and ending of the fiscal year including the publication of an independent audit. The Treasurer shall render a written report at the expiration of the term of office and all records shall be turned over to the successor.

(G) The Treasurer of the Osage Nation shall be appointed by the President with the advice and consent of the Osage National Council.

(H) The President may appoint, with the advice and consent of the Osage National Council, subordinate committees, commissions, boards, tribal officials, delegates, employees not otherwise provided for in this Constitution, and an Executive Cabinet. Salaries, tenure, duties, policies, and procedures will likewise be approved by the Osage National Council. All appointments shall be in writing and in the name and by the authority of the Osage Nation, and signed by the President with the official seal of the Osage Nation affixed.

(I) The President along with the Vice-President and the Executive Cabinet members, or a majority of them, may from time to time, hold and conduct cabinet meetings for ordering and directing the affairs of the Osage Nation according to tribal law.

Article IX.
JUDICIAL DEPARTMENT

SECTION 1. The judicial powers shall be vested in a supreme court and such inferior courts as the Osage National Council may from time to time ordain and establish.

SECTION 2. The judiciary shall exercise jurisdiction over all cases, matters, or controversies arising under this Constitution and the laws, ordinances, regulations, customs, and judicial decisions of the Osage Nation, including such disputes as may be referred by the Osage National Council pursuant to Article VII, unless limited by Federal law.

SECTION 3. The Supreme Court shall consist of a Supreme Court Judge and such inferior court judges as may be established by the Osage National Council.

SECTION 4. The Supreme Court Judge and such inferior court judges shall hold office for the term of four years.

SECTION 5. Any member of the Osage Nation shall be eligible to run for the judiciary provided the member:

(A) has attained the age of 30 years on the date of the election; and

(B) has never been convicted of a felony.

SECTION 6. The Supreme Court and such circuit and inferior court judges shall be compensated at a rate prescribed by the Osage National Council which shall not be diminished or increased during their continuance in office for the term to which most recently elected, but they shall receive no fees or perquisites of office, nor hold any other office of profit or trust under the government of this Nation or any other power, except that no funds from the mineral estate held in trust shall be so expended.

SECTION 7. No judge shall sit on trial on any cause when the parties are connected with the judge. In case all the judges of the court system have an interest in the issue before the court, the Osage National Council may provide by law for the selection of a qualified alternate for the determination thereof, who shall be specially commissioned for the adjudication of such case by the President.

SECTION 8. If a member of the judiciary should die, resign, be removed, or be recalled from office, the Osage National Council shall declare the position vacant. The vacancy 7 shall be filled by appointment made by the President with the advice and consent of the Osage National Council within ten (10) business days. The person who fills the vacant position shall serve out the term of the replaced judge, and shall be sworn into office at the next Osage National Council meeting following the date on which the results of the special election are certified.

SECTION 9. The judiciary shall establish the practice and procedures to be followed in the courts subject to the approval of the Osage National Council.

SECTION 10. All writs and other process shall run "in the name of the Osage Nation" and bear test and be signed by the respective clerks. Indictments shall conclude against the peace and dignity of the Osage Nation.

SECTION 11. In all criminal prosecutions, the accused shall have the right of being heard; of demanding the nature of the accusation; of confronting the witnesses; of having compulsory process for obtaining witnesses in his or her favor, and in prosecutions by indictment or information a speedy public trial; nor shall the accused be compelled to give evidence against himself or herself.

Article X.

RECALL AND REMOVAL

SECTION 1. The recall of any elected official or an officer who has been appointed to complete the term of an elected official of the Osage Nation shall be initiated upon a petition stating the reasons for recall and signed by duly registered electors equal in number to thirty percent (30%) of the number of persons voting in the last regularly scheduled tribal election. Recall petitions shall be submitted to the Election Board, as provided in Article XI, Section 3, which shall make a determination as to the validity of the signatures within ten (10) business days of the receipt of the petition, and a recall election shall be held by the Election Board within thirty (30) days of its determination. An elected official shall be recalled by a majority vote of those casting ballots in the recall election.

SECTION 2. The Osage National Council shall by an affirmative vote of six (6) of the nine (9) members petition the Supreme Court of the Osage Nation to convene and conduct a hearing in the presence of the Osage National Council thirty (30) days from the date the petition is filed, to remove any elected official for any of the following reasons:

(A) Gross misconduct in office:
(B) Conviction of a felony under Federal, state, or tribal law;
(C) Willful neglect of duty as evidenced by excessive absences;
(D) Conviction of any offense under Federal, state, or tribal law involving moral turpitude.

SECTION 3. The petition shall state with specificity the grounds for the proposed removal.

SECTION 4. Any elected official accused of wrongdoing shall be given a copy of the petition and accorded the right to respond to the charges and the right to present witnesses and other evidence in his defense at the hearing convened by the Supreme Court.

SECTION 5. The Supreme Court shall preside over the removal hearing and receive the evidence, provided that in the case of removal of a Supreme Court Judge, the Osage National Council may provide by law for the selection of a judge who shall be specially commissioned to preside in this case. The Osage National Council shall decide by an affirmative vote of six (6) members to remove. The decision of the Osage National Council shall be final and binding on the Osage Nation.

SECTION 6. The matter of impeachment or removal from office of members of the Osage Tribal Council is contained in the Act of June 28, 1906, 34 Stat. 539, and Regulations of the Secretary of the Interior and is not included herein.

Article XI.
ELECTIONS

SECTION 1. General elections to vote for Osage National Council members, President, Vice-President, and Judges of the court system shall be held on June 6, 1994, and on the first Monday in June every second year thereafter at the voting places and in the manner established by tribal law. The members of the Osage National Council, President, Vice-President, and Judges elected at the first election held pursuant to this Constitution shall be installed according to the Osage Governmental Reformation Process Election Regulations on July 18, 1994. Thereafter, installation of elected officials of the Osage Nation shall be prescribed by law.

SECTION 2. Special elections shall be held when called for by the Osage National Council, by this Constitution, or appropriate ordinances.

SECTION 3. At least one-hundred eighty (180) days before each general election, or no less than thirty (30) days before calling a special election, the Osage National Council shall appoint an Election Board. All members of the Election Board must be members and eligible voters of the Osage Nation. The duties, procedures, structure, and composition of the Election Board shall be included in the Election Ordinance.

SECTION 4. In all elections, the Osage National Council shall have the power to prescribe ordinances governing the casting and canvassing of ballots and other necessary details of election procedures.

SECTION 5. All tribal members who are eighteen (18) years of age or older on the date of any tribal election and duly registered to vote, shall be entitled to vote in any election.

SECTION 6. All elections shall be by secret ballot.

SECTION 7. All voters shall be given the opportunity to vote by absentee ballot.

SECTION 8. No candidate for the positions under the Executive and Judicial Departments shall be considered elected unless he or she has received the majority of the votes cast.

Article XII.

OATH OF OFFICE

SECTION 1. All members of the Osage National Council shall be bound to support the Constitution of the Osage Nation and the Constitution of the United States; and to perform the duties of their respective offices with fidelity by stating the following oath or affirmation: "I, _____, do solemnly swear (or affirm, as the case may be,) that I have not obtained my election by bribery, treat, or any undue unlawful means used by myself or others by my desire or approbation for that purpose; that I consider myself constitutionally qualified as a member of the Osage Nation, and that on all questions and measures which may come before me, I will so give my vote, and so conduct myself, as, in my judgment shall appear most conducive to the interest and prosperity of this Nation, and that I will bear true faith and allegiance to the same, and to the utmost of my ability and power, observe, conform to, support, and defend the Constitution of the Osage Nation and the Constitution of the United States. I swear or affirm further, that I will do everything within my power to promote the culture, heritage, and traditions of the Osage Nation."

SECTION 2. Before the President and Vice-President enter on the execution of their office, they shall each take the following oath or affirmation: "I, _____, do solemnly swear or affirm that I will faithfully execute the duties of President (or Vice-President) of the Osage Nation, and will, to the best of my ability, preserve, protect, and defend the Constitution of the Osage Nation and the Constitution of the United States. I swear or affirm further, that I will do everything within my power to promote the culture, heritage, and traditions of the Osage Nation."

SECTION 3. Before the Judges of the Judicial Department enter on the execution of their office, they shall each take the following oath or affirmation: "I, _____, do solemnly swear or affirm that I will faithfully execute the duties of my office, and will, to the best of my ability preserve, protect, and defend the Constitution of the Osage Nation and the Constitution of the United States and the rights of its members. I swear or affirm further, that I will do everything within my power to promote the culture, heritage, and traditions of the Osage Nation."

Article XIII.

SECTION 1. The members of the Osage Nation shall have the right to propose any legislative measure by a petition signed by at least thirty percent (30%) of the registered voters. Each such petition shall contain the entire text of the measure proposed. The petition shall be filed with the President at least sixty (60) days prior to the next election for President at which time it shall appear on the ballot. If such petition is filed more than one (1) year prior to the next election for President, a special election shall be called and conducted. If approved by a majority of those participating in the election, it shall be in full force and effect immediately.

SECTION 2. The Osage National Council by approval of at least six (6) members, may refer any legislative measure to the members of the Osage Nation by directing that said measure be placed on the ballot at the next election for President or by calling for a special election. Decision to refer any matter to the people shall be made at least sixty (60) days prior to the election at which it is presented.

SECTION 3. All petitions for initiative shall be submitted under a cover letter signed by at least three (3) sponsors who are qualified electors of the Osage Nation.

SECTION 4. This Article shall not be applicable to the Osage Tribal Council.

Article XIV.

BILL OF RIGHTS

SECTION 1. There shall be certain inalienable rights which shall not be abridged or denied by any department of the Osage Nation or by any official of the Nation.

SECTION 2. The Osage Nation in exercising powers of self-government shall not:

(A) make or enforce any law prohibiting the free exercise of religion, or abridging the freedom of speech, or of the press, or the right of the people peaceably to assemble and the petition for a redress of grievances;

(B) violate the right of the people to be secure in their persons, houses, papers, and effects against unreasonable search and seizures, nor issue warrants, but upon probable cause, supported by oath or affirmation, and particularly describing the place to be searched and the person or thing to be seized;

(C) subject any person for the same offense to be twice put in jeopardy;

(D) compel any person in any criminal case to be a witness against himself or herself;

(E) take any private property for a public use without just compensation;

(F) deny to any person in a criminal proceeding the right to a speedy and public trial, to be informed of the nature and cause of the accusation, to be confronted with the witness against him or her, to have compulsory process for obtaining witness in his or her favor, and at his or her own expense to have the assistance of counsel for his or her defense;

(G) require excessive bail, impose excessive fines, inflict cruel and unusual punishments, and in no event impose for conviction of any one offense any penalty or punishment greater than imprisonment for a term of one year or five thousand dollars ($5,000) or both;

(H) deny to any person within its jurisdiction the equal protection of its laws or deprive any person of liberty or property without due process of law;

(I) pass any bill of attainder or ex post facto law;

(J) deny to any person accused of an offense punishable by imprisonment the right, upon request, to a trial by jury of not less than six (6) persons;

(K) interfere with the vested property rights that Osage people may have in the Osage mineral estate.

SECTION 3. The Judicial Department of the Osage Nation shall have jurisdiction to enforce and protect the rights delineated in this Article and in other parts of this Constitution.

Article XV.

PROPOSED AMENDMENTS

SECTION 1. Proposed amendments to this Constitution may be initiated by:

(A) A resolution of the Osage National Council adopted by at least six (6) affirmative votes; or

(B) A valid petition submitted to the Osage National Council signed by not less than thirty percent (30%) of the registered voters of the Osage Nation.

SECTION 2. Proposed amendments shall be submitted to a vote of the electorate in an election called for that purpose by the Osage National Council and conducted in a manner prescribed by tribal law.

SECTION 3. Any amendment adopted by a majority of the votes cast in the election shall be submitted to the Secretary of the Interior, or authorized delegate, for approval. If no action is taken within forty-five (45) days following its receipt by the Secretary's authorized delegate, the amendment shall be deemed approved and it shall thereafter be effective.

Article XVI.

ELDERS COUNCIL

SECTION 1. There shall be created by law an Elders Council that will serve in an advisory capacity to the Osage National Council on matters pertaining to cultural, historical, and traditional activities of the Osage people.

SECTION 2. The Elders Council shall be selected by the Osage National Council in a manner to be determined by tribal law.

Article XVII

RATIFICATION OF TITLES AND PRIOR ACTS

SECTION 1. That no inconvenience may arise from the reorganization of the Osage Nation as set forth in this Constitution. It is declared that all process which shall have been issued in the name of the Osage Nation prior to the reorganization herein shall be valid and binding as if issued in the name of the Osage Nation after ratification of this Constitution. It is further declared that all criminal prosecutions or penal actions, which shall have arisen prior to the reorganization herein, shall be prosecuted to judgment as if commenced after ratification of this Constitution. There shall be no ex post facto law.

SECTION 2. That all laws and parts of laws now in force in the Osage Nation, which are not repugnant to this Constitution, shall continue and remain in force until they expire by their own limitation, or shall be amended or repealed by the Osage National Council as provided by Article VII.

SECTION 3. That all fines, penalties, forfeitures, and escheats which shall have accrued to the Osage Nation prior to the reorganization herein shall not be impaired by the reorganization herein, but shall accrue to the Osage Nation as if accrued after the ratification of this Constitution.

SECTION 4. Title to tribal property, which is held by the United States of America in trust for the Osage Nation, shall not be impaired by the reorganization herein, but shall be held by the United States in trust for the reorganized Osage Nation, except that the mineral estate that is held in trust shall be administered by the Osage Tribal Council pursuant to Federal law and royalties derived from the mineral estate shall be collected and distributed pursuant to Federal law including the Act of June 28, 1906, 34 Stat. 539; the Act of March 2, 1929, 45 Stat. 1481; and the Act of August 28, 1957, 71 Stat. 471; as may be amended from time to time by the Federal Congress. All other tribal trust property, including improvements thereon, shall be administered by the Osage National Council.

SECTION 5. The validity of all notes, bonds, loans, contracts and other obligations made by the Osage Nation prior to the reorganization herein shall not be impaired by the reorganization, but shall be the liability of the Osage Nation as if assumed after the ratification of this Constitution.

Appendix 4 **BIA Letter on Osage Citizenship**

U.S. Department of the Interior   Jun 23, 2003
Bureau of Indian Affairs
Washington, DC 20240
Tribal Government Services (TE)
BCCO 03715

  Mr. Leonard M. Maker
  1106 S. Regan
  Hominy, OK 74035
  Dear Mr. Maker:

Thank you for your letters dated May 28, 2003, addressed to Secretary Gale A. Norton and Acting Assistant Secretary—Indian Affairs, Aurene M. Martin, in which you asked the status of the membership criteria for the Osage Tribe, Oklahoma. You specifically wanted to know the validity of the tribal enrollment card which the Osage Tribal Council issues.

You recently wrote an identical letter to the Eastern Oklahoma Region and the Regional Director advised you that the Osage Allotment Act of June 28, 1906 (34 Stat. 539), as amended, authorized the establishment and closing of the Osage Tribe's membership roll. This legislation has not been repealed and remains in effect.

There are no provisions in 34 Stat. 539, its subsequent amendments, or other Acts that provide authority to redefine, alter, or undertake any action to extend tribal membership to descendants of original Osage allottees. In order to extend membership, Congressional action will be needed. The Bureau of Indian Affairs can only recognize action(s) consistent with the provisions of the Act of June 28, 1906.

We suggest that you or your son may wish to contact the student financial aid office to determine the types of assistance (grant, scholarships, loans, work-study, tuition waiver, etc.) that may be available for the 2003–2004 academic year and to ask about the information that you or your son may need to provide, as well as application deadlines. College students, whether members of the 562 federally recognized tribes and Alaska Native villages and corporations or not, in need of financial assistance to attend public or private colleges and universities may be eligible for such funding administered through the student financial aid office located at each campus.

Enclosed is a copy of the Act of June 28, 1906. We are advising our field offices of this letter.

Sincerely,

/s/ Terrance L. Virden

Director, Bureau of Indian Affairs

DEC. 3, 2004

108th Congress

An Act To reaffirm the inherent sovereign rights of the Osage Tribe to determine its membership and form of government.

Be it enacted by the Senate and House of Representatives of the United States of America in Congress assembled,

SECTION 1. REAFFIRMATION OF CERTAIN RIGHTS OF THE OSAGE TRIBE.

(a) FINDINGS.—The Congress finds as follows:

(1) The Osage Tribe is a federally recognized tribe based in Pawhuska, Oklahoma.

(2) The Osage Allotment Act of June 28, 1906 (34 Stat. 539), states that the "legal membership" of the Osage Tribe includes the persons on the January 1, 1906, roll and their children, and that each "member" on that roll is entitled to a headright share in the distribution of funds from the Osage mineral estate and an allotment of the surface lands of the Osage Reservation.

(3) Today only Osage Indians who have a headright share in the mineral estate are "members" of the Osage Tribe.

(4) Adult Osage Indians without a headright interest cannot vote in Osage government elections and are not eligible to seek elective office in the Osage Tribe as a matter of Federal law.

(5) A principal goal of Federal Indian policy is to promote tribal self-sufficiency and strong tribal government.

(b) REAFFIRMATION OF CERTAIN RIGHTS OF THE OSAGE TRIBE.

(1) MEMBERSHIP.—Congress hereby clarifies that the term "legal membership" in section 1 of the Act entitled, "An Act For the division of lands and funds of the Osage Indians in Oklahoma Territory, and for other purposes," approved June 28, 1906 (34 Stat. 539), means the persons eligible for allotments of Osage Reservation lands and a pro rata share of the Osage mineral estate as provided in that Act, not membership in the Osage Tribe for all purposes. Congress hereby reaffirms the inherent sovereign right of the Osage Tribe to determine its own membership,

provided that the rights of any person to Osage mineral estate shares are not diminished thereby.

(2) GOVERNMENT.—Notwithstanding section 9 of the Act entitled, "An Act For the division of lands and funds of the Osage Indians in Oklahoma Territory, and for other purposes," approved June 28, 1906 (34 Stat. 539), Congress hereby reaffirms the inherent sovereign right of the Osage Tribe to determine its own form of government.

(3) ELECTIONS AND REFERENDA.—At the request of the Osage Tribe, the Secretary of the Interior shall assist the Osage Tribe with conducting elections and referenda to implement this section.

Approved December 3, 2004.

Appendix 6 **2005 Osage Government Reform Referendum Results**

Question 1

Option A. The 1906 Osage Allotment Roll should be used as the base roll and thus shall constitute the base membership of the tribe. All lineal descendants of those Osages listed on the 1906 Osage Allotment Roll shall have the right to enroll as members of the Osage Nation, and those enrolled members shall constitute the citizenry.

Or

Option B. A minimum Osage blood quantum requirement shall be used to determine the right to enroll as a member of the Osage Nation and those enrolled members shall constitute the citizenry.

Option A 85.70% 1,414 votes

Option B 14.30% 236 votes

Question 2

Membership of people on the base roll will be subject to challenge by the new government if it is proven that fraudulent measures were used to establish membership into the tribe.

For 79.75% 1,315 votes

Against 20.25% 334 votes

Question 3

An enrolled member of the Osage Nation, can choose to be dually enrolled as a member of another Indian tribe without forfeiting Osage membership.

For 78.44% 1,295 votes

Against 21.56% 356 votes

Question 4

All members of the Osage Nation eighteen (18) years of age and over shall be deemed qualified electors, provided they are duly registered to vote.

For 95.56% 1,571 votes

Against 4.44% 73 votes

Question 5

The newly reformed Osage Nation government will be organized to include legislative, executive and judicial branches with checks and balances among the branches that include veto power granted to the chief executive, a legislative override of an executive veto and no branch shall be permitted to exercise the powers or functions delegated to another branch.

For 90.77% 1,495 votes
Against 9.23% 152 votes

Question 6

The legislative branch, responsible for making the laws of the Osage Nation, shall contain a legislative body composed of 12 representatives who shall select from amongst its members a Speaker of the House and such other officers as deemed necessary. The legislative representatives must be Osage citizens, 25 years of age of older, and all shall be elected at large.

For 90.39% 1,486 votes
Against 9.61% 158 votes

Question 7

Staggered terms shall be established for the legislative body which shall be elected at large by the adult members of the Osage Nation such that 1/2 of the representatives shall serve four year terms following the 2006 election and the other 1/2 of the representatives shall serve six year terms following the 2006 election. When candidates file for office in the 2006 election, they will file for either a four year term or a six year term at their discretion. Thereafter, all legislative representatives will serve four year terms with elections of half of the representatives to be held every two years commencing in 2010.

For 80.32% 1,318 votes
Against 19.68% 323 votes

Question 8

Option A. The newly reformed Osage government is reorganized under one governing constitution of the Osage Nation with one governing body organized into a 3 branch system that does not include the Osage Tribal Council as part of that system. The Osage Tribal Council functions as an independent body with no governmental authority, yet retaining all its present fundamental organization, authority and responsibilities over the Osage mineral estate in accordance with the Osage Allotment Act of June 28, 1906 (sec. 9, 34 Stat. 539).

Or

Option B: The newly reformed Osage government is reorganized under one governing constitution of the Osage nation with one governing body organized into a 3 branch system that does include the Osage Tribal Council as part of that system. The Osage Tribal Council is established as a second chamber of a bicameral, or two house system, within the legislative branch of the newly reformed Osage government. Elected by Osage shareholders, the Osage Tribal Council retains all its present fundamental organization, authority and responsibilities over the Osage mineral estate in accordance with the Osage Allotment Act of June 28, 1906 (sec.9, 34 Stat. 539). All legislative authority, other than that specified to manage the mineral estate, is delegated to a house of representatives elected at large by all adult members of the Osage Nation. A bright line must be drawn between the two houses to clearly delineate duties and responsibilities.

Option A 51.60% 839 votes
Option B 48.40% 787 votes

Question 9

The executive branch, which has responsibility for ensuring that the laws of the Osage Nation are carried out and for the framing of tribal policy, shall have executive power vested in a chief executive and in the chief executive's absence, a deputy chief executive. Both the chief executive and the deputy chief executive must be Osage citizens, age 35 years or older, and shall be elected to serve four years terms by a majority of votes cast by eligible voters in elections of the Osage Nation.

For 93.53% 1,533 votes
Against 6.47% 106 votes

Question 10

Option A. Candidates for the offices of chief executive and deputy chief executive shall be elected as running mates on the same ticket.

Or

Option B. Candidates for the office of chief executive and deputy chief executive shall be elected independently of each other.

Option A 35.85% 584 votes
Option B 64.15% 1,045 votes

Question 11

A Department of Treasury shall be established within the executive branch to oversee fiscal policy and ensure financial accountability within the new government of the Osage Nation. The executive director of the Department of Treasury shall be called the Treasurer of the Osage Nation and shall be appointed by the chief executive of the tribe and confirmed by the legislature. The Treasurer shall accept, receipt for, keep and safeguard all tribal funds as directed by the legislature and shall maintain and provide an accurate record of such tribal funds. The Treasurer shall ensure that an annual financial statement is audited by a Certified Public Accountant and presented to the legislature in a timely manner, and will submit un-audited reports as required.

For 88.89% 1,456 votes

Against 11.11% 182 votes

Question 12

The judicial branch should be responsible for interpreting the laws of the Osage Nation and its powers will include, but not necessarily be limited to, the trial and adjudication of certain civil and criminal matters, the redress of grievances, the resolution of disputes and judicial review of certain holdings and decisions of administrative agencies and of the trial court. Judicial power shall be vested in a Supreme Court of the Osage Nation, a lower Trial Court of the Osage Nation and such lower courts of special jurisdiction and other forums as deemed necessary and authorized by the legislature. There shall be one Chief Justice, who is a citizen of the Osage Nation, licensed to practice law for no less than ten (10) years and at least 40 years of age, and two Justices of the Supreme Court who are licensed to practice law for no less than five (5) years. There shall be one Chief Judge who is a citizen of the Osage Nation, and who has been licensed to practice law for no less than five (5) years and other Associate Judges as deemed necessary by the legislature.

For 88.75% 1,459 votes

Against 11.25% 185 votes

Question 13

Option A. The Chief Justice and Justices of the Osage Nation Supreme Court, along with the Chief Judge of the Osage Nation Trial Court, shall be appointed by the chief executive and confirmed by the legislature. The Chief Justice and Chief Judge, once appointed, shall in turn jointly appoint such Trial Judges as are deemed appropriate for the efficient and proper administration of justice.

Or

Option B. The Chief Justice and justices of the Osage Nation Supreme Court and the Chief Judge of the Osage Nation trial Court shall be appointed by the chief executive and confirmed by the legislature and shall serve one full term prior to standing for retention by a vote of the Osage people. At the conclusion of a full term, each will stand for retention in the next general election and repeat this cycle thereafter. The Chief Justice and the Chief Judge, once appointed, shall in turn jointly appoint such Trial Judges as are deemed appropriate for the efficient and proper administration of justice.

Option A 26.91% 434 votes

Option B 73.09% 1,179 votes

Question 14

All elected officials are subject to removal and/or recall from office for willful neglect of duty, malfeasance in office, habitual drunkenness or drug abuse, inability to meet qualifications to serve, conviction of a felony, a misdemeanor involving moral turpitude or offenses against the Osage Nation committed while in office.

For 97.44% 1,598 votes

Against 2.56% 42 votes

Question 15

Amendments to the constitution may be proposed by the Osage people by citizen's initiative or by the house of representatives in the legislative branch, with a super majority vote. The proposed amendments must go to the citizens of the Osage Nation for approval by vote. If favored by a majority vote of the Osage people, the constitution shall be amended.

For 93.39% 1,540 votes

Against 6.61% 109 votes

Question 16

Tribally owned enterprises shall be managed by boards in which the members are qualified professionals appointed by the Osage Nation legislature. In order to insulate tribal enterprises from politics, no elected official shall be appointed to a tribal enterprise board. The legislature shall maintain general oversight and approve the Annual Plan of Operation for the coming year, including projected budgets, appropriations, major acquisitions, and strategic plans.

For 92.11% 1,517 votes

Against 7.89% 130 votes

PREAMBLE:

We the Wah-zha-zhe, known as the Osage People, having formed as Clans in the far distant past, have been a People and as a People have walked this earth and enjoyed the blessings of Wah-kon-tah for more centuries than we truly know.

Having resolved to live in harmony, we now come together so that we may once more unite as a Nation and as a People, calling upon the fundamental values that we hold sacred: Justice, Fairness, Compassion, Respect for and Protection of Child, Elder, All Fellow Beings, and Self.

Paying homage to generations of Osage leaders of the past and present, we give thanks for their wisdom and courage. Acknowledging our ancient tribal order as the foundation of our present government, first reformed in the 1881 Constitution of the Osage Nation, we continue our legacy by again reorganizing our government.

This Constitution, created by Osage People, hereby grants to every Osage citizen a vote that is equal to all others and forms a government that is accountable to the citizens of the Osage Nation.

We, the Osage People, based on centuries of being a People, now strengthen our government in order to preserve and perpetuate a full and abundant Osage way of life that benefits all Osages, living and as yet unborn.

ARTICLE I—TITLE

This tribe shall hereafter be referred to as The Osage Nation, formerly known as the Osage Tribe of Indians of Oklahoma.

ARTICLE II—TERRITORY AND JURISDICTION

Section 1. *Territory*: The territory of the Osage Nation shall include the Osage Reservation, duly established by the Congress of the United States pursuant to (1) the Treaty between the United States of America and the Great and Little Osage Indians, Sept. 29, 1865, 14 Stat. 687; (2) Article 16 of the Treaty between the United States of America and the Cherokee

Nation of Indians, July 19, 1866, 14 Stat. 799; and (3) the Act of June 5, 1872, ch. 310, 17 Stat. 228 (An Act to Confirm to the Great and Little Osage Indians a Reservation in the Indian Territory), and all other lands under federally-restricted status title to which is held by the Nation or the People, or by the United States in trust on behalf of the Nation or the People, and any such additional lands as are hereafter acquired and similarly held by the Nation or the People or by the United States on behalf of the Nation or the People. Territory is defined as, but is not limited to, air, water, surface, sub-surface, natural resources and any interest therein, notwithstanding the issuance of any patent or right of way in fee or otherwise, by the governments of the United States or the Osage Nation, existing and/or in the future.

Section 2. *Jurisdiction*: The jurisdiction of the Osage Nation shall extend over all persons, subjects, property, and over all activities that occur within the territory of the Osage Nation and over all Osage citizens, subjects, property and activities outside such territory affecting the rights and laws of the Osage Nation.

Nothing in this Article shall be construed to limit or impair the ability of the Osage Nation to exercise its jurisdiction within or without its territory based upon its inherent sovereign authority as a nation of Osage People.

ARTICLE III—MEMBERSHIP

Section 1. *Base Membership Roll*: The base membership of the Osage Nation shall consist of those persons whose names appear on the final roll of the Osage tribe of Indians pursuant to the Act of June 28, 1906 (34 Stat. 539).

Section 2. *Qualifications for Membership*: All lineal descendants of those Osages listed on the 1906 Roll are eligible for membership in the Osage Nation, and those enrolled members shall constitute the citizenry subject to the provisions of this Constitution and to the laws enacted and regulations approved pursuant to this Constitution.

Section 3. *Dual Enrollment*: An enrolled member of the Osage Nation can choose to be dually enrolled as a member of another Indian tribe without forfeiting Osage membership.

Section 4. *Membership Laws*: The Osage Nation Congress shall have the power and is required to regulate membership and maintain a correct roll of all Osages enrolled as members of the Osage Nation. The Osage Nation Congress shall enact laws, not inconsistent with this Constitution, prescribing rules and regulations governing membership, including application and appeal procedures, loss of membership, and the adoption of members.

ARTICLE IV—DECLARATION OF RIGHTS

Section 1. *Popular Sovereignty*: All political power is vested in and derived from the Osage People. All government of right originates with the Osage People, is founded upon their will only, and is instituted solely for the good of the whole.

Section 2. *Self-Government*: The Osage People have the exclusive right of governing themselves as a free, sovereign, and independent nation as done from time immemorial.

Section 3. *Inalienable Rights of Osage Citizens*: There shall be certain inalienable rights, which shall not be abridged or denied by any branch/department of the Osage Nation government or by any official of the government. Furthermore nothing in this Constitution shall be interpreted in a way that would diminish the rights and privileges of any person within the jurisdiction of the Osage Nation. The Osage Nation government in exercising sovereign powers shall not:

A. make or enforce any law prohibiting the free exercise of religion, or abridging the freedom of speech or the press, or the right of the people peaceably to assemble and to petition for redress of grievances;

B. violate the right of the people to be secure in their persons, houses, papers, and effects against unreasonable search and seizures, nor issue warrants, but upon probable cause, supported by oath or affirmation, and particularly describing the place to be searched and the person or thing to be seized;

C. subject any person for the same offense to be twice put in jeopardy;

D. compel any person in any criminal case to be a witness against himself or herself;

E. take any private property for a public use that is not fully justified as being in the best interest of all the people nor take without just compensation;

F. deny to any person in criminal proceeding the right to a speedy and public trial, to be informed of the nature and cause of the accusation, to be confronted with the witnesses against him or her, to have compulsory process for obtaining witnesses in his or her favor, and at his or her own expense to have the assistance of counsel for his or her defense;

G. require excessive bail, impose excessive fines, inflict cruel and unusual punishments, and in no event impose for conviction of any offense any penalty or punishment greater than imprisonment for a term of one year or a fine of five thousand dollars, or both;

H. deny to any person within its jurisdiction the equal protection of its laws or deprive any person of liberty or property without due process of law;

I. pass any bill of attainder or ex post facto law;

J. deny any person accused of an offense punishable by imprisonment the right, upon request, to a trial by jury of not less than six persons.

Section 4. *Remedies*: No person shall be entitled to an award of monetary damages, as a form of relief, in the Osage Trial Court for any violation of these rights; unless the Osage Nation Congress may by law provide for monetary damages as a form of relief for such violations, when relief would best serve the interests of the Osage Nation or that of justice.

Section 5. *Rights of Mineral Royalty Interest Holders*: The Osage Nation Government shall not create any law or ordinance pertaining to the mineral royalties from the Osage Mineral Estate that acts in conflict with Federal law and regulations.

ARTICLE V—DISTRIBUTION OF POWERS OF GOVERNMENT

Section 1. *Governing Powers*: The powers of the government of the Osage Nation shall be vested in three (3) separate branches: the Legislative, the Executive, and the Judicial.

Section 2. *Separation of Powers*: The Legislative, Executive and Judicial branches of government shall be separate and distinct and no person or collection of persons, charged with official duties under one of those branches, shall exercise any power properly vested in either of the others except as expressly provided in the Osage Nation Constitution.

Section 3. *Supremacy Clause*: The Osage Nation Constitution shall be the Supreme law for the Osage Nation over all territory and persons within the jurisdiction of the Osage Nation.

ARTICLE VI—LEGISLATURE

Section 1. *Legislative Power*: The legislative power of the Osage Nation, except for the initiative and referendum powers reserved to the People as provided in this Constitution, is hereby vested in one legislative body to be called the Osage Nation Congress.

Section 2. *Composition*: The Osage Nation Congress shall be composed of twelve (12) representatives to be initially elected at large, by qualified Osage voters, without regard to their district of residency. Nothing within this provision prohibits the Osage Nation Congress from equitably apportioning districts for the election of representatives hereafter.

Section 3. *Term of Office*: For the first election under this Constitution, the twelve (12) positions in the Osage Nation Congress shall be arranged in order to establish a system of staggered terms of office whereby six (6) representatives shall be elected to serve a six (6) year term and six (6) representatives shall be elected to serve a four (4) year term. Thereafter, all members of the Osage Nation Congress shall be elected to four (4) year terms with elections of half of the positions to be held every two (2) years or biennially commencing in 2010. All elected and/or appointed officials of the Osage Nation Congress shall serve until their successors are duly elected and installed.

Section 4. *Qualifications*: Enrolled members of the Osage Nation, who are at least twenty-five (25) years of age on that date of the election, who have never been convicted of a felony, are eligible to serve as members of the Osage Nation Congress.

Section 5. *Disqualifications*: No member of the Osage Nation Congress shall hold any other tribal office or position of profit under the Osage Nation during the term for which the member is elected or appointed. No member of the Osage Nation Congress shall hold any other tribal office under another Indian nation during his/her term of office. The Osage Nation Congress may prescribe further disqualifications.

Section 6. *Vacancies*: Any vacancy in the Osage Nation Congress shall be filled for the unexpired term in such manner as may be provided by law, or, if no provision be made by law, by appointment of the Principal Chief for the balance of the term.

Section 7. *Compensation*: The annual salary and expense allowance of members of the Osage Nation Congress shall be fixed at the first session of the legislature held after the Osage Nation Constitution takes effect. Presiding officers may receive increased compensation for their duties.

Compensation may be increased or decreased by law from time to time thereafter, but no increase or decrease shall be effective until the legislative year following the next general election for members of the Osage Nation Congress.

Section 8. *Election of Officers*: The Osage Nation Congress shall select from amongst its members a Speaker, who shall be the Presiding Officer, and such other officers as deemed necessary. The Speaker and other duly elected officers may vote on all matters before the Osage Nation Congress.

Section 9. *Quorum*: The presence of at least two-thirds (2/3) of the whole number of the members of the Congress shall be necessary to constitute a meeting of the congressional house for the exercise of its powers.

Section 10. *Sessions*: The Osage Nation Congress shall convene twice annually in regular session, so that six (6) months shall not intervene between the last sitting of the Congress and its first sitting in the next session. Regular sessions shall convene on such day and at such time as the Osage Nation Congress shall determine by law.

The first regular congressional session of each year shall be titled the Hun-kah Session and the second regular congressional session of the year shall be titled the Tzi-zho Session. This schedule shall be in honor of the ancient moiety division of Earth and Sky and serves to remind all Osages of the responsibility to bring balance and harmony to the Nation.

At the written request of two-thirds (2/3) of the members, the Speaker shall convene the Osage Nation Congress in special session. The Principal Chief may convene the Osage Nation Congress in special session.

Regular sessions shall be limited to a period of twenty four (24) days, and special sessions shall be limited to a period of ten (10) days. Any session may be extended a total of not more than three (3) days. Such extension shall be granted by the Speaker of the House at the written request of two-thirds (2/3) of the members or may be granted by the Principal Chief.

The Osage Nation Congress shall not adjourn during any session of the legislature for more than three (3) days, Sundays excepted, or to any other place.

The Osage Nation Congress may only meet in the interim, the period of time between two sessions, by Interim Committee(s) to study a particular subject or subjects in order to make recommendations to the next regular session of the legislature.

Section 11. *Rules of Procedure*: The Osage Nation Congress shall adopt uniform rules of procedure for conducting the business of the Congress. The Osage Nation Congress shall keep and publish a journal of its proceedings and the yeas and nays, when taken on any question, shall be entered in the journals. A member may be expelled from the floor for disorderly or contemptuous behavior by a vote of two-thirds (2/3) of all members of the Osage Nation Congress present.

Section 12. *Enactment of Laws:* The Osage Nation Congress shall establish the procedure for enactment of bills into law. No laws shall be made except by statute and no statute shall be enacted except by bill. No bill shall be passed without the concurrence of a majority of the members of the Osage Nation Congress. Each law shall embrace but one subject, which shall be expressed in its title. The enacting clause of each law of the Osage Nation shall be: "Be it enacted by the Congress of the Osage Nation." Every bill that has passed by an affirmative majority vote shall be signed by the presiding officer of the Osage Nation Congress to certify that the procedural requirements for passage have been met and shall be presented forthwith to the Principal Chief for approval.

Section 13. *Presentation of Bills to Principal Chief; Veto:* Every bill passed in conformity to the rules of the Osage Nation Congress shall be presented to the Principal Chief. If approved, the Principal Chief shall sign it and notify the Congress of that fact. If a bill is vetoed by the Principal Chief, it shall be returned with objections to the Osage Nation Congress. The objections shall be entered in the journal. If, after reconsideration, at least three-fourths (3/4) or nine (9) members of Congress vote to pass the bill, it shall become law. Any bill not returned by the Principal Chief within five (5) days, Sundays and holidays excepted, after it is presented becomes a law as if signed by the Principal Chief. Any bill passed during the last three (3) days of a session may be presented to the Principal Chief during the three (3) days following the day of final adjournment, and the Principal Chief may sign or not sign. If not signed, the bill does not become law.

If a bill presented to the Principal Chief contains several items of appropriation of money, he may veto one or more of the items while approving the bill. At the time the bill is signed, the Principal Chief shall append to it a statement of the items vetoed, and the vetoed items shall not take effect. If the legislature is in session, he shall transmit to Congress a copy of the statement, and the items vetoed shall be separately reconsidered. If on reconsideration, any item is approved by three fourths (3/4) of the members elected to Congress, it is a part of the law notwithstanding the objections.

Laws passed by the legislature become effective sixty (60) days after enactment. The Osage Nation Congress may, by concurrence of two-thirds (2/3) of the membership, provide for another effective date.

Section 14. *Presentation of Orders, Resolutions, and Votes to Principal Chief:* Each order, resolution or vote, except such as relate to the business or adjournment of the legislature, shall be presented to the Principal Chief and is subject to a veto with an override provision.

Section 15. *Necessary Laws*: The Osage Nation Congress shall pass all laws necessary to carry into effect the provisions of the Osage Nation Constitution.

Section 16. *Disclosure of Private Interest*: A member of the Osage Nation Congress who has a personal or private interest in any measure or bill, proposed or pending before the legislature, shall disclose the fact and shall not vote thereon.

Section 17. *Power of Removal*: The Osage Congress shall have the power to remove elected and appointed officials of the Osage Nation, and said removal must be conducted in accordance with Article XII of the Osage Nation Constitution.

Section 18. *Public Proceedings*: All proceedings of the Osage Nation Congress shall be open and public, except in cases that require confidentiality. In such cases, an Executive Session may be convened when duly voted upon in an open meeting.

Section 19. *Executive Sessions*: The Osage Nation Congress shall establish procedures to convene an Executive Session of its own members.

Section 20. *Legislative Accountability*: To assist the Osage People in holding their Legislature accountable, at the convening of each regular session of the Osage Nation Congress, the Speaker shall report the legislative priorities of Congress for said session and, at the close of each regular session, report the action taken by Congress.

Section 21. *Legislative Committees, Commissions, etc.*: The Osage Nation Congress may establish and appoint any subordinate commission, committee or other body. Members of the Osage Nation Congress may be appointed to serve on any such body, excepting any and all Tribal Enterprise Boards.

Section 22. *Merit Based Employment System*: The Osage Nation Congress shall establish a system under which the merit principle will govern the employment of persons by the Osage Nation excluding executive staff and other appointed positions serving at the will of the Office of the Principal Chief as described in Article VII, Section 14. The Congress shall include, within the merit principal system, a grievance procedure which must be exhausted before seeking review in the Trial Court. The Congress shall establish laws that define and limit nepotism in tribal government and Tribal Enterprise Board employment.

Section 23. *Annual Budget*: The Osage Nation Congress shall enact, by law, an annual expenditure of funds which shall include an appropriation of operating funds for each branch of the government for each fiscal year. The annual budget shall not exceed projected revenues.

Section 24. *Legislative Referendum*: The Osage Nation Congress and/ or its delegate(s) may voluntarily refer proposed measures to the Osage People for final approval or rejection. The veto power of the Principal Chief shall not extend to measures voted on by the Osage People.

ARTICLE VII—EXECUTIVE

Section 1. *Supreme Executive Power*: The supreme executive power of the Osage Nation is hereby vested in a Principal Chief, who shall be titled "Principal Chief of the Osage Nation," and whose Osage title shall be "Ki-he-kah Dto-dah-ha." These titles shall be reserved exclusively to this office. The Principal Chief shall dutifully support the Constitution and laws of the Osage Nation and shall see that the laws are faithfully executed, administered and enforced.

Section 2. *Term of Office*: The Principal Chief shall be elected by qualified Osage voters at a general election to a term of four (4) years and shall serve until a successor has been elected and installed. The Principal Chief shall be elected by a majority of votes.

Section 3. *Qualifications*: Enrolled members of the Osage Nation, who are at least thirty-five (35) years of age on that date of the election, who have never been convicted of a felony, are eligible to become a candidate for the office of Principal Chief of the Osage Nation.

Section 4. *Disqualifications*: The Principal Chief shall not hold any other office or position of profit under the Osage Nation nor hold any office, be it elected or appointed, under any other tribal government or state, county or federal government.

Section 5. *Composition*: The executive branch shall consist of the elected offices of Principal Chief and Assistant Principal Chief, and all other administrative offices, departments, agencies, and instrumentalities of the Osage Nation including, but not limited to, public trusts, boards, village committees, authorities, and commissions.

Section 6. *Office of Assistant Principal Chief*: There shall be an Assistant Principal Chief, whose Osage title shall be "Ki-he-kah O-wah-ta," who shall have the same qualifications as the Principal Chief and serve for the same term and in the same manner. These titles shall be reserved exclusively to this office. The Assistant Principal Chief shall perform such duties as may be prescribed by Osage law and as may be delegated by the Principal Chief. The Assistant Principal Chief, shall, by virtue of his office, be an ex officio member of the Osage Nation Congress and shall have a right, when in committee of the whole, to join in debate; and, whenever the legislature shall be equally divided, the Assistant Principal Chief shall cast the deciding vote.

Section 7. *Acting Principal Chief*: The Assistant Principal Chief shall serve in the temporary absence of the Principal Chief and when serving will have all the privileges, duties and powers of that office.

Section 8. *Vacancies; Absences*: In the event of a vacancy to the office of Principal Chief for any reason, the Assistant Principal Chief shall succeed to the office for the remaining portion of the four (4) year term to which the Principal Chief was elected.

In the event of a vacancy to the office of Assistant Principal Chief for any reason, the Principal Chief shall appoint a successor to serve for the balance of the term, by and with the advice and consent of the Osage Nation Congress.

Whenever for a period of six (6) months, the Principal Chief has been continuously absent from office or unable to discharge the duties of the office by reason of mental or physical disability, the office shall be deemed vacant. The procedures for determining absence and disability shall be prescribed by Osage law.

Section 9. *Further Succession*: Provision shall be made by Osage law for succession to the office of Principal Chief and for an acting Principal Chief in the event that the Assistant Principal Chief is unable to succeed to the office or act as Principal Chief. In the event that the Assistant Principal Chief is unable to succeed to the office or act as Principal Chief the Speaker of the Congress shall act as Principal Chief.

Section 10. *Compensation*: The annual salary and expense allowance for the offices of Principal Chief and Assistant Principal Chief shall be prescribed by Osage law and shall not be increased or diminished during that term of office.

Section 11. *Veto*: The Principal Chief may veto bills by the Osage Nation Congress. The Principal Chief may, by veto, strike or reduce items in appropriation bills. The Principal Chief shall return any vetoed bills, with a statement of the objection(s), to the Osage Nation Congress.

Section 12. *Communicate with Legislature; Convene Legislature*: The Principal Chief shall communicate to the Osage Nation Congress, by message at the opening of each regular session and at such other times as may be deemed necessary, the condition of the Nation, and shall in like manner recommend such measures as may be deemed desirable. The Principal

Chief may convene the legislature by proclamation, and shall state when assembled, the purpose for which they shall have been convened in a special session whenever the Osage People's interest shall require.

Section 13: *Establish Department of the Treasury*: There shall be established, by Osage law, a Department of the Treasury in the Executive Branch and the Principal Chief shall appoint a Treasurer to act as the Chief Financial Officer and administer fiscal policy and ensure financial accountability of the Osage Nation, by and with the advice and consent of the Osage Nation Congress. The powers and duties of the Treasurer of the Osage Nation shall be prescribed by the Osage Nation Congress and will include the mandate that an annual financial statement for the Osage Nation government be audited by a Certified Public Accountant approved by the Congress or by committee of the Congress and presented to the Congress in a timely manner. The Treasurer shall accept, receipt for, keep and safeguard all tribal funds as directed by the Congress and shall maintain and provide an accurate record of such tribal funds.

Section 14. *Tribal Enterprise Boards*: There shall be established, by Osage law, a Tribal Enterprise Board(s) in the Executive Branch, and the Principal Chief shall appoint qualified professionals to oversee operations of Osage Nation business enterprises, by and with the advice and consent of the Osage Nation Congress. The Osage Nation Congress shall reserve the right to review any action taken by the Board, and may approve the Annual Plan of Operation for the coming year. No Osage Nation elected official may be appointed to such Board.

Section 15. *Appointments*: The Principal Chief may appoint executive staff, in accordance with the budget approved by the Congress. The Principal Chief shall also appoint, subject to advice and consent by the Osage Nation Congress, the members of each board, commission or other instrumentality in the executive branch whose election or appointment is not provided by this constitution or by law. All appointees shall serve at the pleasure of the Principal Chief and shall be exempt employees, not subject to the Merit System established at Article VI, Section 22.

Should the legislature be in regular session, the Principal Chief shall submit for confirmation the name of an appointee within forty-eight (48) hours after the appointment is made. Failure of the Osage Nation Congress to confirm the appointment, prior to the end of the session, shall constitute rejection.

If the legislature is not in regular session, the Principal Chief may make interim appointments, which shall expire at the end of the next regular session, unless submitted to and confirmed by the Osage Nation Congress during that session.

A person not confirmed by the Osage Nation Congress shall not be appointed to the same office during any recess of the legislature.

Section 16. *Removal Power*: The Principal Chief may remove from office a person appointed by the Principal Chief's office, except a person appointed for a term fixed by this Constitution or by Osage law. Removal shall be conducted in accordance with Article XII of the Osage Nation Constitution. If the legislature is not in session when the Principal Chief desires to remove an officer, the Principal Chief shall call a special session for consideration of the proposed removal. The session may not exceed two days in duration.

Section 17. *Offices and Records of Executive Officers*: The Principal Chief, Treasurer and other Executive Officers shall keep the public records, books and papers at the seat of government in a manner relating to their respective offices as prescribed by Osage law.

Section 18. *Seal of the Osage Nation*: There shall be a seal of the Osage Nation which shall be officially used by the Principal Chief and shall be called the Great Seal of the Osage Nation.

ARTICLE VIII—JUDICIARY

Section 1. *Judicial Powers*: The Judicial powers of the Osage Nation are hereby vested in one Supreme Court, in a lower Trial Court and in such inferior Courts as the Osage Nation Congress may ordain and establish for the development, maintenance and administration of the Tribal Justice System. The judicial branch shall be responsible for interpreting the laws of the Osage Nation and its powers will include, but not necessarily be limited to, the trial and adjudication of certain civil and criminal matters, the redress of grievances, the resolution of disputes and judicial review of certain holdings and decisions of administrative agencies and of the Trial Court.

Section 2. *Appellate Jurisdiction*: The appellate jurisdiction of the Supreme Court may extend to all cases of law and equity. The Supreme Court, by appropriate order, may hear appeals, compel inferior Courts or their officials to act in accordance with the law, and exercise such other jurisdiction as may be conferred by statute. The Supreme Court shall promulgate rules and procedures relating to original and appellate jurisdiction. Decisions of the Supreme Court shall be published and indexed and shall be final.

Section 3. *Composition of Supreme Court; Qualifications*: The Supreme Court shall consist of one Chief Justice and two Associate Justices. Any member of the Osage Nation, who is at least forty (40) years of age and duly licensed to practice law for no less than ten (10) years, is eligible for the office of Chief Justice. Anyone duly licensed to practice law for no less than five (5) years, is eligible for the office of Associate Justice. The Justices shall serve until their successors are duly appointed and installed.

Section 4. *Disqualification*: Judicial officers shall not hold any other office or position of profit under the Osage Nation.

Section 5. *Jurisdiction of Trial Court*: The Trial Court shall have original jurisdiction, not otherwise reserved to the Supreme Court, over all cases and controversies arising under the Constitution, laws, and customs and traditions of the Osage Nation. Any such case or controversy arising within the jurisdiction of the Osage Nation shall be filed in Trial Court before it is filed in any other court, unless otherwise provided in this Constitution. This grant of jurisdiction by the Osage People shall not be construed to be a waiver of the Osage Nation's sovereign immunity.

Section 6. *Composition of Trial Court; Qualifications*: The Trial Court shall consist of one Chief Judge and, as deemed necessary and appropriate, additional Associate Judges. Any member of the Osage Nation, duly licensed to practice law for no less than five (5) years, is eligible for the office of Chief Judge.

Section 7. *Appointment of Chief Justice, Associate Justices and Chief Judge*: The Principal Chief shall appoint the Chief Justice and Associate Justices of the Osage Nation Supreme Court, as well as the Chief Judge of the Trial Court, by and with the advice and consent of the Osage Nation Congress. After serving one term of four (4) years, each will stand for retention by a vote of the qualified Osage electors and at the expiration of each four (4) year term thereafter.

Section 8. *Appointment of Associate Judges*: Once appointed and installed, the Chief Justice and Chief Trial Court Judge may jointly appoint such subordinate judges as are necessary and proper to carry into effect matters in which the Judicial Department is empowered to act now or in the future.

Section 9. *Conflict of Interest*: Any Justice or Judge of the Osage Nation who appears to have a direct personal or financial interest in any matter before the judiciary shall recuse himself/herself. Any party who believes that a Judge or Justice may have a personal or financial interest in the issues before the court, may challenge the participation of that Judge or Justice.

Section 10. *Compensation*: Supreme Court Justices and Trial Court Judges shall be reasonably compensated. No increase or decrease in compensation shall take effect until after the next General election or appointment to that office.

Section 11. *Administration*: The Chief Justice of the Osage Nation Supreme Court shall be responsible for the budget and the administration of all courts.

ARTICLE IX—OATH OF OFFICE

All elected and appointed officers of the Osage Nation, before entering upon the duties of their offices, shall take and subscribe to the following oath or affirmation:

"I, _____ (name), do proudly swear (or affirm) to carry out the responsibilities of the office of _____ (name of office) to the best of my ability, freely acknowledging that the powers of this office flow from the Osage People and Wah Kon Tah. I further swear (or affirm) always to place the interest of all Osages above any special or personal interests, and to respect the right of future generations to share the rich historic and natural heritage of our Osage People. In doing so, I will always uphold and defend the Constitution of the Osage Nation, so help me God."

The foregoing oath shall be administered by a member of the Osage Nation Judiciary.

ARTICLE X—CODE OF ETHICS

Section 1. *Purpose*: Recognizing the desire of the Osage people to establish a government that is fair and equitable to all people; elected or appointed tribal officials and employees of the Osage Nation, putting aside their personal or private interest, shall strive for the common good of the Osage People and shall administrate fair and equal treatment of all persons, claims, and transactions petitioning before the Osage Nation Government.

Section 2. *Compliance with Law and Regulations*: In the performance of their duties, all officials and employees of the Osage Nation shall comply with all laws and regulations of the Osage Nation not in conflict with this Constitution.

Section 3. *The Conduct of Tribal Officials and Employees*: All tribal officials and employees of the Osage Nation shall avoid even the appearance of impropriety in the performance of their duties. Officials and employees shall refrain from abusive conduct, personal charges, or verbal affronts upon the character, motives, or intents of other officials or Osage citizens.

Tribal officials and employees shall not hinder or obstruct the proper administration of the Osage Nation government in the administration of their duties.

Section 4. *Conflicts of Interest*: In order to assure independence and impartiality, tribal officials and employees are prohibited from using public positions to influence or otherwise effect government decisions for personal gain. Tribal officials and employees shall fully and in a timely manner disclose any conflicts, real or apparent, that might be seen to influence their judgment in the performance of their duties. Tribal officials and employees shall abstain from participation in deliberations or decision-making where any conflicts are deemed to exist.

Section 5. *Gifts and Public Favor*: Tribal officials and employees shall not accept any special advantage of services or opportunities for personal gain, by virtue of public office, that is not available to the Osage People. Tribal officials and employees shall not accept any gift, favor, or promise of future benefit for themselves or their relatives in exchange for preferential treatment.

Section 6. *Use of Tribal Resources*: Tribal officials and employees shall refrain from the use of tribal resources when not acting in an official capacity.

Section 7. *Advocacy*: All official delegates of the Osage Nation shall accurately represent the official policies and positions of the Osage Nation government to the best of their abilities. When called upon to provide their own individual opinions or positions, all such delegates shall state explicitly that such information is not representative of the position of any administrative body within the Osage Nation government and shall not allow such an inference to occur.

Section 8. *Independence of Boards and Commissions*: Tribal officials and employees shall refrain from using tribal positions to improperly influence the deliberations, administrations, or decisions of established board or commission proceedings.

Section 9. *Political Subdivisions*: The Osage Nation Code of Ethics shall be applicable to all political subdivisions of the Osage Nation including members of the boards, commissions and other bodies.

Section 10. *Provisions for Violations*: The Osage Nation Congress shall enact provisions for violations of the above stated code.

ARTICLE XI—CITIZEN INITIATIVE, REFERENDUM AND RECALL

Section 1. *Citizen Initiative and Referendum*: The Osage People may propose and enact laws by the initiative or reject acts of the Osage Nation Congress by the referendum.

Section 2. *Application of Initiative, Referendum or Recall*: An initiative or referendum is proposed by an application containing the bill to be initiated or the act to be referred. The application shall be signed by not less than (100) one hundred qualified Osage voters as sponsors and shall be filed with the person authorized by Osage law to receive the same. The application shall be certified, if found in proper form. Denial of certification shall be subject to judicial review.

Section 3. *Petition for Initiative or Referendum*: After certification of the application, a petition containing a summary of the subject matter shall be prepared by the person authorized by Osage law to do so for circulation by the sponsors. If signed by qualified Osage voters who are equal in number to at least (15) fifteen percent of the electorate, it may be filed.

Section 4. *Initiative Election*: An initiative petition may be filed at any time. The person authorized by Osage law to do so shall prepare a ballot title and proposition summarizing the proposed law, and shall place them on the ballot for the first election held after adjournment of the legislative session following the filing. If, before the election, substantially the same measure has been enacted, the petition is void.

Section 5. *Referendum Election*: A referendum petition may be filed only within ninety (90) days after adjournment of the legislative session at which the act was passed. The person authorized by Osage law to do so shall prepare a ballot title and proposition summarizing the act and shall place them on the ballot for the first election held after adjournment of that session.

Section 6. *Enactment and Rejection*: If a majority of the votes cast on the proposition favor its adoption, the initiated measure is enacted. If a majority of the votes cast on the proposition favor the rejection of an act referred, it is rejected. The person authorized by Osage law to do so shall certify the election returns. An initiated law becomes effective ninety (90) days after certification, is not subject to veto by the Principal Chief, and may not be repealed by the Osage Nation Congress within two (2) years of its effective date. It may be amended at any time. An act rejected by referendum is void thirty (30) days after certification. Additional procedures for the initiative and referendum may be prescribed by Osage law.

Section 7. *Restrictions*: The initiative shall not be used to dedicate revenues, make or repeal appropriations, create courts, define the jurisdiction of courts or prescribe their rules, or enact local or special legislation. The referendum shall not be applied to dedications of revenue, to appropriations, or to laws necessary for the immediate preservation of the public peace, health, or safety of the Osage People. No article, section, or provision of the Osage Nation Constitution shall be amended except as provided in Article XX of this Constitution.

Section 8. *Recall*: All elected and/or appointed officials of the Osage Nation are subject to recall by the qualified Osage voters. The grounds for recall of a judicial officer shall be established by the Osage Nation Supreme Court. The grounds for recall of an officer other than a judge are serious malfeasance or nonfeasance, during the term of office, in the performance of the duties of the office or a conviction, during the term of office, of a felony or conviction of a misdemeanor involving moral turpitude. After certification of the Application, as set forth in Section 2 of this Article, a petition for recall shall be prepared by the person authorized by Osage law to do so and the petition shall set forth the specific conduct that may warrant recall. A recall petition may not be issued for circulation by the sponsors until the Osage Nation Supreme Court has determined that the facts alleged in the petition are true and are sufficient grounds for issuing a recall petition. A recall petition must be signed by qualified Osage voters who are equal in number to at least fifteen (15) percent of the electorate. Upon a determination by the person authorized by Osage law to so determine that a petition has been signed by at least the minimum number of eligible voters, a recall election must be conducted in the manner provided by Osage law. The incumbent shall continue to perform the duties of the office until the recall election results are officially declared and, unless the incumbent declines or no longer qualifies, the incumbent shall without filing be deemed to have filed for the recall election. A recall election may not occur less than six (6) months before the end of the officer's term. An officer who is removed from office by a recall election or who resigns from office after a petition for recall issues may not be appointed to fill the vacancy that is created. Additional procedures and grounds for recall may be prescribed by the Osage Nation Congress.

ARTICLE XII—REMOVAL

Section 1. *Grounds for Removal*: All elected and appointed officers of the Osage Nation shall be subject to removal from office for cause, including but not limited to willful neglect of duty, malfeasance in office, habitual abuse of alcohol or drugs, inability to meet qualifications to serve, conviction of a felony or conviction of a misdemeanor involving moral turpitude while in office.

Section 2. *Rules and Procedures*: Removal of Osage Nation Officers shall originate in the Osage Nation Congress, except as otherwise provided in the Osage Nation Constitution. The motion for removal shall list fully the basis for the proceeding and must be approved by a two-thirds (2/3) vote of the members. Trial on removal shall then be conducted by the Osage Nation Congress with the accused afforded due process and an opportunity to be heard. An Osage Nation Supreme Court Justice, designated by the Supreme Court, shall preside at the trial. Concurrence of five-sixths (⅚) of the members of the Osage Nation Congress is required for a judgment of removal. The judgment shall not extend further than to removal from office and disqualification to hold and enjoy any office of honor, trust or profit in the Osage Nation, but shall not prevent proceedings in the courts on the same or related charges.

The Osage Nation Congress may prescribe additional rules and procedures that are necessary to implement the provisions of this Article.

ARTICLE XIII—SUFFRAGE AND ELECTIONS

Section 1. *Qualified Voters*: All enrolled members of the Osage Nation who shall have attained the age of eighteen (18) years and are registered to vote as provided by Osage law shall be qualified to vote under the authority of this Constitution.

Section 2. *Election Code*: The Osage Nation Congress shall enact an election code governing all necessary election procedures.

Section 3. *Election Board*: The Osage Nation Congress shall enact a law creating an Election Board that shall be charged with conducting both General and Special Elections.

Section 4. *General Elections*: General Elections shall be held on the first Monday in June commencing in 2006 and next in 2010 and every even numbered year thereafter.

Section 5. *Special Elections*: Special Elections may be held as provided by Osage law. Special Elections shall provide ample notice to Osage voters as provided by Osage law.

Section 6. *Contested Elections*: Contested elections shall be determined by a Trial Court of the Osage Nation in such manner as shall be prescribed by Osage law.

Section 7. *Secret Ballots*: All elections shall be conducted by secret ballot, and a majority of the votes cast shall determine the action or result thereon unless otherwise provided by this Constitution or Osage law.

ARTICLE XIV—VILLAGES

Section 1. *Recognized Villages*: The recognized villages of the Osage Nation are: (a) the Grayhorse Indian Village, (b) the Pawhuska Indian Village, and (c) the Hominy Indian Village.

The Osage Nation Congress recognizes and respects that each village has its own traditions, customs, and history.

Section 2. *Reserved Status*: The Grayhorse Indian Village, the Pawhuska Indian Village and the Hominy Indian Village shall be reserved exclusively for the use and benefit of the Osage Indians pursuant to the act of June 28, 1906 (34 Stat. 539), as amended by the act of June 24, 1938 (52 Stat. 1034).

Section 3. *Governance*: The laws enacted by the Osage Nation Congress apply with equal force to all territory located within the jurisdiction of the Nation, including the three villages, and to the extent any action taken by a village is inconsistent with the laws of the Nation, such action shall be deemed void.

ARTICLE XV—NATURAL RESOURCES
AND MINERALS MANAGEMENT

Section 1. *General Authority*: The legislature of the Osage Nation shall provide for the utilization, development and conservation of all natural resources within the territory of the Nation for the maximum benefit of the Osage People.

Section 2. *Osage Mineral Estate*: The oil, gas, coal, and/or other minerals within the boundaries of the Osage Reservation are hereby reserved to the Osage Nation pursuant to the Act of June 28, 1906 (34 Stat. 539), as amended, and is hereby designated the Osage Mineral Estate.

Section 3. *Osage Mineral Royalties*: The right to income from mineral royalties shall be respected and protected by the Osage Nation through the Osage Minerals Council formerly known as the Osage Tribal Council and composed of eight (8) members elected by the mineral royalty interest holders.

Section 4. *Management of the Osage Mineral Estate*: The mineral estate of the Osage Reservation is reserved to the Osage Nation. The government of the Osage Nation shall have the perpetual obligation to ensure the preservation of the Osage Mineral Estate. The government shall further ensure that the rights of members of the Osage Nation to income derived from that mineral estate are protected.

To discharge those obligations, the Osage Nation hereby creates a minerals management agency, designated the Osage Minerals Council, consisting of members of the Osage Nation who are entitled to receive mineral royalty income from the Osage Mineral Estate, as provided by federal law. Only Osage mineral royalty interest holders shall be entitled to vote in electing the Osage Minerals Council.

The Osage Minerals Council is recognized by the Osage Nation government as an independent agency within the Osage Nation established for the sole purpose of continuing its previous duties to administer and develop the Osage Mineral Estate in accordance with the Osage Allotment Act of June 28, 1906, as amended, with no legislative authority for the Osage Nation government.

As an independent agency within the Osage Nation, the Osage Minerals Council may promulgate its own rules and regulations as long as such rules and regulations are not inconsistent with the laws neither of the Osage Nation nor with the rules and regulations established by the United States Congress in the 1906 Allotment Act.

The Osage Minerals Council shall have the power to consider and approve leases and to propose other forms of development of the Osage Mineral Estate. Mineral leases approved and executed by the Council shall be deemed approved by the Osage Nation unless, within five (5) working days, written objection is received from the Office of the Principal Chief that the executed lease or other development activity violates Osage law or regulation. Any dispute that arises through this process may be heard before the Supreme Court of the Osage Nation Judiciary.

All leases or other forms of agreement for development of the Osage Mineral Estate shall comply with applicable federal law and all laws and regulations of the Osage Nation. The Osage Minerals Council shall exercise the administrative authority delegated under this Constitution, the laws of the Osage Nation, and as permitted by federal law.

Section 5. *Preservation of Hunting and Fishing*: Hunting and fishing and the taking of game and fish are a valued part of our heritage that shall be forever preserved for the Osage People and shall be managed by Osage law and regulation for the public good.

ARTICLE XVI—OSAGE CULTURE AND LANGUAGE

Section 1. *Preservation of Linguistic and Cultural Lifeways*: The Osage People have the inherent right to preserve and foster their historic linguistic and cultural lifeways.

The Osage Nation shall protect and promote the language, culture and traditional ways of the Osage People.

ARTICLE XVII—OSAGE HEALTH, EDUCATION, AND WELFARE

Section 1. *Health Care*: The Osage Nation shall provide for the protection and advancement of a health care system for the Osage People by the ongoing development of services for the treatment, management and prevention of illnesses and chronic diseases, and of services that promote mental and physical well-being.

Section 2. *Care of the Elders*: The Osage Nation shall provide for the security of Osage elders by establishing and promoting programs to contribute to their economic, physical, and social well-being.

Section 3. *Care of Our Children*: The Osage Nation shall provide for the care and safety of Osage children by establishing and promoting programs that contribute to protecting, nurturing, and developing the minds, bodies and spirits of our children.

Section 4. *Education*: The education of Osage People is recognized as being essential to building a prosperous and self-determining society. The Osage Nation shall protect and promote education by providing for and supporting a system of high quality early childhood learning programs for its children, advocating on behalf of Osage students for improvements in the public elementary and secondary school systems within the Osage Reservation through intergovernmental agreements, and developing effective tribal education programs that allow Osage students to obtain the skills and resources necessary for a post-secondary education.

ARTICLE XVIII—RESERVED POWERS

The powers enumerated in this Constitution are not exclusive, and the remaining sovereign powers of the Osage Nation are reserved to the Osage People. Adoption of this Constitution does not constitute an agreement on the part of the Osage Nation to limit the exercise by the Osage Nation of any right or power it may otherwise be entitled to exercise.

ARTICLE XIX—SOVEREIGN IMMUNITY

Section 1. *Immunity of Osage Nation from Suit*: As a sovereign Indian nation, the Osage Nation and all administrative offices, departments, agencies, and instrumentalities of the Osage Nation shall be immune from suit or process in any forum except to the extent that the Osage Nation Congress expressly waives its sovereign immunity. The Osage Nation's sovereign immunity shall extend to officials and employees of the Osage Nation when acting within the scope of their duties and authority.

ARTICLE XX—AMENDMENT OF CONSTITUTION

Section 1. *Amendment by Legislature*: Amendments to this Constitution may be proposed by the Osage Nation Congress. Proposed amendments agreed to by five-sixths (⅚) of the members in Congress shall be put before the Osage People for their approval or rejection at the next general election, except when the legislature shall order a special election for that purpose.

If at least sixty-five percent (65%) of Osage electors voting on a proposed amendment approve the same, it shall become part of the Constitution and shall abrogate or amend existing provisions of the Constitution at the end of thirty (30) days after the date of the election at which it was approved.

Section 2. *Amendment by Petition*: Amendments may be proposed to this Constitution by petition of the qualified electors of the Osage Nation. Every petition shall include the full text of the proposed amendment, and be signed by qualified electors of the Osage Nation equal in number to at least twenty-five (25%) percent of the electorate. Such petitions shall be filed with the person authorized by law to receive the same at least ninety (90) days before the election at which the proposed amendment is to be voted upon. Any such petition shall be in the form, and shall be signed and circulated in such manner, as prescribed by Osage law. The person authorized by law to receive such petition shall upon its receipt determine, as provided by law, the validity and sufficiency of the signatures on the petition, and make an official announcement thereof at least sixty (60) days prior to the election at which the proposed amendment is to be voted upon.

Any amendment proposed by such petition shall be submitted, not less than ninety (90) days after it was filed, to the Osage electors at the next general election. Such proposed amendment, existing provisions of the Constitution which would be altered or abrogated thereby, and the question as it shall appear on the ballot shall be published in full as provided by Osage law. Copies of such publication shall be prominently posted in each polling place, at tribal administration offices, and furnished to news media as provided by Osage law.

The ballot to be used in such election shall contain a statement of the purpose of the proposed amendment, expressed in not more than one hundred (100) words, exclusive of caption. Such statement of purpose and caption shall be prepared by the person who is so authorized by Osage law, and shall consist of a true and impartial statement of the purpose of the amendment in such language as shall create no prejudice for or against the proposed amendment.

If the proposed amendment is approved by sixty-five percent (65%) of the electors voting on the question, it shall become part of the Osage Constitution, and shall abrogate or amend existing provisions of the Constitution at the end of thirty (30) days after the date of the election at which it was approved. If two or more amendments approved by the electors at the same election conflict, that amendment receiving the highest affirmative vote shall prevail.

Section 3. *No Veto Power*: No proposal for amendment of the Osage Nation Constitution adopted in either manner provided by this article shall be subject to veto by the Principal Chief.

ARTICLE XXI—SEVERABILITY

If any provision of the Osage Nation Constitution shall, in the future, be declared invalid or unconstitutional by the Osage Nation Judiciary, the invalid portions shall be severed and the remaining provisions shall remain in full force and effect.

ARTICLE XXII—SAVINGS CLAUSE

Section 1. *Savings Clause*: All laws, resolutions, ordinances and acts of the Osage Nation, formerly known as the Osage Tribe of Indians of Oklahoma, taken before the effective date of this Constitution, including elections and terms of office, shall remain in full force and effect to the extent that said action is consistent with the Osage Nation Constitution and until said laws, resolutions, ordinances and acts are altered by the Osage Nation government, as organized under this Constitution, after the effective date of this Constitution.

Section 2. *Continuity of Governmental Authority and Jurisdiction*: Upon the adoption of this Osage Nation Constitution by a vote of the Osage people, and the election of the members of the Osage Nation Congress and the Executive Officers, all powers, rights, responsibilities, and obligations of a government of, by, and for the Osage people shall pass from the Osage Tribal Council to the Osage Nation government established by this Constitution.

All officers of the Osage Nation, formerly known as the Osage Tribe of Indians of Oklahoma, on the effective date of this Constitution shall continue to perform the duties of their offices in a manner not repugnant of this Constitution until those officers are superseded by newly elected or appointed officers as organized under this Constitution.

Until the Osage Nation Supreme Court and Trial Court provided for in Article VIII of this Constitution are organized and established, the existing courts of the Osage Nation, formerly known as the Osage Tribe of Indians of Oklahoma, its jurisdiction, and the judicial system shall remain as constituted before the effective date of this Constitution, in a manner consistent with this Article.

ARTICLE XXIII—RATIFICATION OF CONSTITUTION

This Constitution, when ratified by a majority vote of the qualified voters of the Osage Nation voting in an election called for that purpose by the Osage Government Reform Commission, shall be effective from the date of approval by the Osage People. It shall be signed by the Principal Chief, the Assistant Principal Chief, members of the 31st Osage Tribal Council and the Osage Government Reform Commission, and sacredly preserved as the fundamental law of the Osage Nation.

Notes

Introduction

1. Personal Communication, June 1, 2005. I used a video camera throughout my research, and most of the quotes in this book are from transcriptions made of meetings or interviews. Only occasionally, such as in this discussion, when I was not recording, were the quotes taken from my notes. All quotes from interviews, meetings, and personal conversations have a date, and the community meetings are also referenced as to their location. When I am referencing a conversation that happened either informally or during a formal interview, I refer to it as a Personal Communication. Even though most people I interviewed did not request anonymity, I have only used the names of the major public figures, particularly those people whose position would not allow their statements to remain anonymous.

2. Ōmae, *End of the Nation State*.

3. Brubaker, "Migration, Membership, and the Modern Nation-State," 77.

4. Burton, *After the Imperial Turn*.

5. Simpson, "Paths toward a Mohawk Nation," 119.

6. Berggren et al., *Why Constitutions Matter*, 12.

7. This approach takes inspiration from various works in political anthropology, including Williams, *Stains on My Name*; Joseph and Nugent, *Everyday Forms of State Formation*; Alonso, "Politics of Space, Time, and Substance"; Palay, "Toward an Anthropology of Democracy"; Simpson, *To the Reserve and Back Again*; and Lambert, *Choctaw Nation*.

8. Roseberry, "Hegemony and the Language of Contention," 358.

9. Burton, *After the Imperial Turn*, 6.

10. Nagan and Hammer, "The Changing Character of Sovereignty in International Law and International Relations," 20.

11. Wolfe, "Settler Colonialism and the Elimination of the Native," 388.

12. Smith, *Everything You Know about Indians Is Wrong*, 27.

13. Mbembe, *On the Postcolony*, 66.

14. Stoler, *Carnal Knowledge and Imperial Power*, 1–2.

15. For more information on Osage ribbon work, see Bailey and Swan, *Art of the Osage*; Callahan, *The Osage Ceremonial Dance I'n-Lon-Schka*.

16. For discussion of artwork as a statement of indigenous sovereignty, see Rickard, "Uncovering/Recovering."

17. For a parallel usage of the term "entanglement," see Thomas, *Entangled Objects*.

18. Dirks, *Colonialism and Culture*, 15.

19. Burton, *After the Imperial Turn*, 85.

20. Haraway, "Situated Knowledges."

21. See Hacking, "Making Up People," for further discussion of the classification of people within the human sciences.

22. Haraway, *Modest_Witness@Second_Millennium.FemaleMan_Meets_Onco Mouse*, 273.

23. Lesser, *Pawnee Ghost Dance Hand Game*, xxii.

24. Medicine, *Learning to Be an Anthropologist and Remaining Native*, 291.

25. Deloria, *Custer Died for Your Sins*, quoted in Medicine, *Learning to Be an Anthropologist and Remaining Native*, 290.

26. Medicine, *Learning to Be an Anthropologist and Remaining Native*, 177.

27. Simpson, "On Ethnographic Refusal," 126.

28. Simpson, *To the Reserve and Back Again*, 11.

29. Lambert, *Choctaw Nation*, 11.

30. Ibid., 15.

31. Ibid., 10.

32. Many academics, including other anthropologists, political scientists, literary critics, and historians, have influenced my understanding and presentation of the 2004–6 Osage reform process. Their work will be cited throughout this book.

33. Lemont, *American Indian Constitutional Reform*, 88–89.

34. Medicine, *Learning to Be an Anthropologist and Remaining Native*, 290.

35. Delgado and Stefancic, *Critical Race Theory*, 3.

Chapter 1

1. Rollings, *Unaffected by the Gospel*.

2. Ibid.

3. Jackson, *Letters of the Lewis and Clark Expedition*, 200.

4. Ibid., 201.

5. Rollings, *Unaffected by the Gospel*.

6. Burns, *A History of the Osage People*.

7. Kappler, *Indian Treaties, 1778–1883*, 878.

8. Deloria and Lytle, *American Indians, American Justice*.

9. Little is known about the circumstances surrounding the 1861 Constitution. This is a topic that needs further research.

10. Beede, "Osage Agency, Indian Territory," 92.

11. Wilson, *The Underground Reservation*.

12. Warrior, *Tribal Secrets*, 75.

13. Ibid.

14. Freeman, "Report of Osage Agency," 241.

15. Burns, *A History of the Osage People*.

16. Ibid.

17. Wilkins and Lomawaima, *Uneven Ground*.

18. Prucha, *Great Father*.

19. This effort began in the late 1860s, in the peace commissions that followed the Civil War. At the Okmulgee Council, there was an effort to block allotment once and for all, but President Grant had the language changed, allowing for later

allotment, if the nations agreed. See Denson, *Demanding the Cherokee Nation*; and Genetin-Pilawa, *Confining Indians*.

20. Wilson, *Underground Reservation*.

21. Many different arguments have been made about why the Osage were able to negotiate such a beneficial allotment: because of the preexisting minerals leases, because it was the personal project of Chief James Bigheart, or simply because of the "steadfast resistance" Osage showed toward allotment. See Moore, "The Enduring Reservations of Oklahoma," 95; Baird, *Osage People*, 70; and Wilson, *Underground Reservation*, 97. More research is needed on the exact reasons behind the uniqueness of Osage allotment and the Mineral Estate.

22. Burns, *A History of the Osage People*.

23. Skibine, "Cautionary Tale of the Osage Indian Nation."

24. As recently as February 2011, Kugee Supernaw, a second-term Osage Nation representative to Congress, wrote, "We know that tribes that do not have a functioning language and culture, and a land base may face termination in the future." Supernaw, "Notes to the Nation," 1. While this was part of his larger argument for his bill to buy more lands throughout the reservation, he does not provide any citation for this argument but just assumes the connections among language, culture, land, and recognition.

25. 457 F.Supp. 1318, 1324.

26. 640 F.2d 269 [1981].

27. Osage National Council letter to Osage tribesmen, date unknown.

28. Personal Communication, July 20, 2004.

29. *Fletcher v. United States*, 116 F.3d 1315.

30. Pawhuska Community Meeting, January 19, 2006.

31. Warrior, *People and the Word*.

32. Leonard Maker, Personal Communication, August 2, 2011.

33. Jorgensen, *Rebuilding Native Nations*.

34. Ibid., 17.

35. Personal Communication, December 29, 2004.

36. Personal Communication, August 2, 2011.

37. Ibid.

38. Lemont, *American Indian Constitutional Reform*.

39. Ibid.

40. Personal Communication, July 20, 2004.

41. Personal Communication, May 12, 2005.

42. Personal Communication, May 23, 2005.

43. OTC Committee Meeting, February 7, 2005.

44. Personal Communication, July 30, 2006.

45. Lemont, *American Indian Constitutional Reform*.

46. Ibid.

47. Maker, "Osage Government Reform Project Comprehensive Plan," 8.

48. Personal Communication, July 20, 2004.

49. Ibid.

50. Osage News, "Meet the Osage Government Reform Commission."

51. Personal Communication, May 12, 2005.

52. OGRC Business Meeting, May 23, 2005.

53. For a good discussion of the conditions necessary for relationship building among negotiators, see Haberfeld, "Process of Constitutional Reform."

54. OGRC Business Meeting, June 20, 2005.

55. Meeting for Osage employees, November 7, 2005.

56. Lemont, *American Indian Constitutional Reform*, 238.

57. Negotiated rulemaking was first outlined in the 1980s as part of an effort to increase stakeholder participation in federal lawmaking. Usually a federal agency works with various interest groups in person to negotiate the terms of a proposed law or administrative rule. While this process often consumes far more resources than other rulemaking procedures, it does bring different groups to the lawmaking table. See Haberfeld, "Process of Constitutional Reform."

58. Lemont, *American Indian Constitutional Reform*.

59. Ibid.

60. Maker, "Osage Government Reform Project Comprehensive Plan."

61. Skiatook Community Meeting, May 12, 2005.

62. Personal Communication, July 11, 2006.

63. Hominy Community Meeting, February 28, 2006.

64. Personal Communication, December 28, 2010.

65. Only one question produced little consensus, question six, which read, "Do you prefer the Minerals (Section 9) Council be permanently integrated in the new Government?" To this question, 37 percent answered yes, 45 percent answered no, and 18 percent were undecided.

66. Priscilla Iba, Personal Communication, November 5, 2011.

67. Personal Communication, July 30, 2006.

68. Preamble Writing Meeting, January 30, 2006.

69. While my primary role in the 2004–6 reform was to document the process, from time to time I was also a participant. In addition to sending in a questionnaire about the reform process and voting in all of the Osage elections, I, on occasion, also gave advice. Sometimes this advice was solicited and taken seriously and other times it was neither.

70. Preamble Writing Meeting, January 30, 2006.

71. In February 2006, shortly before the passage of the 2006 Constitution, the Osage Shareholders Association (OSA) sent out a mailing to all Osage annuitants. In the letter, it listed seven reasons why people should "Vote No for a Better Future," including "insufficient protection of Tribal membership," "insufficient protection of the Osage Mineral Estate," "more power to the government at the expense of the people," "more power to the chief," "more power to the tribal courts," "less power to the National Congress," and "lack of popular participation in the reform process." Under each of these, the association included a short explanation. On March 1, the Osage Government Reform Commission (OGRC) responded with its own mailer with the same seven categories and its response. The November 2005 referendum vote drew 1,670 voters, and the March 2006 ratification of the constitution drew

2,182. While the total number of people who were eligible for Osage citizenship is estimated to be between 12,000 and 16,000, in February 2006, there were only 5,755 people with Osage membership cards, many of whom were under the eligible voting age. Osage News, "Membership Needs to Hear from YOU!" Part of the reason for the low number of membership cards was that it was a new process, with most people only having Certificate Degree of Indian Blood (CDIB) cards from the BIA. Another reason was that many people of Osage descent had moved away from the reservation and had lost all contact with the Osage Nation. In comparison, 55.3 percent of the voting-age population turned out for the 2004 presidential election, and 37.1 percent voted in the 2006 federal election. Federal Election Commission, "National Voter Turnout in Federal Elections." Thus the Osage election was on par with the average turnouts for federal election.

72. Participants in this forum made frequent complaints that the document was poorly written and gave too much authority to the executive branch. The primary concern of the members of the OSA, however, always revolved around protecting their authority over their headrights. Also evident in these discussions is the significant role that they thought the U.S. government should play in Osage life.

73. Lemont, *American Indian Constitutional Reform*.

Chapter 2

1. Departments during this time included the Boys and Girls Club, CDIB Membership, Child Support Services, Child Care/Day Care Program, Community Health Representatives Program, Clinical/Medical Services, Counseling Center, Cultural Center, Education Department, Environmental and Natural Resources, Fitness Center, Food Distribution Center, Gaming Commission, Gaming Enterprise Board, Head Start Program, Historic Preservation, Home Health Care, Housing Department, Human Resources Department, Language Department, Law Enforcement Department, Osage Tribal Museum, Osage Data, Planning Office, Prevention Programs, Properties, Social Services Agency, Temporary Assistance to Needy Families Program, Tax Commission, Title VI Department, Transportation Improvement Program, and Women, Infant, and Children Program.

2. In order to take more control of the process by which the BIA awarded CDIB cards, the 31st Osage Tribal Council (2000–2004) contracted with the BIA and created the CDIB Department within the Osage Nation. This department was intended to help Osage fill out the necessary paperwork, but ultimately it was still the BIA that determined the criteria for the card and approved all cards issued. This card is not equivalent to citizenship in the American Indian nation, which is handled separately with its own criteria determined by the nation. To receive an Osage CDIB card, one has to prove descent from someone listed on the BIA's 1906 allotment roll.

3. Personal Communication, July 1, 2005.

4. OGRC Business Meeting, June 27, 2005.

5. Burton, *After the Imperial Turn*, 196.

6. See Kauanui, *Hawaiian Blood*; and Baker, *Anthropology and the Racial Politics of Culture*; Barker, *Native Acts*; Wolfe, "Race and the Trace of History."

7. See Garroutte, *Real Indians*; Hamill, *Going Indian*; Kauanui, *Hawaiian Blood*; Meyer, "American Indian Blood Quantum Requirements"; Strong and Van Winkle, "Indian Blood"; and Sturm, *Blood Politics*.

8. Latour, "On the Partial Existence of Existing and Nonexisting Objects," 255.

9. Mathews, *The Osages, Children of the Middle Waters*, 53.

10. La Flesche, *War Ceremony and Peace Ceremony of the Osage Indians*, 83–84.

11. Rollings, *The Osage*. For further discussion of the practice of adoption and the historical transformation of outsiders within American Indian communities, see Strong, "Transforming Outsiders"; and Perdue, *"Mixed Blood" Indians*.

12. Burns, *A History of the Osage People*.

13. McGee, "The Siouan Indians."

14. For an in-depth history of blood, see Meyer, "American Indian Blood Quantum Requirements."

15. Stoler, *Carnal Knowledge and Imperial Power*, 24.

16. One of the key contributors to these understandings of racialized bodies was the geologist Samuel G. Morton. Borrowing from phrenological theories of his day, including those of eighteenth-century German physiologist and physical anthropologist Johann Friedrich Blumenbach, Morton began the collection and classification of human skulls in 1830. By comparing the various weights of lead shot required to fill human skulls, Morton was able to locate older concepts of "savagery" within the body itself. Bieder, *Science Encounters the Indian*.

17. Stoler, *Carnal Knowledge and Imperial Power*.

18. For further discussion of the differences among understandings of Indian and black blood, see Baker, *From Savage to Negro*.

19. Jefferson, *Writings of Thomas Jefferson*, 467.

20. Ibid.

21. Mathews, *The Osages, Children of the Middle Waters*, 307.

22. Ibid.

23. Kappler, *Indian Treaties, 1778–1883*, 268.

24. Ibid., 684.

25. Mathews, *The Osages, Children of the Middle Waters*.

26. Burns, *A History of the Osage People*; Mathews, *The Osages, Children of the Middle Waters*; Wilson, *The Underground Reservation*.

27. Ibid., 327.

28. Harris, *Whiteness as Property*, describes the way property came to be associated with whiteness, to the exclusion of both blacks and American Indians. Removal displaced Indians from the land without the equivalent level of compensation that would have been given to whites; and allotment, with its individual distribution of land to each Indian individual, was based on the assumption that Indians could be made into whites by forcing them into property ownership.

29. Price Annual Report of the Commissioner of Indian Affairs to the Secretary of the Interior for the Year 1884, XXVII.

30. In some cases, the federal government did go as far as to impose a blood quantum on tribal nations. For a discussion of how issues of blood were imposed

on indigenous Hawaiians, see Kauanui, *Hawaiian Blood*; for its impact on the Comanche, see Foster, *Being Comanche*.

31. Commissioner of Indian Affairs, *Report of the Commissioner of Indian Affairs to the Secretary of the Interior*, 34.

32. Ibid. A "patent in fee" means that the land was owned outright and no longer had any federally imposed restrictions on its use or sale. "Competency" became the legal term, meaning that the Indian had been deemed capable of handling his own affairs and could thus be issued a patent in fee.

33. Wilson, *Underground Reservation*; Burns, *A History of the Osage People*; Warrior, *People and the Word*; McAuliffe, *Bloodland*.

34. Vaux, "Appendix A. Report on the Osage Indians, Oklahoma," 341.

35. For further discussion of these issues, particularly surrounding miscegenation, see Scheick, *The Half-Blood*; White, *Children of the French Empire*; Biolsi, *Deadliest Enemies*; Basson, *White Enough to Be American*; Simms, "Miscegenation and Racism"; and Chludzinski, *Fear of Colonial Miscegenation*.

36. Vaux, "Appendix A. Report on the Osage Indians, Oklahoma," 350.

37. Sells, *Reports of the Department of the Interior*, 3.

38. Ibid., 4.

39. Ibid., 5.

40. For further discussion of the development of racial attitudes, particularly around mixed-blood Indians in the nineteenth century, see Perdue, *"Mixed Blood" Indians*.

41. Spruhan, "Indian as Race and Indian as Political Status," 29.

42. Osage Tribal Museum, "About the Osage Tribal Museum."

43. Personal Communication, February 4, 2005.

44. Garroutte, *Real Indians*.

45. See O'Nell, *Disciplined Hearts*; Sturm, *Blood Politics*; and Garroutte, *Real Indians*.

46. Hill, "Language, Race, and White Public Space."

47. Meyer, "American Indian Blood Quantum Requirements," 241.

48. Ibid., 244.

49. Wolfe, "Settler Colonialism and the Elimination of the Native."

50. Kauanui, *Hawaiian Blood*, 9.

51. Personal Communication, February 4, 2005.

52. Garroutte, *Real Indians*; Sturm, *Blood Politics*.

53. Sturm, *Blood Politics*, 100.

54. Personal Communication, August 20, 2005.

55. Pawhuska Community Meeting, April 22, 2005.

56. Ibid.

57. Lambert, *Choctaw Nation*, 200.

58. Personal Communication, February 4, 2005.

59. Personal Communication, October 17, 2005.

60. In 1905, *Waldron v. United States* set the precedent that recognized American Indian nations' inherent authority to determine their own citizenship standards.

61. OGRC Business Meeting, August 18, 2005.

62. Personal Communication, July 20, 2004.

63. Cook-Martín and FitzGerald, "Liberalism and the Limits of Inclusion."

64. Harris, "Whiteness as Property," 1730.

65. Chin et al., "Arizona Senate Bill 1070."

66. The Osage Tribal Council approved the official election codes for the referendum in a unanimous vote on September 28, 2005.

67. OGRC Business Meeting, August 18, 2005.

68. Strong and Van Winkle, "Indian Blood," 562.

69. Ibid.

70. Allen, "Blood (and) Memory," 111.

71. Pipestem, "How Do Vizenor and Momaday Use Imagination?"

72. Osage Government Reform Commission, "OGRC Message Board."

73. Kauanui, *Hawaiian Blood*, 9.

74. Malkki, "National Geographic," 28.

75. Rifkin, "Romancing Kinship," 27.

76. Personal Communication, February 4, 2005.

77. Tulsa Writing Retreat, January 6, 2006.

78. OGRC Drafting Meeting, January 23, 2006.

79. 2006 Osage Nation Constitution, 2.

Chapter 3

1. Dombrowski, *Against Culture*.

2. Urban, *Metaculture*.

3. Strickland, "Absurd Ballet of American Indian Policy"; Dombrowski, *Against Culture*; Medicine, *Learning to Be an Anthropologist and Remaining Native*; Strum, *Blood Politics*; Garroutte, *Real Indians*; Smith, *Everything You Know about Indians Is Wrong*; Barker, *Native Acts*.

4. Deloria, *Custer Died for Your Sins*, 81–82.

5. On anthropology, American Indians, and culture, see Strickland, "Absurd Ballet of American Indian Policy"; Dombrowski, *Against Culture*; Medicine, *Learning to Be an Anthropologist and Remaining Native*; and Baker, *Anthropology and the Racial Politics of Culture*.

6. Dirks, *Colonialism and Culture*, 3–4.

7. Bruyneel, *Third Space of Sovereignty*, xvii.

8. To see how this played out in U.S. American Indian policy, particularly the Indian Reorganization Act, see Spruhan, "Indian as Race and Indian as Political Status"; and Rifkin, *When Did Indians Become Straight*.

9. Vizenor defines "survivance" as "more than survival, more than endurance or mere response; the stories of survivance are an active presence." This is part of his larger argument that the "Indian" is an invention of the white man and that only upon moving past such a construction can Indians escape domination. Vizenor, *Fugitive Poses*, 15.

10. Dombrowski, *Against Culture*, 186.

11. Smith, *Everything You Know about Indians Is Wrong*, 6.

12. Lyons, *X-Marks*, 186.

13. Ibid., 188.

14. Of course, as with Deloria, Vizenor, and Smith, mentioned above, many American Indian peoples are skeptical of the cultural entanglement and its consequences. See also Strickland, "Absurd Ballet of American Indian Policy"; Medicine, *Learning to Be an Anthropologist and Remaining Native*; Lambert, *Choctaw Nation*; and Simpson, "On Ethnographic Refusal."

15. Simpson, "On Ethnographic Refusal."

16. Tulsa Community Meeting, May 5, 2005.

17. Osage Sovereignty Day speech, February 4, 2005.

18. Ibid.

19. Osage Nation Language Department, "Mission Statement."

20. Personal Communication, July 14, 2005.

21. The term "informal leaders" is used throughout this chapter to describe the nonpolitical leaders who are in charge of activities viewed as cultural, such as the Language Revitalization Program, the *In-lon-Schka* dances, or the Native American Church meetings.

22. Callahan, *Osage Ceremonial Dance*.

23. Ibid., 21.

24. Personal Communication, July 18, 2006.

25. Ibid.

26. Ibid.

27. This is not an uncommon connection. See Sturm, *Blood Politics*; and Garroutte, *Real Indians*.

28. Winders, "Bringing Back the (B)order."

29. Personal Communication, November 19, 2005.

30. Hominy Community Meeting, February 28, 2006.

31. Writing Retreat, January 7, 2006.

32. The term "traditional people" here refers to the informal leaders discussed throughout this chapter.

33. Writing Retreat, January 7, 2006.

34. At the time of this writing, the criteria for federal recognition included the following: continuous recognition as an American Indian entity since 1900, existence as a distinct community with political control from historical times to the present, and a governing document with citizenship criteria composed of descendants of a historical Indian tribe who are not citizens of any other recognized tribe and who are not part of a tribe terminated by the government (25 C.F.R. 83.7).

35. Tulsa University Legal Training Session, May 19, 2005.

36. Osage Nation Planning Office, *Osage Government Reform Project Comprehensive Plan*, 14.

37. Leonard Maker, Personal Communication, July 20, 2004.

38. Native Nations Institute Seminar, March 27, 2005.

39. Ibid.

40. Lemont, *American Indian Constitutional Reform*, 3.

41. Ibid., 4.

42. Ibid.

43. Povinelli, *Cunning of Recognition*.

44. Using the extensive writings of Francis La Flesche, Garrick A. Bailey, a citizen of the Omaha tribe who conducted research on the Osage around the turn of the twentieth century, pieced together a picture of Osage cosmology and tribal organization. See Bailey and La Flesche, *The Osage and the Invisible World*.

45. Tulsa University Legal Training, May 19, 2005.

46. Bailey and La Flesche, *The Osage and the Invisible World*, 40.

47. Tulsa University Legal Training, May 19, 2005.

48. For a similar critique of culture, see Dombrowski, *Against Culture*.

49. 1994 Osage Nation Constitution, 12. From 1994 until 1997, the Osage operated a constitutional government created from the court case *Fletcher v. United States*, in which Judge James O. Ellison mandated a constitutional referendum process. The 10th Circuit Court of Appeals in Denver, Colorado, overturned this constitution, arguing that Ellison's mandate had violated the sovereign immunity of the Osage Tribal Council.

50. Bailey and La Flesche, *The Osage and the Invisible World*.

51. Personal Communication, February 7, 2006.

52. Mathews, *The Osages, Children of the Middle Waters*, 53.

53. Ibid.

54. Burns, *A History of the Osage People*; Warrior, *People and the Word*.

55. Bailey and La Flesche, *The Osage and the Invisible World*, 6.

56. Warrior, *Tribal Secrets*, 74.

57. Personal Communication, May 24, 2005.

58. Personal Communication, January 1, 2006.

59. Rifkin, *When Did Indians Become Straight*.

60. Lyons, *X-Marks*, 3.

61. OTC Committee Meeting, August 22, 2005.

62. Personal Communication, August 22, 2005.

63. Ibid.

64. OGRC Business Meeting, February 6, 2006.

65. OGRC Business Meeting, September 12, 2005.

66. Writing Retreat, January 7, 2006.

67. Ibid.

68. Ibid.

69. Ibid.

70. 2006 Osage Nation Constitution, 17.

71. Ibid., 5.

72. In the Preamble to the 2006 Osage Nation Constitution, there are several additional places where the old ways are honored.

73. Jorgensen, *Rebuilding Native Nations*, xiii.

Chapter 4

1. Burns, *A History of the Osage People*.

2. Grayhorse Community Meeting, January 12, 2006.

3. Wilson, *Underground Reservation*.

4. Weyler, *Blood of the Land*.

5. Moore, "The Enduring Reservations of Oklahoma."

6. Subcommittee of the Committee on Indian Affairs, "Division of Lands and Moneys of the Osage Tribe of Indians."

7. Harmon, *Rich Indians*.

8. The 2,230th share of the Mineral Estate was granted to a white woman for her lifetime because of her service to the Osage Nation. There were only 2,229 Osage listed on the roll. For more on the 1906 roll, see Wilson, *Underground Reservation*.

9. Ibid.

10. Federal Bureau of Investigation, "Osage Indian Murders."

11. Harmon, *Rich Indians*, 197.

12. Ibid.

13. Ibid., 199.

14. Ibid.

15. Myers, "Osage Nation, U.S., Settle Legal Battle."

16. Public Law 108-431, December 3, 2004.

17. Grayhorse Community Meeting, January 12, 2006.

18. Ibid.

19. Osage Shareholders Association, "OSA Charter."

20. Osage Shareholders Association Meeting, August 29, 2005.

21. Ibid.

22. Tsosie, "Conflict between the Public Trust and the Indian Trust Doctrines."

23. "Treaty with the Osage, 1808."

24. *Cherokee Nation v. Georgia*, 30 U.S. (5 Pet.) at 17, 20 (1831).

25. *Seminole Nation v. United States*, 316 U.S. 286, 296–97 (1942).

26. *United States v. Mitchell*, 463 U.S. 206 (1983).

27. See *Lone Wolf v. Hitchcock*, 185 U.S. 553 (1903), for a full description of Congress' plenary power.

28. DuVal, *Native Ground*, 8.

29. Pawhuska Community Meeting, April 4, 2005.

30. Government Reform Meeting, September 26, 2005.

31. The Osage Nation applies for many grants each year, most of which are federally funded. Grant funds support a range of activities, including Osage language preservation, Head Start equipment, housing-related expenses, drug use prevention, senior services, road repair, and youth summer workforce employment and training. Some of these funds are specifically earmarked for American Indian nations; others are open to any organization performing specific duties.

32. Pawhuska Community Meeting, January 19, 2006.

33. Personal Communication, February 4, 2005.

34. Personal Communication, May 23, 2005.

35. Skiatook Community Meeting, May 12, 2005.

36. OGRC Business Meeting, July 6, 2005.

37. Bartlesville Community Meeting, April 28, 2005.

38. Hominy Community Meeting, January 16, 2006.

39. Personal Communication, September 12, 2005.

40. Crum, "Re: Thank You/Comments."

41. Crum, "Galen Crum."

42. Redcorn, "White Hair Stills the Wind," http://www.osageshareholders.org/disc51_frm.htm.

43. *Jech v. United States*, 09-CV-818 (USDC ND/OK 2009), 19.

44. Ibid., 9.

45. Skibine, "Cautionary Tale of the Osage Indian Nation," 821.

46. 871 F.2d 924 (10th Cir. 1989).

47. Emphasis added.

48. Personal Communication, August 26, 2005.

49. The potential funds for this donation came from the Osage Nation's S-510 fund, which was originally created in 2006 when a non-Indian donated land in Kansas to the Osage Nation with the stipulation that any funds from the land go to Osage annuitants. Shaw, "U.S. Solicitor General Advises Supreme Court."

50. "Re: Black & White World."

51. Ibid.

52. Southside Osage, "Re: Thanks."

53. Ibid.

54. Lemont, *American Indian Constitutional Reform*.

Chapter 5

1. For further discussion of sovereignty's link to state governments, see Hannum, *Autonomy, Sovereignty, and Self-Determination*; Mair, *Primitive Government*; and Gledhill, *Power and Its Disguises*.

2. Alfred, *Peace, Power, Righteousness*.

3. Moreton-Robinson, *Sovereign Subjects*; Trask, *From a Native Daughter*.

4. Bruyneel, *Third Space of Sovereignty*.

5. Nagan and Hammer, "The Changing Character of Sovereignty in International Law and International Relations," 5.

6. The Treaty of Westphalia (1648) is recognized as formally establishing the nation-state system in place of the hierarchical structure at the time, which was dominated by the pope.

7. Lambert, *Choctaw Nation*, 18. See also Cattelino, *High Stakes*.

8. Lambert, *Choctaw Nation*, 17.

9. Ibid.

10. Bruyneel, *Third Space of Sovereignty*, xvii.

11. Personal Communication, February 4, 2005.

12. Osage Sovereignty Day speech, February 4, 2005.

13. Ibid.

14. Ibid.

15. Personal Communication, July 20, 2004.

16. Tulsa Community Meeting, May 5, 2005.

17. OGRC Business Meeting, March 21, 2005.

18. "Harvard Project on American Indian Economic Development."

19. Dallas Community Meeting, November 12, 2005.

20. Personal Communication, February 4, 2005.

21. OGRC Business Meeting, March 21, 2005.

22. Personal Communication, March 23, 2005.

23. Osage Sovereignty Day speech, February 4, 2005.

24. Personal Communication, May 23, 2005.

25. 2006 Osage Nation Constitution, 2.

26. Ibid.

27. The Major Crimes Act (18 U.S.C. 1153) is one of the clearest examples of the federal government's assertion of authority over American Indian nations. Passed in 1885, this act placed seven crimes, including murder and robbery, under the jurisdiction of the federal government when committed by or against Indians within reservation boundaries.

28. 2006 Osage Nation Constitution, 2.

29. For an in-depth look at the underground reservation, see Wilson, *Underground Reservation*.

30. For more on patchwork reservations, see Biolsi, "Imagined Geographies."

31. 2006 Osage Nation Constitution, 3.

32. Pawhuska Community Meeting, March 21, 2006.

33. "Osage County Rancher Found Dead at Home," http://www.examiner-enterprise.com/articles/2007/11/07/news/news129.txt.

34. "Osage Rez or Osage County," 1.

35. For more on the growing reaction to Indian national sovereignty, see Corntassel and Witmer, *Forced Federalism*; Mason, *Indian Gaming*; and Bruyneel, *Third Space of Sovereignty*.

36. Flies-Away, "My Grandma, Her People, and Our Constitution," 153.

37. Brubaker, "Migration, Membership, and the Modern Nation-State."

38. Cited in Crum, "Daily Oklahoman Editorial."

39. Proud Osage, "Internalization of Oppressor, a Legacy of Colonialism."

40. Congress founded the National Indian Gaming Commission in 1988 under the Indian Gaming Regulatory Act (25 U.S.C. 2701 *et seq.*), which set out to provide standards by which Indian nations could be held accountable when conducting gaming on Indian lands. The purpose of the commission is to enforce those standards.

41. Coleman, "Formal Opinion of the National Indian Gaming Commission," 5.

42. Ibid., 6.

43. Ibid., 7.

44. See Mason, *Indian Gaming*.

45. 498 U.S. 505.

46. Bays, "Tobacco Compacts and Motor Fuel Contracts in Oklahoma."

47. As Bays writes, "State legislation created incentive for smoke shop operators to lobby their tribal governments to sign tobacco compacts. . . . Prior to 1992 smoke shops were essentially unregulated, untaxed, and unduly harassed. After 1992, smoke shops began to gain legitimacy, and many grew and expanded." Ibid., 191.

48. Associated Press, "Oklahoma, Tribes, Sign Pacts on Indian Sales of Tobacco," 10B.

49. Bays, "Tobacco Compacts and Motor Fuel Contracts in Oklahoma," 191.

50. For an in-depth critique of the compacting process, see Corntassel and Witmer, *Forced Federalism*.

51. "Osage Nation Stands by Smoke Shop Owners and Tobacco Compact," 6.

52. Those smoke shops near the border were able to negotiate a lesser rate to stay competitive since the states bordering Oklahoma had lower tax rates.

53. Adcock, "Rule Squeezes Smoke Shops."

54. Hinton, "Governor Signs New Tobacco-Tax Rule."

55. Ruckman, "Tribes Unite against Tobacco Pact Woes," 8.

56. Gray, "Letter to the Governor."

57. "Tribe Is Going to Federal Court over State Compact," 4.

58. "Osages to Pursue Reservation Suit," 1.

59. Hinton, "Change Sought on Tax Stamps."

60. For a full discussion of these cases, see Mason, *Indian Gaming*.

61. Pitchlyn, "Osage Nation v. State of Oklahoma," 3.

62. *Osage Nation v. State of Oklahoma Ex Rel.* (10 Cir. No. 03-5162) (2007), 27.

63. Moore, "The Enduring Reservations of Oklahoma," 95.

64. See also Baird, *Osage People*; Wilson, *Underground Reservation*; and Burns, *History of the Osage People*.

65. Strickland, "Absurd Ballet of American Indian Policy," 217.

66. Personal Communication, February 3, 2009.

67. Personal Communication, November 22, 2010.

68. "U.S.: Rez Case Not Worthy," 11.

69. Ibid.

70. Ibid.

71. Ibid.

72. Gray, "Nation Building in Native America and in Egypt."

73. Ibid.

74. Ibid.

Bibliography

Adcock, Clifton. "Rule Squeezes Smoke Shops." *Tulsa World*, April 3, 2008. http://www.tulsaworld.com/news/article.aspx?articleID=20080403_1_A1_hSome38061.

Agamben, Giorgio. *Homo Sacer*. Stanford: Stanford University Press, 1998.

Alfred, Taiaiake. *Peace, Power, Righteousness: An Indigenous Manifesto*. Cambridge: Oxford University Press, 2009.

Allen, Chadwick. "Blood (and) Memory. American Literature." *American Literature* 71, no. 1 (1999): 93–116.

Alonso, A. M. "The Politics of Space, Time, and Substance: State Formation, Nationalism, and Ethnicity." *Annual Review of Anthropology* 23 (1994): 379–405.

Anderson, Benedict. *Imagined Communities*. London: Verso, 1993.

Arendt, Hannah. *On Revolution*. New York: Penguin, 2006.

Associated Press. "Oklahoma, Tribes, Sign Pacts on Indian Sales of Tobacco." *Dallas Morning News*, June 9, 1992.

Bailey, Garrick, and Francis La Flesche. *The Osage and the Invisible World: From the Works of Francis La Flesche*. Norman: University of Oklahoma Press, 1995.

Bailey, Garrick, and Daniel C. Swan. *Art of the Osage*. Seattle: University of Washington Press, 2004.

Baird, David. *The Osage People*. Phoenix: Indian Tribal Series, 1972.

Baker, Lee D. *Anthropology and the Racial Politics of Culture*. Durham: Duke University Press, 2010.

———. *From Savage to Negro: Anthropology and the Construction of Race, 1896–1954*. Berkley: University of California Press, 1998.

Barker, Joanne. *Native Acts: Law, Recognition, and Cultural Authenticity*. Durham: Duke University Press, 2011.

Basson, Lauren. *White Enough to Be American? Race Mixing, Indigenous People, and the Boundaries of State and Nation*. Chapel Hill: University of North Carolina Press, 2008.

Bays, Brad. "Tobacco Compacts and Motor Fuel Contracts in Oklahoma." In *The Tribes and the States*, edited by Brad A. Bays and Erin Hogan Fouberg, 181–210. Lanham: Rowman and Littlefield, 2002.

Beede, Cyrus. "Osage Agency, Indian Territory." In *Annual Report of the Commissioner of Indian Affairs to the Secretary of the Interior*, 90–95. Washington, D.C.: Government Printing Office 1877.

Berggren, Niclas, Nils Karlson, and Joakim Nergelius, eds. *Why Constitutions Matter*. New Brunswick: Transaction Publishers, 2002.

Berry, Carol. "Who Is 'Indian' Varies by Definition." *Indian Country Today*, February 16, 2010. http://www.indiancountrytoday.com/national/plains/84239852.html.

Bieder, Robert. *Science Encounters the Indian, 1820–1880: The Early Years of American Ethnology.* 1st ed. Norman: University of Oklahoma Press, 1986.

Biolsi, Thomas. *Deadliest Enemies: Law and the Making of Race Relations On and Off Rosebud Reservation.* 1st ed. Berkeley: University of California Press, 2001.

————. "Imagined Geographies: Sovereignty, Indigenous Space, and American." *American Ethnologist* 32, no. 2 (2005): 239–59.

Brubaker, Rogers. "Migration, Membership, and the Modern Nation-State: Internal and External Dimensions of the Politics of Belonging." *Journal of Interdisciplinary History* 41, no. 1 (2010): 61–78.

Bruyneel, Kevin. *The Third Space of Sovereignty: The Postcolonial Politics of U.S.-Indigenous Relations.* Minneapolis: University Of Minnesota Press, 2007.

Burns, Louis. *A History of the Osage People.* 1st ed. Fallbrook, Calif.: Ciga Press, 1989.

Burton, Antoinette. *After the Imperial Turn: Thinking with and through the Nation.* Durham: Duke University Press, 2003.

Callahan, Alice. *The Osage Ceremonial Dance I'n-Lon-Schka.* Norman: University of Oklahoma Press, 1990.

Cattelino, Jessica. *High Stakes: Florida Seminole Gaming and Sovereignty.* Durham: Duke University Press, 2008.

Chin, G. J., C. B. Hessick, T. M. Massaro, and M. L. Miller. "Arizona Senate Bill 1070: A Preliminary Report on Legal Issues Raised by Arizona's New Statute Regulating Immigration." *Arizona Legal Studies Discussion Paper* 10-24 (2010): 1–58.

Chludzinski, Katrina. "The Fear of Colonial Miscegenation in the British Colonies of Southeast Asia." *The Forum: Cal Poly's Journal of History* 1, no. 1 (June 1, 2009). http://digitalcommons.calpoly.edu/forum/vol1/iss1/8.

Clifford, James. *The Predicament of Culture.* Cambridge: Harvard University Press, 1988.

Coleman, Penny. "Formal Opinion of the National Indian Gaming Commission Regarding the Osage Reservation." Letter written to Assistant Solicitor of the Department of the Interior Richard Meyers, July 28, 2005.

Commissioner of Indian Affairs. *Annual Report of the Commissioner of Indian Affairs to the Secretary of the Interior.* Washington D.C.: Government Printing Office, 1906.

Cook-Martín, David, and David FitzGerald. "Liberalism and the Limits of Inclusion: Race and Immigration Law in the Americas, 1850–2000." *Journal of Interdisciplinary History* 41, no. 1 (2010): 7–25.

Corntassel, Jeff, and Richard C. Witmer. *Forced Federalism: Contemporary Challenges to Indigenous Nationhood.* Norman: University of Oklahoma Press, 2008.

Crum, Galen. "Daily Oklahoman Editorial." *Osage Shareholders Association*, July 14, 2007. http://www.osageshareholders.org/disc50_frm.htm.

————. "Galen Crum." *Galen Crum Homepage*, December 11, 2010. http://www.galencrum.com/2001.html.

————. "Re: Daily Oklahoman Editorial." *Osage Shareholders Association*, July 15, 2007. http://www.osageshareholders.org/disc50_frm.htm.

————. "Re: Thank You/Comments." *Osage Shareholders Association*, October 22, 2006. http://www.osageshareholders.org/disc51_frm.htm.

Delgado, Richard, and Jean Stefancic. *Critical Race Theory: An Introduction*. New York: New York University Press, 2001.

Deloria, Vine. *Custer Died for Your Sins: An Indian Manifesto*. Norman: University of Oklahoma Press, 1988.

Deloria, Vine, Jr., and Clifford M. Lytle. *American Indians, American Justice*. Austin: University of Texas Press, 1983.

Denson, Andrew. *Demanding the Cherokee Nation: Indian Autonomy and American Culture, 1830–1900*. Lincoln: University of Nebraska Press, 2004.

Dirks, Nicholas. *Colonialism and Culture*. Ann Arbor: University of Michigan Press, 1992.

Dombrowski, Kirk. *Against Culture: Development, Politics, and Religion in Indian Alaska*. Lincoln: University of Nebraska Press, 2001.

DuVal, Kathleen. *The Native Ground: Indians and Colonists in the Heart of the Continent*. Philadelphia: University of Pennsylvania Press, 2007.

Federal Bureau of Investigation. "Osage Indian Murders," n.d. http://foia.fbi.gov/foiaindex/osageind.htm.

Federal Election Commission. "National Voter Turnout in Federal Elections: 1960–2004." *Information Please Database*, 2007. http://www.infoplease.com/ipa/A0781453.html.

Feit, Harvey. "James Bay Crees' Life Projects and Politics: Histories of Place, Animal Partners, and Enduring Relationships." In *In the Way of Development: Indigenous Peoples, Life Projects, and Globalization*, edited by Mario Blaser, Harvey A. Feit, and Glenn McRae, 92–110. London: Zed Books and the Canadian International Development Research Centre, 2004.

Flies-Away, Joseph Thomas. "My Grandma, Her People, and Our Constitution." In *American Indian Constitutional Reform and the Rebuilding of Native Nations*, edited by Eric D. Lemont, 144–65. Austin: University of Texas Press, 2006.

Foster, Morris. *Being Comanche: A Social History of an American Indian Community*. Tucson: University Of Arizona Press, 1991.

Freeman, H.B. "Report of Osage Agency." In *Annual Report of the Commissioner of Indian Affairs*, 241–5. Washington, D.C.: Government Printing Office, 1894.

Garroutte, Eva. *Real Indians: Identity and the Survival of Native America*. Berkeley: University of California Press, 2003.

Genetin-Pilawa, C. Joseph. *Confining Indians: Power, Authority, and the Colonialist Ideologies of Nineteenth-Century Reformers*. Ann Arbor: ProQuest/UMI, 2011.

Gledhill, John. *Power and Its Disguises: Anthropological Perspectives on Politics*. 2nd ed. London: Pluto Press, 2000.

Gramsci, Antonio. *Selections from the Prison Notebooks*. New York: International Publishers, 1971.

Gray, Jim. "Letter to the Governor." *Osage News* 3, no. 2 (February 2006): 7, 10.

————. "Nation Building in Native America and in Egypt." *Facebook*, February 8, 2011. http://www.facebook.com/home.php#!/note.php?note_id=184125264 961422.

Gregory, Derek. *The Dictionary of Human Geography.* 5th ed. Malden, Mass.: Blackwell, 2009.

Haberfeld, Steven. "The Process of Constitutional Reform." In *American Indian Constitutional Reform and the Rebuilding of Native Nations*, edited by Eric D. Lemont, 252–71. Austin: University of Texas Press, 2006.

Hacking, Ian. "Making Up People." In *Reconstructing Individualism: Autonomy, Individuality, and the Self in Western Thought*, edited by Thomas C. Heller, David E. Wellbery, and Morton Sosna, 222–36. Palo Alto: Stanford University Press, 1987.

Hamill, James. *Going Indian.* Urbana: University of Illinois Press, 2006.

Hannum, Hurst. *Autonomy, Sovereignty, and Self-Determination: The Accommodation of Conflicting Rights.* Rev. ed. Philadelphia: University of Pennsylvania Press, 1996.

Haraway, Donna. *Modest_Witness@Second_Millennium.FemaleMan_Meets_OncoMouse: Feminism and Technoscience.* New York: Routledge, 1997.

————. "Situated Knowledges: The Science Question in Feminism and the Privilege of Partial Perspective." *Feminist Studies* (1988): 575–99.

Harmon, Alexandra. *Rich Indians: Native People and the Problem of Wealth in American History.* Chapel Hill: University of North Carolina Press, 2010.

"The Harvard Project on American Indian Economic Development," 2010. http://hpaied.org/about-hpaied/overview.

Hill, Jane H. "Language, Race, and White Public Space." *American Anthropologist* (1998): 680–89.

Hinton, Mick. "Governor Signs New Tobacco-Tax Rule." *Tulsa World*, April 8, 2006.

Jackson, Donald. *Letters of the Lewis and Clark Expedition, With Related Documents, 1783–1854.* 2nd ed. Urbana: University of Illinois Press, 1978.

Jefferson, Thomas. *The Writings of Thomas Jefferson.* Vol. 4. New York: John C. Riker, 1854.

Jorgensen, Miriam. *Rebuilding Native Nations: Strategies for Governance and Development.* Tucson: University of Arizona Press, 2007.

Joseph, Gilbert M., and Daniel Nugent, eds. *Everyday Forms of State Formation: Revolution and the Negotiation of Rule in Modern Mexico.* Durham: Duke University Press, 1994.

Kappler, Charles. *Indian Treaties, 1778–1883.* New York: Interland Publishing, 1972.

Kauanui, J. Kēhaulani. *Hawaiian Blood: Colonialism and the Politics of Sovereignty and Indigeneity.* Durham: Duke University Press, 2008.

La Flesche, Francis. *War Ceremony and Peace Ceremony of the Osage Indians.* Bulletin 101. Washington, D.C.: Smithsonian Institution of American Ethnology, 1939.

Lambert, Valerie. *Choctaw Nation: A Story of American Indian Resurgence.* Lincoln: University of Nebraska Press, 2007.

Latour, Bruno. "On the Partial Existence of Existing and Nonexisting Objects." In *Biographies of Scientific Objects*, edited by Lorraine Daston, 247–69. Chicago: University Of Chicago Press, 2000.

Lemont, Eric D. *American Indian Constitutional Reform and the Rebuilding of Native Nations*. Austin: University of Texas Press, 2006.

Lesser, Alexander. *The Pawnee Ghost Dance Hand Game: Ghost Dance Revival and Ethnic Identity*. Lincoln: University of Nebraska Press, 1996.

Lyons, Scott. *X-Marks: Native Signatures of Assent*. Minneapolis: University of Minnesota Press, 2010.

Mair, Lucy. *Primitive Government*. Bloomington: Indiana University Press, 1977.

Maker, Leonard. "Osage Government Reform Project Comprehensive Plan." February 21, 2005.

Malkki, Liisa. "National Geographic: The Rooting of Peoples and the Territorialization of National Identity among Scholars and Refugees." *Cultural Anthropology* 7, no. 1(1992): 24–44.

Mason, W. Dale. *Indian Gaming: Tribal Sovereignty and American Politics*. Norman: University of Oklahoma Press, 2000.

Mathews, John Joseph. *The Osages, Children of the Middle Waters*. Norman: University of Oklahoma Press, 1961.

Mbembe, Achille. *On the Postcolony*. Berkeley: University of California Press, 2001.

McAuliffe, Dennis. *Bloodland: A Family Story of Oil, Greed, and Murder on the Osage Reservation*. San Francisco: Council Oak Books, 1999.

McGee, W. J. "The Siouan Indians: A Preliminary Sketch." In *Smithsonian Bureau of Ethnology, 15th Annual Report, 1893–1894*, 157–204. Washington, D.C.: Government Printing Office, 1897.

Medicine, Beatrice. *Learning to Be an Anthropologist and Remaining Native: Selected Writings*. Urbana: University of Illinois Press, 2001.

Meyer, Melissa. "American Indian Blood Quantum Requirements: Blood Is Thicker Than Family." In *Over the Edge Remapping the American West*, edited by Valerie J. Matsumoto and Blake Allmendinger, 231–49. Berkeley: University of California Press, 1999.

Moore, John. "The Enduring Reservations of Oklahoma." In *State and Reservation: New Perspectives on Federal Indian Policy*, edited by Robert L. Bee and George P. Castile, 92–109. Tucson: University of Arizona Press, 1992.

Moreton-Robinson, Aileen. *Sovereign Subjects: Indigenous Sovereignty Matters*. Crows Nest, Australia: Allen and Unwin, 2008.

Myers, Jim. "Osage Nation, U.S., Settle Legal Battle." *Tulsa World*, October 22, 2011. http://www.tulsaworld.com/news/article.aspx?subjectid=335&article id=20111022_16_A1_WASHIN293151.

Nagan, Winston, FRSA, and Craig Hammer. "The Changing Character of Sovereignty in International Law and International Relations." *Columbia Journal of Transnational Law* 43 (2004–5): 141–88.

Ōmae, Ken'ichi. *The End of the Nation State: The Rise of Regional Economies*. New York: Free Press, 1995.

O'Nell, Theresa. *Disciplined Hearts: History, Identity, and Depression in an American Indian Community*. Berkeley: University of California Press, 1996.

"Osage County Rancher Found Dead at Home: Surber was Outspoken Activist," November 7, 2007. http://www.examiner-enterprise.com/articles/2007/11/07/news/news129.txt.

Osage Government Reform Commission. "OGRC Message Board." *Osage Government Reform*, 2005.

Osage Nation Language Department. "Mission Statement of the Osage Nation Language," 2004.

"Osage Nation Stands by Smoke Shop Owners and Tobacco Compact." *Osage News*, 3, no. 1 (2006): 3, 6.

"Osage Rez or Osage County." *Bigheart Times*, June 7, 2007.

"Osages File in U.S. Supreme Court." *Bigheart Times*, October 28, 2010.

"Osages to Pursue Reservation Suit." *Bigheart Times*, December 18, 2008.

Palay, Julia. "Toward an Anthropology of Democracy." *Annual Review of Anthropology* 31 (2002): 469–96.

Perdue, Theda. *"Mixed Blood" Indians: Racial Construction in the Early South*. Athens: University of Georgia Press, 2005.

Pitchlyn, Gary. "Osage Nation v. State of Oklahoma." *Osage News*. November 2004: 3.

Pipestem, Veronica. "How Do Vizenor and Momaday Use Imagination?" Unpublished seminar paper. Norman: University of Oklahoma, 2005.

Povinelli, Elizabeth A. *The Cunning of Recognition: Indigenous Alterities and the Making of Australian Multiculturalism*. Durham: Duke University Press, 2002.

Price, H. *Annual Report of the Commissioner of Indian Affairs to the Secretary of the Interior for the Year 1884*. Washington, D.C.: Government Printing Office, 1884.

Proud Osage. "Internalization of Oppressor, a Legacy of Colonialism." *Osage Shareholders Association*, July 16, 2007. http://www.osageshareholders.org/disc50_frm.htm.

Prucha, Francis Paul. *The Great Father: The United States Government and the American Indians*. Abridged ed. Lincoln: University of Nebraska Press, 1986.

Redcorn, Talee. "White Hair Stills the Wind." *Osage Shareholders Association*, November 30, 2006. http://www.osageshareholders.org/disc51_frm.htm

"Re: Daily Oklahoman editorial." *Osage Shareholders Association*, July 16, 2007. http://www.osageshareholders.org/disc50_frm.htm.

"Re: Black & White World." *Osage Shareholders Association*, September 30, 2010. http://www.osageshareholders.org/disc68_frm.htm.

Rickard, Jolene. "Uncovering/Recovering: Indigenous Artists in California." In *Art/Women/California 1950–2000*, edited by Diana Burgess Fuller and Daniela Salvioni, 143–60. Berkeley: University of California Press, 2002.

Rifkin, Mark. "Indigenizing Agamben: Rethinking Sovereignty in Light of the 'Peculiar' Status of Native Peoples." *Cultural Critique* 73 (2009): 88–124.

———. "Romancing Kinship: A Queer Reading of Indian Education and Zitkala-Sa's American Indian Stories." *GLQ: A Journal of Lesbian and Gay Studies* 12, no. 1 (2006): 27–59.

———. *When Did Indians Become Straight? Kinship, the History of Sexuality, and Native Sovereignty*. Oxford: Oxford University Press, 2011.

Rollings, Willard Hughes. *The Osage: An Ethnohistorical Study of Hegemony on the Prairie-Plains*. Columbia: University of Missouri Press, 1992.

———. *Unaffected by the Gospel: Osage Resistance to the Christian Invasion, 1673–1906: A Cultural Victory*. Albuquerque: University of New Mexico Press, 2004.

Roseberry, William. "Hegemony and the Language of Contention." In *Everyday Forms of State Formation*, edited by Gilbert M Joseph and Daniel Nugent, 355–65. Durham: Duke University Press, 1994.

Ruckman, S. E. "Tribes Unite against Tobacco Pact Woes." *Osage News* 3, no. 2 (February 2006): 8.

Scheick, William J. *The Half-Blood: A Cultural Symbol in 19th Century American Fiction*. Lexington: University Press of Kentucky, 1980.

Sells, Cato. *Reports of the Department of the Interior*. Washington, D.C.: Government Printing Office, 1918.

Shaw, Shannon. "Bill Seeking Audit of Osage Property in Kansas Fails." *Osage News*, May 2011.

———. "U.S. Solicitor General Advises Supreme Court Not to Hear Osage Reservation Case." *Osage News*, May 31, 2011. http://osagenews.org/article/us-solicitor-general-advises-supreme-court-not-hear-osage-reservation-case.

Shohat, Ella. "Notes on the 'Post-Colonial.'" *Social Text* (1992): 99–113.

Simms, Ellen. "Miscegenation and Racism: Afro-Mexicans in Colonial New Spain." *Journal of Pan African Studies* 2, no. 3 (2008): 228–54.

Simpson, Audra. "On Ethnographic Refusal: Indigeneity, 'Voice,' and Colonial Citizenship." *Junctures* (December 9, 2007): 67–80.

———. "Paths toward a Mohawk Nation: Narratives of Citizenship and Nationhood in Kahnawake." In *Political Theory and the Rights of Indigenous Peoples*, edited by Eric Lemont, 113–36. Cambridge: Cambridge University Press, 2000.

———. "To the Reserve and Back Again: Kahnawake Mohawk Narratives of Self, Home, and Nation." Ph.D. diss., McGill University, 2003.

Skibine, Alex Tallchief. "The Cautionary Tale of the Osage Indian Nation Attempt to Survive Its Wealth." *Kansas Journal of Law and Public Policy* 9 (1999): 815–45.

Smith, Paul Chaat. *Everything You Know about Indians Is Wrong*. Minneapolis: University of Minnesota Press, 2009.

Southside Osage. "Re: Thanks." *Osage Shareholders Association*, October 5, 2010. http://www.osageshareholders.org/disc68_frm.htm.

Spruhan, Paul "Indian as Race and Indian as Political Status: Implementation of the Half-Blood Requirement under the Indian Reorganization Act, 1934–1945." *Rutgers Race & Law Review* 8 (2006): 27–49.

Stoler, Ann. *Carnal Knowledge and Imperial Power: Race and the Intimate in Colonial Rule*. Berkeley: University of California Press, 2002.

———. *Imperial Formations*. 1st ed. Santa Fe: School for Advanced Research Press, 2007.

Strickland, Rennard. "The Absurd Ballet of American Indian Policy or American Indian Struggling with Ape on Tropical Landscape: An Afterword." *Maine Law Review* 31 (1979): 213–21.

Strong, Pauline Turner. "Transforming Outsiders: Captivity, Adoption, and Slavery Reconsidered." In *A Companion to American Indian History*, edited by Philip J. Deloria and Neal Salisbury, 339–56. Malden, Mass.: Blackwell, 2002.

Strong, P. T., and B. Van Winkle. "'Indian Blood': Reflections on the Reckoning and Refiguring of Native North American Identity." *Cultural Anthropology* 11, no. 4 (1996): 547–76.

Sturm, Circe Dawn. *Blood Politics: Race, Culture, and Identity in the Cherokee Nation of Oklahoma*. Berkeley: University of California Press, 2002.

Subcommittee of the Committee on Indian Affairs. "Division of Lands and Moneys of the Osage Tribe of Indians: Hearing on H.R. 1478." 58th Congress, 3rd Session, January 20, 1905.

Supernaw, Kugee. Letter. "Notes to the Nation," March 7, 2010. Notes to the Nation email list.

———. Letter. "Notes to the Nation," February 7, 2011.

"Target Date for a Wrap on Trust Case: 2012." *Bigheart Times*, May 13, 2010.

Thomas, Nicholas. *Entangled Objects: Exchange, Material Culture, and Colonialism in the Pacific*. Cambridge: Harvard University Press, 1991.

Trask, Haunani-Kay. *From a Native Daughter: Colonialism and Sovereignty in Hawai'i*. Honolulu: University of Hawai'i Press, 1999.

"Treaty with the Osage, 1808," 7 Stat. 107. *Indian Affairs: Laws And Treaties*. Vol. 2, *Treaties*, November 10, 1808. http://digital.library.okstate.edu/kappler/vol2/treaties/osa0095.htm.

"Tribe Is Going to Federal Court over State Compact." *Osage News*, March 2006, 4.

Tsosie, Rebecca. "Conflict between the Public Trust and the Indian Trust Doctrines: Federal Public Land Policy and Native Indians." *Tulsa Law Review* 39 (2003): 271.

Urban, Greg. *Metaculture: How Culture Moves through the World*. Minneapolis: University of Minnesota Press, 2001.

"U.S.: Rez Case Not Worthy." *Bigheart Times*, June 2, 2011.

Vaux, George. "Appendix A. Report on the Osage Indians, Oklahoma." In *Reports of the Department of the Interior*. Washington, D.C.: Government Printing Office, 1918.

Vizenor, Gerald. *Fugitive Poses: Native American Indian Scenes of Absence and Presence*. Lincoln: University of Nebraska Press, 1998.

Warrior, Robert Allen. *The People and the Word: Reading Native Nonfiction*. Minneapolis: University of Minnesota Press, 2005.

———. *Tribal Secrets: Recovering American Indian Intellectual Traditions*. Minneapolis: University of Minnesota Press, 1995.

Weil, Patrick. "Access to Citizenship: A Comparison of Twenty-five Nationality Laws." In *Citizenship Today: Global Perspectives and Practices*, edited by Thomas Alexander Aleinikoff, Douglas B. Klusmeyer, and T. Alexander Aleinikoff, 17–35. Washington D.C.: Carnegie Endowment for International Peace, 2001.

Weyler, Rex. *Blood of the Land: The Government and Corporate War against First Nations*. Gabriola Island, B.C.: New Catalyst Books, 2007.

White, Owen. *Children of the French Empire: Miscegenation and Colonial Society in French West Africa, 1895–1960*. New York: Oxford University Press, 1999.

Wilkins, David E., and K. Tsianina Lomawaima. *Uneven Ground: American Indian Sovereignty and Federal Law*. Norman: University of Oklahoma Press, 2002.

Williams, Brackette. *Stains on My Name, War in My Veins: Guyana and the Politics of Cultural Struggle*. Durham: Duke University Press, 1991.

Wilson, Terry P. *The Underground Reservation: Osage Oil*. Lincoln: University of Nebraska Press, 1985.

Winders, Jamie. "Bringing Back the (B)order: Post-9/11 Politics of Immigration, Borders, and Belonging in the Contemporary US South." *Antipode* 39, no. 5 (2007): 920–42.

Wolfe, Patrick. "Race and the Trace of History." In *Studies in Settler Colonialism*, edited by Fiona Bateman and Lionel Pilkington, 272–96. New York: Palgrave Macmillan, 2011.

———. "Settler Colonialism and the Elimination of the Native." *Journal of Genocide Research* 8, no. 4 (2006): 387–409.

Index

Bailey, Garrick A., 91, 94, 152, 230 (n. 44)
Barnett, Hepsi: and Osage reform process, 32, 35–37, 42, 97, 137–38; and Maker, 36, 43; and constitutional writing, 43–44, 137; and Osage citizenship, 65; and Osage sovereignty, 135, 137–38
Bays, Brad, 233 (n. 47)
Beede, Cyrus, 21
Belonging: notions surrounding, 2; and culture, 78, 99
Bigheart, James (Osage Chief), 23, 103, 223 (n. 21)
Biological traits, and Osage identity, 3, 4, 50, 63–64, 67, 83
Blacks: "polluting" nature of African blood, 54; and U.S. citizenship, 67
Blood: American Indians defined by, 51, 55, 56, 58–59, 64–65, 68–69; contested history of, 51–52; and colonial process, 52, 63, 69; and race, 53, 55, 59, 61–62, 65, 73, 77; and civilization, 53–54, 55; blood mixing, 54–55, 58; and allotment policy, 55–56, 226–27 (n. 30); and blood quantum, 62, 65, 226–27 (n. 30); and blood memory, 68–69; and heterosexuality, 70. *See also* Osage blood
Blumenbach, Johann Friedrich, 226 (n. 16)
Branstetter, Jerri Jean, 34
Bruyneel, Kevin, 79, 133
Bureau of Indian Affairs (BIA): letters on Osage citizenship, 26, 28, 115, 124, 125, 187–88; and Certificate Degree of Indian, 49, 51, 225 (n. 2); and self-government compacts, 109, 110, 111; and Osage Mineral Estate, 127. *See also* Office of Indian Affairs
Burke Act of 1906, 56
Burns, Louis, 53, 55
Burton, Antoinette, 5, 50, 221 (n. 19)

Callahan, Alice, 83
Carlisle Indian School, 20
Casinos: and Osage Nation, 24, 27, 67, 103, 137, 145, 146–47; and Osage Tribal Council, 24, 27, 110
Cattelino, Jessica, 132
Certificate Degree of Indian Blood (CDIB), 33, 48, 49, 51, 67, 225 (n. 71)
Cherokee Constitution (1839), 21
Cherokee Nation, 64, 112, 148, 149
Cherokee Nation v. Georgia (1831), 112
Chickasaw Nation, 148
Chippewa treaty of 1826, 54–55
Choctaw Nation: and sovereignty, 12–13, 132; and constitutional reforms, 38–39; and tuberculosis treatments, 57; and citizenship requirements, 65; and compacting, 148
Civilization: and U.S. acquisition of Indian land, 20; and allotment policy, 22; and blood, 53–54, 55; and competency, 56
Civil War, peace commissions of, 222 (n. 19)
Clark, William, 19
Class, and culture, 79
Code of Federal Regulations (CFR): and governing Osage villages, 23–24; and distribution of Osage Mineral Estate proceeds, 113–14, 122, 124
Colonial conquest: and nation-state, 4; and racism, 50–51; and culture, 78
Colonial Indian schools, 20
Colonial process: ongoing nature of, 6, 8, 46, 51, 132; and American Indian nations, 7, 11, 20; and destruction of American Indian governments, 20; and blood, 52, 63, 69; and racism, 53, 56, 57–58, 61, 65; and blood mixing, 54; and culture, 73–74, 77, 78–79, 80, 89; and Osage culture, 82–83, 86; and Osage oil, 103–4, 106, 112, 141; and Osage

Mineral Estate, 105, 106, 107, 114–15; and sovereignty, 131, 132, 133, 136, 139, 141. *See also* Settler colonialism

Conner, Joe L., 30, 34

Constitutional writing: and nationalism, 5; process of, 8; and entanglement, 9; and Osage government, 21, 22; and Osage reform process, 31, 43–45; and Osage Government Reform Referendum, 38, 191–96; and Barnett, 43–44, 137; and Osage Government Reform Commission's writing retreat, 43–45; and preamble, 44–45; and Osage culture, 80, 82, 88–90, 91; and Osage Mineral Estate, 106; and Osage authority, 139, 140, 141

Constitutions, and contestation, 4–5, 6, 39, 131. *See also specific constitutions*

Cornell, Stephen, 28

Critical race theory, 15

Crum, Galen, 121–22, 126, 127

Culture: and entanglement, 8, 73, 77, 78, 79, 80, 87, 89, 99, 229 (n. 14); and colonial histories, 9; and U.S. termination of American Indian nations, 24, 85, 86–87; and blood, 64; and colonial process, 73–74, 77, 78–79, 80, 89; static notions of, 74, 77, 78, 79, 80, 87, 91, 93, 96, 98; stereotypes of, 76–77; of American Indians, 76–79, 80, 85, 89, 96, 99; complexity of, 77; and authenticity, 77, 78, 79, 87; and anthropology, 77–78, 79; and ideal types, 78; and assimilation, 85, 89, 95. *See also* Osage culture; Osage identity

Currey, Melissa, 114

Curthoys, Ann, 8

Curtis Act (1897), 152

Daily Oklahoman editorial, 144–46

Daniels, Anthony, 24–25

Daniels, Tony, 30, 34, 83–84

Dawes General Allotment Act (1887), 22, 23, 152

Declaration of Sovereignty and Independence by the People of the Osage Nation, 130–31, 133–34, 139

Deloria, Vine, Jr., 11, 20, 78, 229 (n. 14)

Dennison, Gene, 2, 3, 117

Dennison, George Orville ("Bus"), 2, 3, 104

Diffraction patterns, 11

Dirks, Nicholas, 8, 78

Dombrowski, Kirk, 79

DuVal, Kathleen, 112

Egypt, 154

Ellison, James O., 230 (n. 49)

Elsberry, James, 81

Entanglement: and power dynamics, 6–7; and Osage Mineral Estate, 8, 9, 24, 103, 105, 106, 113, 123; and Osage reform process, 8, 10, 18, 24; and Osage blood, 8, 55, 59, 62, 70, 73; and culture, 8, 73, 77, 78, 79, 80, 87, 89, 99, 229 (n. 14); and situated perspectives, 10; and trade, 19; and Osage government, 20–21, 97; and indigenous body, 51; and civilization, 56; and blood quantum, 62–63, 64; and lineal descent, 70; and Osage culture, 86, 87, 95; and Osage sovereignty, 132, 136, 145, 153; and American Indian national sovereignties, 147, 149

Ethnographic refusal, 80

European Union, 4

FBI, 95, 105

Fletcher, Billy Sam: and Osage reform process, 26, 30, 34, 84, 108–9, 120, 138; and Osage citizenship, 50; and Osage Shareholders Association, 108–10; and Osage sovereignty, 135, 138–39

Office of Indian Affairs' termination of, 22, 24, 25, 26, 138; federal suit on, 25; organization for reinstatement of, 25–26; and Osage authority, 94; and tripartite government, 99, 116; and sovereignty, 139; text of, 161–69

Osage Nation Constitution (1994): court-mandated negotiation of, 26, 34; appeals court's extinguishing of, 27; and Council of Elders, 91, 97; and tripartite government, 99, 116; and Osage Shareholders Association, 108; text of, 170–86

Osage Nation Constitution (2006): debates surrounding, 4, 5–6, 9–10, 18, 41–42; and nodes of entanglement, 8; cultural markers excluded from, 9; and government structure, 42; and Osage citizenship, 42, 71, 72; Preamble to, 44–45, 230 (n. 72); and Osage Mineral Estate, 45, 114, 120, 124, 128, 154, 224 (n. 71); amendment process, 46; and Osage blood, 52, 154; ratification of, 72, 224–25 (n. 71); and Osage culture, 74, 98–99, 154; and culture, 78, 80; and Osage sovereignty, 86, 131, 139–40, 141, 142, 154; and tripartite government, 99; challenges to, 114, 121–22, 126–27, 128, 142; and Osage authority, 128, 143; text of, 197–220

Osage Nation Organization (ONO): and Osage citizenship, 3; formation of, 24–25, 104

Osage News, 35

Osage oil: and colonial process, 103–4, 106, 112, 141; market for, 105; and Osage reform process, 110

Osage reform process (2004–6): evolution of, 2; and Osage sovereignty, 3–4, 9, 46, 83, 86, 131, 132, 135, 136, 138; and nationalism, 4, 7; ethnography of, 5–6, 12; and colonial

process, 6; and entanglement, 8, 10, 18, 24; and Osage Shareholders Association, 14, 45–46, 108, 114, 115, 116, 224–25 (n. 71), 225 (n. 72); insecurity of, 17; and Osage Tribal Council, 27, 28–29, 31–32, 35, 84, 88–89, 115, 119, 125, 136; and Osage Mineral Estate, 32–33, 38, 43, 46, 83, 100, 102–3, 106, 109, 110, 113, 117, 118; control of, 34; and Osage culture, 35, 46, 73–74, 80, 81–82, 86, 87, 88–93, 99; Osage public's support for, 38, 117; and community meetings, 39–42, 43, 65; and annuitants, 102–3, 106–7, 109, 111, 114–15, 117, 118, 119, 120, 121; debates on change, 107–20, 128; and definition of the Osage, 135. *See also* Osage Government Reform Commission; Public Law 108-431

Osage ribbon work, 7, 155

Osage Shareholders Association (OSA): and Osage reform process, 14, 45–46, 108, 114, 115, 116, 224–25 (n. 71), 225 (n. 72); and Osage Mineral Estate, 45, 103, 108, 111, 113, 121, 127–28; and Fletcher, 108–10; and off-reservation annuitants, 120–21; online discussion forum of, 120–23, 126, 127–28, 145; meetings of, 141

Osage sovereignty: and Osage reform process, 3–4, 9, 46, 83, 86, 131, 132, 135, 136, 138; and Osage citizenship, 66, 139, 140; and Osage culture, 79, 86; and Osage Mineral Estate, 106; and Osage authority, 128, 131–32, 133, 134, 135, 136, 137, 139, 140, 141, 143, 153–54; Declaration of Sovereignty and Independence by the People of the Osage Nation, 130–31, 133–34, 139; and land, 139, 140, 141, 142, 143, 146–47, 151–53; and water rights,

associated with, 57–58; and blood quantum, 61, 62, 64

White settlement: and allotment policy, 22, 23, 56, 58; and boundaries of American Indian nations, 59; and Osage Mineral Estate, 103; and Osage sovereignty, 142, 151

Wilson, Carrie, 95

Wilson, Terry P., 21, 55

Wolf, Eric, 79

Wolfe, Patrick, 6

Wright, George, 105–6

X-marks, 95

www.ingramcontent.com/pod-product-compliance
Lightning Source LLC
Chambersburg PA
CBHW030645270326
41929CB00007B/213